Paddle Quest

Canada's Best Canoe Routes

Edited by
Alister Thomas

The BOSTON
MILLS PRESS

Canadian Cataloguing in Publication Data
Main entry under title:
Paddle quest : Canada's best canoe routes
ISBN 1-55046-311-X

1. Canoes and canoeing – Canada – Guidebooks.
2. Canoeists – Canada – Biography. 3. Canada – Guidebooks.
I. Thomas, Alister, 1953–

GV776.15.A2P32 2000   971.1'22'0971   C00-930593-9

Published in 2000 by
Boston Mills Press
132 Main Street
Erin, Ontario
N0B 1T0
Tel 519-833-2407
Fax 519-833-2195
e-mail books@bostonmillspress.com
www.bostonmillspress.com

An affiliate of
Stoddart Publishing Co. Limited
34 Lesmill Road
Toronto, Ontario, Canada
M3B 2T6
Tel 416-445-3333
Fax 416-445-5967
e-mail gdsinc@genpub.com

Distributed in Canada by
General Distribution Services Limited
325 Humber College Boulevard
Toronto, Canada M9W 7C3
Orders 1-800-387-0141 Ontario & Quebec
Orders 1-800-387-0172 NW Ontario
    & other provinces
e-mail cservice@genpub.com

Distributed in the United States by
General Distribution Services Inc.
PMB 128, 4500 Witmer Industrial Estates
Niagara Falls, New York 14305-1386
Toll-free 1-800-805-1083
Toll-free fax 1-800-481-6207
e-mail gdsinc@genpub.com
www.genpub.com

Front cover photograph by Chris Harris.
Back cover photograph by Don Standfield.

Design by Joseph Gisini/Andrew Smith Graphics Inc.

Printed in Canada

THE CANADA COUNCIL | LE CONSEIL DES ARTS
FOR THE ARTS | DU CANADA
SINCE 1957 | DEPUIS 1957

*We acknowledge for their financial support of our publishing program the Canada
Council, the Ontario Arts Council, and the Government of Canada through the
Book Publishing Industry Development Program (BPIDP).*

To the memory of
Malcolm Thomas (1957–1978),
a paddler and a brother.

Contents

SECTION TWO: 25 Distinguished Paddler Profiles

SECTION THREE: A River Landscape for Canada

Preface
Paddling Voices

*P*ADDLE QUEST ATTEMPTS TO PLY INTRIGUING WATERS. THE FIRST SECTION contains accounts of great canoe trips — lake and river, freshwater and salt-water, wilderness and urban, placid and harrowing — from all ten provinces and three territories. (The stories in this book were written prior to April 1, 1999, when the Northwest Territories were divided, with Nunavut in the east and the Northwest Territories in the west.) The second section features profiles of paddlers — many known only in their own region or province, some with national recognition, and a few who have transcended borders. The third section is a bold blueprint for riverine stewardship.

The Poet, Voyager, Adventurer and Explorer in All of Us

Accomplished paddlers from across Canada were asked to write about their favourite trips. These 37 trips are featured in the first section of *Paddle Quest*. Not surprisingly, all the trips describe a purpose in the motion, a clear course to follow, and a true sense of journey. Canoeing as a means of travel is both self-powered and empowering. But the experience is the key.

In "Confessions of a Know-It-All, or Why Take a Clinic," Sheena Masson describes a revelation she had while on the waterways in Nova Scotia: "Over the weekend I realized what a skilled solo paddler can do — move the canoe sideways, pirouette around the paddle, and turn gracefully with a little forward momentum. Meditation in motion. If whitewater paddling is slam dancing, solo flatwater paddling is ballet. I had discovered another way to have fun instead of just crossing the lake."

More often than not, canoeing is the conduit to heightened perception, as well as a sense of renewal. There can be a feeling of flow to the wild and to a deep sense of being — a spiritual connectedness, an immersion. Bruce and Carol Hodgins and their extended paddling family have felt and enjoyed this experience. Bruce writes, "In haunting memory, the landscape of the Lady Evelyn keeps drawing me back for canoe voyages of both the dreaming and the physical. Often more appropriately called the Trout Streams, its waters are as close to mountain flows as the Canadian Shield in Ontario can deliver.

The Lady Evelyn has so many small, often unnavigable rapids, so many captivating, high yet small falls, and such rugged Precambrian shorelines and heights. It has such rocks, such white and red pine stands, such cedar, such lily pads, such shallows, such depths, such sunsets, and such portages. I simply must recanoe and reimagine its mysteries."

In order to see what similarities and differences, themes and concerns run throughout *Paddle Quest's* canoe stories, a content analysis was undertaken by Calgary researcher Ann Dahlberg. (Happily, this task renewed her interest in paddling.) Dahlberg's analysis revealed four distinct streams of experience: Poet, Voyager, Adventurer and Explorer. Of course, common currents run through all four streams. There's the contrast between pristine, isolated nature and civilization. There's an awareness of the history of the route, and with it a sense of timelessness. There's a sense of passing through the wilderness and that the land belongs to the flora and fauna. Because these trips are favourites, they are often revisited, and in this way there is personal renewal. (Alex Hall, who has paddled the Thelon River more than 40 times, must be extremely renewed.) One of the strongest common elements is that each trip described here touched its author deeply.

Stream I: POETS ⌐ From Quetico and the French River, in Ontario, to the South Nahanni River, in the Northwest Territories, the Poets describe the canoeing experience as vital to their existence — rejuvenating and rewarding. Sheila Archer on Saskatchewan's Churchill River: "Then I am walking out of the boreal darkness late on a September night, the roar of the distant rapids blowing over the lake. The island I'm on is surrounded by brilliant northern lights, a sky so beautiful I cannot stand up . . . Now it is the morning and there are eagles circling over the channels downstream. The early sun begins to heat the black slope of rock slanting down into the bay. I walk down from the tent and plunge into the river. . . ."

Each of the Poets describes a close relationship with the land. Their descriptions are filled with memories as well as new delights. There are also sensory and historical relationships, and personal revelations. Their trips are reflective and self-defining. And since these trips are often shared with others, the experience becomes a community one. In describing the out-of-the-way places in Algonquin Park, David Pelly writes: "That's why it remains the smaller, less-travelled lakes that draw me back. That's where I find peace. That's where I see old-growth white pine so large that it takes four of us to link hands around its girth. That's where I feel the bond to wild places that stirs deep within us all. For those who know it, the Park provides that primeval connection. It is a steady, reliable friend — a place that is always there waiting for your next visit, a place that never disappoints. Ralph Bice, in his nineties, the last of the Park's old-time guides and trappers, summed it up nicely: 'Anyone who knows Algonquin Park will be disappointed when they get to heaven.'"

Stream II: VOYAGERS ⟿ From the William River and Bowron Lakes in the West to Harp Lake, Labrador, and north to the Yukon, the Voyagers emphasize the land and nature, while de-emphasizing the canoe and paddling. After a visit by a silver-tipped barrenland grizzly on the Thelon, Max Finkelstein writes: "It was an apt finale for a magical trip — and a reminder that we were merely visitors here. It was our presence that had interrupted the bear on his regular river patrol. The bear didn't invade our camp; rather, it was we who had intruded on his domain."

For Voyagers the landscape is dynamic and ever-changing. They learn to read the land, taking in and experiencing what it has to offer. They are filled with exploration and discovery. There is a sense of achievement. Each traveller can look back and see growth over the course of the trip. They also realize that no trip is ever the same way twice. After a 24-hour solo trip in the tame wilds north of Peterborough, Gwyneth Hoyle writes: "I had been alive in every fibre of my body, all senses alert, even while I slept . . . It had been an exhilarating and totally satisfying trip."

Stream III: ADVENTURERS ⟿ Stephan Kesting's solo trip from the Seal River to the town of Churchill, on Hudson Bay, and Laurel Archer's whitewater kicks on British Columbia's Kicking Horse River both focus on the personal challenge of the Adventurer. Some stories depict triumph, others defeat, but all impart important lessons learned — the waters warrant respect and demand technical skill. In a surrealistic account of a trip from Shefferville to Ungava Bay, Gino Bergeron writes: "Running down from the land of the Montagnais and the Naskapis to the seas of the Inuit, the George River represents, for me, the road to the Far North. A trip that flows over 600 kilometres allows me to visit the meanders and undertows of my fears."

For these Adventurers there is often a transformation from defensive to offensive whereby various paddling skills become second nature, as does the art of reading and listening to the river. Relating a nighttime trip down the Ottawa River, Paul Mason explains that he and his paddling partner will be able to see the rapids "by the light of our white knuckles." A little later he says, "It was now 10:30 P.M. and we were becoming quite adept at sensing the different waves and currents, and reading the rapids by moonlight."

Stream IV: EXPLORERS ⇋ From Ric Driediger's account of Saskatchewan's Drinking River to Kevin Redmond's description of Newfoundland's Main River, the Explorers have varied reasons for and needs to paddle. They combine an awe for the pristine land and the nature of the water with its challenges, rewards, and surprises. About a trip into the Land of the Midnight Sun in the Yukon, Paula Zybach writes: "At 2:00 A.M. the pilot has just off-loaded us on Bonnet Plume Lake, where we proceeded to set up camp. Being further north and earlier in the season than any previous trip caught us laughing at ourselves. The first thing unpacked was a good flashlight, complete with new batteries. It would be weeks before night would return to this region. That weight in the barrel should have been chocolate." A paddler after my own heart.

For Explorers there's a deep appreciation for the untouched or barely touched land. It is an opportunity to view extreme and varied landscapes. These expeditions allow the Explorers to interact unobtrusively with nature and wildlife. "For those who love to travel by canoe, it is rare that any trip is not memorable. Naturally it is often the most recent trip that you recall most vividly and fondly," writes Shawn Hodgins about a trip on the Snare and Coppermine rivers in the Northwest Territories. "Some trips, however, stay etched in your memory for a much longer period of time. A whole combination of factors lead to this — companionship and group dynamics, to physical challenge, scenic beauty, and natural resources such as the weather. Ironically, hardships, while not necessarily enjoyed at the time, may be remembered fondly afterwards. A lengthy trip may also be much more vivid. Time gives you much opportunity for reflection."

These are four types of paddling voices I've heard. I'm sure you've heard them, too. Each voice is individual and unique, yet all are unanimous in their descriptions of the joys and pleasures of paddling. Perhaps a timeless voice that will always be with us best describes this rapture. "The first thing you must learn about canoeing is that the canoe is not a lifeless, inanimate object; it feels very much alive, alive with the life of the river. Life is transmitted to the canoe by currents of air and the water upon which it rides. The behavior and temperament of the canoe is dependent upon the elements: from the slightest breeze to a raging storm, from the smallest ripple to a towering wave, or from a meandering stream to a thundering rapid," wrote Bill Mason in *Path of the Paddle*. And from *Song of the Paddle*: "I was elated with my new-found freedom. I was no longer just listening to the song. I was singing it!"

Paddling is as much an inner journey as it is an adventure of discovery.

Paddler Profiles

In the middle section of this book are 25 profiles of people for whom paddling is profound. There are legends: Eric Morse and Omer Stringer. There are families: Hodgins, Peake, McGuffin and Mason. Some are from Atlantic Canada: Roger Pearson, Steve Cook, John B. Hughes and "Miramichi" Bill Palmer. Some are from the West: Brian Creer, Mark Lund, Ric Driediger and Bill Brigden. Some are from the North: Alex Hall, Neil Hartling and Ken Madsen. And some are from central Canada: Claudia Kerckhoff-van Wijk, George Luste, James Raffan, Wally Schaber, Mark Scriver, Kevin Callan, Hap Wilson and Kirk A.W. Wipper. Each has made outstanding contributions to the paddling community.

Stewardship

The anchor story of the book's third section is entitled "A National Waterway Management Plan — The Blueprint for Preserving Canada's Wild Rivers," authored by Wally Schaber, founder of Black Feather Wilderness Adventures. He believes we are living through the last decade of wilderness travel. He also believes rivers are the life forces that link all wilderness in Canada with our fresh- and saltwater coastlines. "Rivers offer pathways for journeys of discovery through all the natural regions of Canada, and even offer journeys that are metaphors for life itself," he explains. "So why don't Canadians preserve more rivers? Is it because we lack the willpower or foresight?"

Wally steps up and presents a complete waterway preservation system, which includes a river in each of the 15 ecozones and many of the ecoregions of Canada, as well as a river in each of the 15 major watersheds. In addition to a vital natural history, each of these rivers must have a significant cultural, historic and/or recreational component. And each candidate should be chosen because of its existing (or post-restoration potential) use to support the wildlife and aquatic populations indigenous to the area. As he explains, "The ultimate goal is to have the rivers link our 15 terrestrial ecozones with our five marine ecozones. It would mean our landscapes and seascapes would be united by a common bond — flowing water."

Ken Madsen knows all about flowing water. He was instrumental in helping save the Tatshenshini River in northern B.C. In the Stewardship section, Ken offers a step-by-step plan to launch your own conservation campaign. "Sometimes I feel like shouting, 'Screw it!' I have a list of secret streams buried in the wilderness where I can retreat from bulldozers; canyons where even the most zealous developer can't find me. But wild places are being hunted down like passenger pigeons were during the 1800s, and my conscience won't let me hide forever," he writes. "Strange things happen to those who 'get involved' in river conservation issues."

Waterway stewardship would not be complete without including the Canadian Heritage Rivers System (CHRS). "Canada's river heritage is threatened," says Max Finkelstein. "We are changing our rivers. Damming them, paving their banks, poisoning their waters, destroying the vital, yet fragile, ribbon of their shorelines, bulldozing the human heritage along their banks."

Max explains the important role and objectives of the CHRS, and then suggests how all of us can get involved. "Heritage River status does not guarantee that a river will not be degraded or changed. But it is the best opportunity available to ensure that our rivers flow to the future, unpolluted and rich in life and human heritage."

Alister Thomas
Calgary, Alberta

Acknowledgments

THIS BOOK WOULD NOT HAVE BEEN POSSIBLE WITHOUT THE ASSISTANCE of and direction by Joseph Agnew, former executive director of the Canadian Recreational Canoeing Association, and John Denison and Noel Hudson of Boston Mills Press.

Thanks also to Tina and Jeff Forster for their preliminary design work, and to Joseph Gisini of Andrew Smith Graphics for the final product.

Much gratitude to my wife, Gae VanSiri; my parents, Bettie and Keith; and my brother, Kevin, for support and encouragement.

Most of all, I appreciate the time and effort that all the paddler-authors put into getting their stories just right. Please take a bow.

And to all of the people I have paddled with in the past, and to those I will paddle with in the future — see you in the back eddy.

37 Outstanding Canoe Trips

Terra Nova River

Main River

Nova Scotia Waterways

The Five Islands

P.E.I.'s North Shore

Nepisiguit River

Moisie River

Harp Lake

Ottawa River

Rideau Waterway

George River

The Kawarthas

Soper River

Algonquin Park

L'Eau Claire River

French River

Lady Evelyn River

Steel River

Hudson Bay

Quetico

Thelon River

Snare-Coppermine Rivers

Morse River

William River

MacFarlane River

Churchill River

Souris River

Bennet Plume River

South Nahanni River

Spatsizi and Stikine Rivers

Drinking River

Kicking Horse River

Highwood River

Bowron Lakes

Sheep River

Yukon River

Tatshenshini River

Section One

37 Outstanding Canoe Trips

Main River
A Short But Complete River Experience
Kevin Redmond

MY FIRST IMPRESSION OF THE MAIN RIVER CAME FROM THE ACCOUNTS of two paddlers who were flown in to the headwaters in June and paddled half the river in a lone canoe before realizing they were in over their heads, so to speak. After a night's rain that raised the water level several metres, they capsized at the start of a canyon — 23 kilometres long with an average gradient of 10 metres per kilometre. They survived the capsize, and recognizing their good luck, they left everything — canoe and gear — to walk the 15 kilometres to the end of the river. But the following September they flew back, collected their gear, and with the water at more reasonable levels, completed the trip in their canoe. The legend of the Main had begun.

Located in western Newfoundland, the Main is one of the most diverse and challenging rivers anywhere, despite the fact that it is just 57 kilometres long. The first designated Heritage River in the province, the Main makes a riveting impression that brings paddlers back again and again.

Overcoming the obstacles on a canoe trip always makes for a good story, and our first trip to, and then down, the Main is no exception. The plane that is to take us from the Atlantic Ocean to the headwaters, on the Great Northern Peninsula, is over a day late. It seems the pilot crashed the day before! While we wait, one of our party hooks and lands a prize Atlantic salmon, allowing us to forget the delay for a little while. But anxiety levels are up again when our 22-year-old pilot doesn't know how to properly attach the canoe to the strut of the Beaver. When the first flight is three times later than it should be, you can guess what goes through our minds. As it turns out, the pilot has become lost, but he gets back on track after plugging in his electronic navigation system. Fortunately, our descent of the Main by canoe proves not nearly as stressful.

The headwaters of the Main River consist of four ponds on top of the Long Range Mountains. A short hike from our drop-off point provides a view of Gros Morne, the second highest peak in Newfoundland. The geology of this area illustrates the theory of global plate tectonics and is the primary reason Gros Morne was designated a World Heritage Site by UNESCO in 1987.

Generally a barren rockscape intertwined with lichens, mosses, and stunted tuckamore trees (they rarely exceed a metre in height yet are hundreds of years old), the land is reminiscent of the arctic barrenlands.

The royal-blue water of each pond reflects scattered snowbanks along the shoreline. We soon discover that corn snow mixed in weak lemonade — made from clear, unpolluted river water — is quite refreshing in the warm sunshine. A light breeze picks up and carries away the swarms of blackflies. With the wind at our backs, it's not long before the fourth pond is behind us, and we enter the rock garden.

This section is an 8-to-10-kilometre-long whitewater paradise. At high water it is a run-and-gun fun run in open boats — the river drops close to 100 metres with no falls or portages. In moderately low water, however, there is a lot of getting in and out of the canoe, which can be fun and challenging in its own right. On the bright side, low water here means the canyon further downstream is runnable.

The Big Steady Beckons

As the boulder garden flattens out we enter the "Big Steady." The river's still water reflects a tall virgin forest, each tree symmetrical and perfectly spaced, as if traced with an artist's brush against the afternoon's steel-blue sky. Frequent flooding and spring ice break-up keep the mature forest in the Big

Steady clear of most undergrowth and permanent vegetation. The marshes, bogs and grasslands here are the seasonal nesting grounds of most of the waterfowl found in insular Newfoundland — black ducks, green-winged teal, goldeneye, red-breasted mergansers, loons and Canada geese. The lush meadows of the Big Steady also attract moose in such large numbers that their population density in this area is among the highest in the province.

Camped on an island in the middle of the Big Steady, we sit around a tiny campfire after supper. The air is quiet and the water still. We spot a caribou having a drink of water. Then a cow moose and her calf, barely a couple of weeks old, cross the river no more than 15 metres west of our camp. To the south, a Canada goose and her eight goslings swim silently past a gaggle of ducklings on the opposite shore. A few minutes later, two loons banter back and forth as their echoes rebound between the distant bumper hills of the Main's infamous canyon. All of this is heard and seen in the space of half an hour. Admission is free. All you have to do is watch and wait while nature's web unfolds before your eyes and ears.

This serenity is broken for a moment when, as dusk overtakes the setting sun, we prepare to evade the persistent swarms of blackflies with the hilarious "Harry Butt Shuffle," named after Newfoundland's own canoeing reprobate, Harry Butt. With one partner poised to open the tent zipper, the "shuffler" runs as fast as possible around the tent to dodge the flies and then on cue dives into the tent, free of the pesky pests. Once inside our sleeping bags it's difficult to sleep. The images of this first day leave the heart pounding and the mind looking forward to the days to come.

Before leaving the pristine waters and forests of the Big Steady, we explore Paradise Pool, which is surrounded by domed bogs dominated by sedge, sweet gale and leather leaf. We take a quick trip to a quiet brook that connects with a series of gullies. After passing nesting Canada geese, we stop to fish. Each cast brings more lunch — pan-size brook trout. Alive with fish and wild game, this tiny string of water is an ideal side trip in peak nesting season. But our fishing exploits are far from over. Back on the river at the start of the canyon, we meet up with a run of Atlantic salmon. The first one weighs 20 kilograms. That's all we need for food, but the thrill of catching Atlantic salmon is so great that a fishing derby ensues, with each fish soon released back to the river.

The canyon looms. Looking down the canyon, the bottom appears to fall out of the river. Visibility is restricted by both the river's steep gradient and the heavily wooded, V-shaped walls that rise sharply up 300 metres. The days are made short by the shadows cast down from the towering canyon walls. In contrast to the upper part of the river, there are few good campsites to be found along these steep walls. Wildlife is also less apparent. Class II and III rapids await us as the river drops 250 metres over the next 15 kilometres to the Atlantic Ocean. Here, a paddler requires a high level of skill, experience and luck, since a simple mistake can easily result in a long, nasty swim and/or a broached canoe. As would be expected, the difficulty of running the canyon in high water goes up a notch or two. And while in the confines of this canyon, getting out to scout is almost impossible. Instead, there are lots of opportunities to pull into eddies in order to rest and plan your next few metres of ecstasy. For the whitewater enthusiast, a day's paddle in the canyon of the Main River is sure to bring a smile.

Despite its short length, the Main is a complete river that includes a tundra-like watershed, tall virgin forests, wild game, and frothing white rapids. The Main River offers challenges, entertainment, and charm.

POSTSCRIPT: In 1989 Kruger Pulp and Paper built a bridge across the Main River about 15 kilometres from the river mouth to access the province's last virgin timber. As part of the business deal, an environmental assessment of the access road and bridge was waived. The access road opened up the Main River valley to timber harvesting and other resource extraction for the first time. This road also allows access to the Main River canyon. There is much pain in the thought of 80,000 cords of timber a year being logged well into the twenty-first century. The final management plan protects only a narrow reserve area around the Main, leaving room for resource extraction within 100 metres of the river. This puts the Main River's pristine nature at peril.

Terra Nova River
Barrens, Bogs and Boreal Forests

Jim Price

WE LANDED ON THE GLASSY HEADWATER LAKE UNDER SPARKLING SUN-shine. Although it was June and the sun's rays penetrated our skin, the remnants of snow along the water's edge were instant reminders that winter had not long since given up its hold on the upper plateau. I was here in the southeastern portion of central Newfoundland as part of a reconnaissance team checking out the area's potential as part of the proposed Bay du Nord Wilderness Reserve. (The reserve became a reality in March 1990.) It was our task to view possible conflicts between forestry and mineral potential, as well as to assess the potential of the Terra Nova River as a canoe route and provide a preliminary sense for the importance of the upper Terra Nova region to the proposed Wilderness Reserve.

After a quick lunch, we hiked the 1.5-kilometre divide over the upper pond of the Bay du Nord watershed, which is the start of the Bay du Nord River — another amazing wilderness canoe trip. Here, in the middle of the Middle Ridge Wildlife Reserve, caribou and moose were feeding quietly in the warm afternoon sunshine as loons and black ducks flew overhead. The average elevation is about 300 metres above sea level, with nearby Mt. Sylvester reaching 376 metres. We were in the heart of the Central New-foundland Forest Ecoregion, with its black spruce, trembling aspen and white birch. The ground cover was punctuated with mosses, lichens, bunchberries, starflowers and twinflowers, while the nearby bogs were dominated by deer-grass, Labrador tea, sheep laurel and blueberries.

After we returned to the Terra Nova system and had an early supper, we considered moving downstream. We were a group of six and most of us wanted to move on, but a few individuals were content to lie back in the sun and enjoy the tranquil setting of this wilderness haven. This proved to be a huge mistake!

We awoke the next morning to the howls of an arctic wind and the crackle of ice pellets against our tents. Some of the group had risen earlier, lit a fire and tried to get themselves a cup of coffee. It was a wasted effort, as powerful gusts of wind blew the fire out and scattered the ashes everywhere. We decided to break camp hastily and head to Nanedock Lake, about 8 kilometres away, on empty stomachs. My bow partner and I had only one set of gloves between us, and it was so cold that we had to alternate — one would wear the right and the other the left, and after about five minutes we would switch. This worked quite well and before we knew it we were in the shelter of an old trapper's cabin on Nanedock Lake.

After a hot breakfast and a few comments about how cozy it would have been to stay in the cabin the night before, we moved on downriver. The Terra Nova was high and several rapids had to be lined. This was a topic for further discussion and disagreement. In each successive case the same two canoeists would opt to portage or line in complete opposition to the consensus of the rest of the group. This contrarian point of view finally caught up with them when they decided to haul their canoe over a 3-metre-high waterfall. While the rest of us ferried across the river to the more easily lined side, they prepared to lower their canoe down over the rocks.

Canoe as Lip on Waterfall

The rest of us were about 200 metres downstream around the bend when one of them appeared, waving frantically, and shouting that something was wrong. He explained that when they lifted the bow up on the rocks, the stern had been swept out into the current and had caught on a rock on the lip of the falls. With the bow and stern both stuck on solid rock, the canoe quickly caught an upstream edge, swamped, and began to take on the appearance of downstream "V." We all ran upriver, and the sight around that bend was frightening. The borrowed Grumman was completely submerged and was now forming a lip on the waterfall.

Using as levers long poles cut from the forest, we managed to pry the canoe loose and haul the heavily laden craft to the safety of the calm pool below the falls. With the wet gear unloaded several of us "jumped out" the bulges in the hull and then applied an emergency layer of duct tape. This got us to the next campsite, where more permanent repairs were made.

That night, around the warmth of the campfire, it was decided that from then on it was "all for one and one for all." Everyone would stick together and line or portage on the same side of the river. The tripping camaraderie improved immensely, and the two contrarians were very thankful for how we handled the situation and how we got them out of an otherwise serious predicament.

When we reached Lake St. John, about 60 kilometres from the start of our trip, there was a fair wind blowing and we had to wait several hours at the head of the lake. This wait proved beneficial, for by the time we landed, several members of our wet group had started to exhibit the first signs of hypothermia. We quickly got a blazing fire going, and within a short time everyone was sipping hot tea and drying out wet clothes. When the wind died down, the two in the repaired canoe elected to hug the shoreline rather than proceed directly across the lake as we did.

Because of this delay, it was very late when we started to look for a camp-site. The water was extremely high and many of the suitable campsites were flooded out. We had to go back from the river and hack out a campsite among the stunted spruce.

This middle section of the Terra Nova River valley has been the scene of extensive forestry operations. In the early 1900s a European group planned and began construction of a pulp mill at Glovertown near the mouth of the river. Because of financial difficulties the project was aban-doned, but the concrete ruins of the partially constructed mill remain today. This business failure, however, did not save the valley from exploitation. In the 1940s lumber mills were set up on Terra Nova Lake and the lumber was shipped out by rail to major Newfoundland centres. It was not until the 1950s that pulpwood was harvested in the upper reaches of the river valley. This pulpwood was driven downriver to the railhead at Terra Nova village and then shipped to the paper mill at Grand Falls–Windsor. This activity ceased many years ago, but the network of roads and wooden dams is a reminder of these past operations.

Beginning at the outlet of Lake St. John, known locally as John's Pond, the character of the Terra Nova River changes. Calm steadies are interspersed with enjoyable short rapids. Mollyguajeck Falls is the only major obstacle in this section and can be easily portaged on the north side. We passed through many small ponds connected by short stretches of river. These ponds are very intricate, with numerous projecting points that make navigation difficult. After a while the river becomes deep and sluggish with occasional stretches of faster current, boulders, and the odd shallow area. Further downstream, several short portages are required around small ledges and, at low water, wading your canoe through boulder gardens is the order of the day.

The last section of the Terra Nova flows about 23 kilometres from the village of Terra Nova to Spencer's Bridge on the Trans-Canada Highway. This section parallels but never enters Terra Nova National Park and is the most challenging for both open and closed boats alike. Several Class IV and V rapids, along with a 5-metre runnable waterfall, are sufficient to get the

adrenaline flowing. For the most part, portaging is easy, and many of the rapids can be lined. On this, the last day of our trip, the weather cleared and sun shone for the first time since our landing. About 5 kilometres upriver from the Trans-Canada Highway, there is a spectacular canyon complete with a 20-metre waterfall cascading directly off the cliffs into the river. A short but strenuous climb down the gorge enabled us to paddle past curtains of white-water plunging from the cliffs. We pulled out at Spencer's Bridge, near Glovertown, with an increased sense of camaraderie and accomplishment.

Our repaired canoe delivered its two paddlers safely to the end of the Terra Nova River but has never seen another trip.

Today, the Bay du Nord Wilderness Reserve is Newfoundland's largest protected area — 2,895 square kilometres of rugged country with wild rivers, boreal forest, bogs and barrens. In it, the provincial government protects two provincial ecoregions that provide a home for an estimated 15,000 woodland caribou, eastern Newfoundland's largest Canada goose population, and a diversity of other wildlife.

Moisie River

The Nahanni of the East

Kevin Redmond

MEMORIES MAY VARY FOR THOSE WHO PADDLE "THE NAHANNI OF THE East," but its impact and spell are indelible. The Moisie River will never leave you. And just getting there is an adventure. For us, from insular Newfoundland, it included a two-day drive, two separate ferries, and a day on the train from Sept-Îsles to the put-in at Lac de Mille, 25 kilometres south of Labrador City and the headwaters of the Moisie.

As we stood alone among our three weeks' worth of provisions and gear, our last link with civilization chugged away. Or so we thought. We believed that after spending 24 hours on the train we would not see or hear another one until the last portion of the trip. A rainbow arched across the sky as we set up camp that night. Later, asleep in our tent, no more than a metre and a half from the railbed, we were awakened by a distant rumble. As the noise came closer, the ground trembled while a 250-car ore train passed by, causing our tent to ruffle, stretch and contort like never before. We couldn't escape. With the tent door facing the track, all we could do was sit and wait until the train passed.

The great paradox was that during the next couple of mornings we were awakened very early by the sounds of wildlife. Consequently, we created a "Moisie Time Zone" by pushing our watches two hours ahead. This meant the sun rose at 7:30 A.M. Moisie time. It worked for us. Later, this early rise gave us the opportunity to make some distance when the wind was lighter.

As we crossed the Québec–Labrador border, which is the height-of-land between Lac de Mille and Menistouc Lake, there was a unique sense of presence. Here, the water flows in opposite directions. The eastern edge flows to Labrador and the western lip drops into Québec, creating a tiny brook just wide enough for a canoe. Surrounded by metre-high grasses, this small rivulet opened up to a sandy delta littered with wolf tracks, and then the crystal clear water of Lake Menistouc. Unfortunately, the first kilometre of Lake Menistouc was so shallow we couldn't paddle. Instead, we dragged our canoes across the sandy bottom toward the illusive lake ahead of us.

After being windbound on Lac Opocopa for several hours, we paddled into the night until a spectacular thunder and lightning storm forced us to make camp. Each flash of lightning converged with the distant midnight sunset, creating an eerie orange halo in the sky. Very early the next morning we were awakened by a swishing noise followed by a splash. A beaver was having fun sliding down the riverbank and into the river no more than a metre and a half from our tent.

Later that morning the air was cool and the water still. Two canoes, paddling side by side, entered Lake Felix. A muskrat, carrying a fresh alder branch in its teeth, swam undaunted within a paddle's length of our canoes. As we paddled across the lake, the loons called back and forth over the calm waters. In the distance, the mouth of the Moisie River beckoned. Here, the still waters and serenity of Lake Felix were transformed into a ceaseless roar of rapids and a series of portages that would have left the hardiest voyageur tired and spent.

The longest and hardest portages are from the beginning of the Moisie to the confluence of the Pekans River. Most portages, some up to 1.5 kilometres long, are steep and rocky. But the portage at the Pekans was park-like with rich golden sand beneath a tall stand of symmetrical spruce trees 100 to 120 metres high. Ripe bakeapples (in August) along the portage quenched our thirst and left a sweet taste to remember.

Lost Canoe

As the Moisie's gradient levels out, portages become easier and less frequent. The deep, winding river valley collects more water as the river becomes wider, creating a greater variety of channels with more opportunities to line or run, rather than portage. On one occasion, after portaging one canoe over and around house-sized boulders, we decided to line the second canoe through the Class IV rapids. Unfortunately the 60 metres of stern rope came up short, so we had to let go of the painter or get pulled into the rapid. We watched helplessly as the out-of-control canoe dropped into a hole and disappeared. Luckily, it washed out after a few tense seconds, and we were able to retrieve it by hopping into the first canoe that we had portaged.

With the wider river and a variety of channels, paddling 6 kilometres of continuous rapids, including 900 metres of Class III whitewater, is not uncommon. It is amazing that in stretches like this you quickly forget about the bugs and portages you battled and swore at to get this far.

During a typical day on the Moisie, the wildlife can include a black bear and her cub, moose, ducks, porcupines, osprey and lots of salmon. Camping

on a sandy beach in the shadow of a sheer 200-metre rockface, we began to miss the roar of the rapids that had been with us for the past week. After settling in, we discovered bear tracks just 20 metres downstream. Later, in the middle of the night, we were awakened by the sound of an animal. With great fear, we got up and pointed a flashlight on what appeared to be dark, shiny black bear fur. To our relief, it was only a porcupine chewing a paddle shaft.

Along the last 150 kilometres of the river there are a number of private fishing camps. Despite the fact we were paddling during the first two weeks of August, there were still plenty of salmon migrating up the river. While we had lunch overlooking one pool, we counted more than a hundred of these spectacular orange beauties. The Moisie is known as one of the best salmon rivers in North America, with fish running up to 22 kilograms. For many paddlers who enjoy fishing, the Moisie has it all.

The last rapid on the river, Train Trestle Rapid, was originally scouted from the train on our way to the start of this trip. It's amazing how dramatically your perception of the rapid changes when, in your canoe, you are 30 metres closer. Paddling this last rapid without incident left us with mixed feelings of joy and emptiness. We were happy to have successfully completed the trip, but we also had a hollow feeling, knowing we were about to leave this majestic river.

These are but a few nuggets from the Moisie. We are certain that in your travels along this waterway you will discover your own best memories, and perhaps some of ours. For those who paddle the Moisie, it will always remain "the Nahanni of the East."

Harp Lake
The Labrador Experience

James Cottrell and Bob Henderson

WITH OUR CANOES STRAPPED ONTO THE PONTOONS OF THE RATHER nostalgic-looking single-engine 1953 Otter, we pushed away from the Goose Bay–Happy Valley dock and coasted out into the bay. Taxiing out to the west end, we pivoted to face east, then, with a heavy torque of the engine, we ploughed through the water. Our young French pilot, from Labrador City, worked the instruments like a heavy crane operator. Manually winding down the flaps and pushing on the throttle while pulling hard on the steering column, it was as if he were actually prying the plane off the water. Suddenly, freed from the grasp of the water's surface, we began to rise up, making a smooth and steady climb. We were on our way to mysterious Harp Lake.

With noses pressed against the scratched Plexiglas window, we watched in wonder as the unfamiliar landscape passed by below. But once we identified Grand Lake, the giant pieces of the Labrador puzzle came together. We spotted the mouth of the Naskapi River, the river mouth Leonidas Hubbard had missed back in 1903. He died on the Susan River, which was just below our left wing. A little further on, we spotted Seal Lake, a destination for trappers from the North West River. Our minds raced with the significance of our journey. This land's past is scattered with portage trails and stories of struggles and celebrations. In 1911 H. Hesketh Pritchard called this land "menacing wilderness" and "a dreary prospect," but around the same time Mina Hubbard, Leonidas's wife, called it "the strength-giving presence of an understanding friend."

In 1535 Jacques Cartier called Labrador "the land that God gave Cain," and it is a cornucopia of travelling delights: rushing rivers and high plateau lakes speckled by dwarf tamaracks, eskers and fiord-like lakes, sweeping river valleys, and mysterious coastal inlets.

Like many canoeists, we find that much of the joy in travelling comes in the planning of a trip, especially in the initial focus of place. A mixture occurs, intellectual anticipation and the idea of consequence combining with desire and impulse. For us, this happened during the winter of 1990 when we circled Harp Lake–Adlatok River as a possible trip for 1992. Everything from that point on became a ritualistic odyssey.

We dug for maps and wrote letters to the very few friends and canoe-tripping associates who could tell us about their own first-hand experiences in Labrador. Herb Pohl, Bob Davis, Neil MacKay and George Luste contributed information and anecdotes. We came to call it "The Labrador Experience." We then contacted our old tripping friends, Dave Taylor and Jimmi Steward, to round out our foursome.

The plane's pace was unbearable: too slow in exposing the full view of Harp Lake, but too fast for me to absorb all the details of the land below. The land was creased by a massive crevice running on a diagonal from the northeast. We crossed over the lake, viewing the full 65 kilometres of its length. Beneath us, it appeared as if the earth had been violently ripped apart, leaving a long shoreline of 300-metre cliffs that drop straight down into deep, black water.

In the distance we could see a silken waterfall, our outflow to the Adlatok River, and snow-capped mountains. The old plane banked counter-clockwise and dropped into the canyon. With the engines off, we sank silently, dropped softly onto the calm water, and glided into the first of only three small bays on the entire lake. We taxied to a sandy beach, and four of us jumped out onto the pontoons. It was perfect. I didn't know where to look first. Everything was so unusual and so beautiful. It was as if we had dropped from the sky and landed on one of those glossy colour photographs in an expensive coffee-table book of locations too spectacular to be true. We stood in awe, our jaws agape and eyes smiling. Eventually, we forced ourselves out of the stupor long enough to unload the plane.

We waved a grateful goodbye to our pilot, who really wanted to join us, and the trusty Otter lifted off and disappeared beyond the escarpment. Suddenly I was wet from Bob's splash as he took a celebratory plunge into the lake. We were actually here.

At first Harp Lake seemed very still, almost tomb-like, but slowly we became familiar with the quiet ecology of the lake. Even hearing the sound of a small hermit thrush, intimate and satisfying, was an event to be celebrated, as its solitary song rose up in a private recital just for us. On our first paddle up the feeder river to the southwest of the lake, we watched with great excitement as a large trout swam leisurely under our canoe. There seemed to be so much space for all of nature's events to be played out with clarity and fullness.

Experiment in Time

From our camp, set high atop a soft deposit of glacial sand, we spent the first night absorbing our new surroundings. The next morning, with no clouds and no wind, our tripping instincts told us to travel, but it was agreed that this trip was an experiment in time — time for travelling and time for exploring. As a result, despite perfect travelling conditions, we swam (a loose term to describe frenetic plunges into icy water), we fished and, after a late breakfast, we pushed off in our canoes in search of a route up the escarpment to see the high country of Labrador. Four tries — two foolish, one on scree, and one too steep — were attempted before we found an ascendable foothold.

After a 300-metre climb, we finally had our first full view of the interior beyond and the lake below. As we turned to look back, we were rewarded with a panoramic view of deep cobalt water framed by skyscraping walls of rock and covered with a canopy of Aegean blue sky. There was an overwhelming sense of space. Here on top it was a different world, an undulating plateau of erratics (oddly placed boulders, remnant deposits of the glacial gods), and the endearing stout spruce and tamarack.

We let our eyes explore and come to terms with the scale of this strange land. In one direction, the slope of land was steady and regular. In another direction, a mess of topography seemed to crash and rise up beyond our view. Down on the lake we were always looking up, trying to get perspective, but up here we got a sense of releasing space. In Labrador, size is everything. Yet it is only realized in its contrast to the singleness of its tiny components. The grand design of nature seems more apparent with the single bird, the lone spruce forcing its way out of a bald rock, and the daring boulder that seems to be standing on its toes, teetering on the edge of a cliff. We watched a ptarmigan with great interest. We'd seen lots of ptarmigans before, but this one was in Labrador. Here, watching it was like participating in a meeting.

The next seven days were spent setting a very unconventional pace. Instead of paddling like voyageurs at 60 strokes per minute and covering the most number of miles possible, we were here to explore Harp Lake slowly.

Maybe what made this travel philosophy attainable was the fact that we paddled and hiked under perfect blue skies and on windless water. Fortunately, we were never to see it through adverse conditions. A capricious system would have made it treacherous to paddle, especially with its steep embankments and scant shelter. If that had been the case, we probably would have quickly dropped our philosophical pretentiousness and paddled like mad to escape the entrapment of a 65-kilometre wind tunnel.

We coasted silently, marvelling at the sheer height of the cliff walls above us and their dramatic continuation deep into the water below. As we paddled along we watched as the dark surface of the lake reflected an occasional snow embankment, mirroring it to create a strange Rorschach ink-blot image.

Paddling under the heat of the midday sun, we were cooled by the air-conditioning effect of the frigid water. But occasionally a breeze would pick up, hitting us with a wave of hot air, like the opening of a large oven door. We surmised that it was some form of thermal inversion, the result of air

being baked on the high rock faces above us and, defying the laws of thermo-dynamics, flipping hot for cold, a gush would swoop down and slam against us. One minute we would be bundled up in jackets and caps, while the next we would be stripped to the bone and basking in the heat of a brief, strange African sirocco-like wind.

Ice Floes

According to our maps, midway up the lake we were supposed to find a deep river re-entry point with a possible campsite off to the east side. If this did not materialize we would have to paddle upriver in search of enough turf to pitch camp. Cruising down the lake, we strained our eyes for a break in the northern escarpment, while at the same time we debated whether the white form that stretched across the surface of the water was actually solid ice or simply a mirage of heat and water vapour playing a nasty trick. As we pad-dled closer, we passed a couple of large ice floes and our doubts about a mirage dwindled. But as we paddled and paddled, they never did get any closer. The floes did not block our route, and before we could fully convince ourselves of their non-existence, our turn-off appeared, and we were soon off Harp Lake and heading upriver. Waiting for us was yet another perfect site as the cliffs gave way to long, sandy eskers, steep hills and a verdant forest of spruce. We would camp and explore here for a few days.

It was a lovely, calm evening when the tracks of our canoes last rippled the waters of Harp Lake. We pulled up onto a stony beach on the eastern end, and from there gazed back southwest over the solitary scene out of which we had travelled. Tomorrow we would push into the short, fast river that would wash us out of Harp onto the Adlatok River. The cliffs would give way and we would enter open forest, long eskers, hills, wind, bugs and current. There would be days of hikes, days of endless lining through icy-cold waters, and evenings trapped in our tents, held at bay by the mosquitoes and blackflies. Beyond that, the coast and all its uncertainties — tides, pack-ice, and whale-backed islands that would confuse us by their scale and common shape.

For now, however, we sat back enjoying bellies full of delicious lake trout. It would be difficult to leave Harp Lake, knowing that we would prob-ably never see it again, knowing that we had, in a sense, stumbled onto a lake that offered all the treasures of real discovery. We never did see any indica-tion of past travellers. In Harp we found a paradise of vertical grandeur and calm reflective waters. We shared a joint feeling of privilege, that nature had permitted us to be among the very few to view one if its special treasures.

The Five Islands
Like Pearls on a String in Nova Scotia's Minas Basin

Scott Cunningham

I CRAWLED OVER THE SCARP EDGE ONTO A PLATEAU OF DENSE BRAMBLES and stunted spruce so characteristic of this inhospitable coast and set about seeking my fortune. But the rambling search produced only ragged pants, scratched flesh and the rotting remains of a few boards, hints of previous human activity. When left alone, nature rapidly reclaims what is rightly hers, and she had all but obliterated the traces of earlier diggings. My gold fever waned, along with the daylight, and I lay along the cliff edge and savoured the panorama below. The currents raced among the reefs and islands and invaded the banks of mud and sand, chasing the clamdiggers into their boats and back to the mainland. Only the canoe remained, securely tethered to the rocks underneath and rising by the minute. I was alone.

From the beginning of local storytelling, the Five Islands have been cloaked in as much mystery as the fog that claims them well past spring. Inaccessible and forbidding, they are aberrations in an otherwise tame world of sandy beach and mud flat, bastions of legend and myth. According to the Mi'kmaqs, they were born when the Indian demigod Gloscap hurled enormous boulders at his archenemy, the beaver, who had dammed the Bay of Fundy and flooded his garden. Later, in the days of pirates and privateers, these waters were scoured for potential safe havens and possibly as a hiding places for ill-gotten loot — as an old map indicated was the case of Long Island. Such were the boyhood fantasies that drew me to these spooky islands.

Arranged like pearls on a string, the Five Islands reach out 6 kilometres from the tip of Economy Mountain in Nova Scotia's Minas Basin. They all betray their forms in their names: Diamond, Long, Egg and Pinnacle. Only Moose has attracted debate, with some suggesting that it resembles the head of the animal, while others see it as the moose's back as it breaks the surface. Diamond and Egg are unassailable (at least for mere mortals such as I), Long and Pinnacle can be climbed only with considerable difficulty, but Moose, closest to the mainland, will welcome you willingly. Farther west are other basalt remnants that lead the way out of the bay — the Brothers, Partridge and Spensor's Island, the birthplace of the mystery ship *Mary Celeste*.

Moose Island was the only one of the five ever to be inhabited and carries with it the most tangible tale of intrigue. Early in the 1800s John Ruff, a Scotsman, settled this outpost with his family. He cleared much of the forest and established a modest mixed farm, supplying the coastal village with produce, wood and charcoal. He was reputed to be a hard, cruel person, and rumours circulated that he abused his wife and children. When he died a violent death, suspicions arose that he had been murdered by his sons, but a controversial trial led to their acquittal. Afterwards the family moved to the mainland, carrying the unresolved mystery with them. Legend has it that John Ruff's spirit walks the overgrown fields in search of vengeance on misty, moonless nights.

Power of the Tides

I returned to these secretive islands of my youth with the uncertainty bred by earlier innocence only partly dissipated. They were closer to shore than I had imagined but retained the aura of obscure invincibility. I was warned not to take a canoe. I was reminded of the tides and of a schoolmate who, while out duck hunting, had been surrounded and carried away. For if any place symbolizes the tremendous power of tidal movement, it is the Bay of Fundy. Twice a day, billions of tons of saltwater surge into this funnel separating the provinces of Nova Scotia and New Brunswick. In the upper reaches they create the highest tides on Earth. Around these islands they can exceed 14 metres!

Such a phenomenon is taken lightly at one's own peril. From my vantage point on Long Island, I could follow the chimerical patterns of the currents as they swept over open bars, dancing and swirling, constantly modifying abstract patterns before finally settling down in deepening water. The expansive flats, surrounding and connecting islands, disappeared into the clouded ripples and eddies of an ever-changing seascape, which rolled right up to the hayfields.

The incessant attack of water (and, in winter, ice) has gradually taken a toll on the exposed shoreline. Soft sandstone and glacial till are readily removed and distributed in beaches and bars that are seldom the same one year to the next. Even the resistant basalt has been cut and moulded. Pinnacle Island, once surrounded by a ring of spires (depicted in old paintings), now has only a few monolithic towers at its western tip. Caves and arches continue

to etch into the cliffs behind the huge blocks that girdle the base.

At low tide you can walk around all the islands, and between some of them — as if the waters had parted. All that's missing are the columns of chariots following a fleeing people. Seaweed, shellfish and crustaceans of all types clutter and colour the bed, an open-air laboratory for biology students and naturalists.

With the ocean and its effects so omnipresent, it may be difficult to imagine its being otherwise. However, it was, and radically so. Millions of years ago, when the days were shorter and the atmosphere was of another composition, our world would have been unrecognizable. The continents gathered together as one massive supercontinent, where they remained for eons, jostling for position. When the individual plates of the Earth's crust finally began to shift apart again, a large rift valley opened, extending all the way down to what was to become the eastern seaboard of North America. The sands and silts of adjoining mountains (e.g., the Appalachians) accumulated, and when climatic change emptied the rivers and dried the lakes, the particles oxidized into the reddish-brown colour so characteristic of the landscape today. It became an arid desert. As continental migration progressed, faults and fissures cracked the earth's surface. Volcanic eruptions repeatedly spewed forth lava until layers of dark basalt hundreds of metres thick covered the entire valley floor. The northern edge of this tectonic plate slipped ahead, and debris continued to accumulate on the bed of the future bay. When the continents finally pulled apart and the sea entered, the process of erosion began with a vengeance, augmented in recent geological time by the Ice Age. The large tidal range developed about 5,000 years ago.

Another remnant of this tortuous geological past is found within the frozen lava. Jasper, agate and amethyst will yield to the keen eye or sharp rock pick, along the base of the basalt scarp. Expanding gasses formed chambers in the liquid rock, into which minerals found their way and crystallized into colourful networks. Each year, in August, a rockhound festival is held in nearby Parrsboro, where you can buy and sell, or forage with the experts.

Dinosaur Discovery

The Five Islands also unveiled a new chapter in the tale of evolution. In July 1985, Neil Shubin, a biologist from Harvard, was relaxing under a rock outcrop at McCoys Brook, opposite the Five Islands, when he glanced at the cliffs above. What he saw etched into the sandstone was to become part of the world's largest collection of Triassic–Jurassic fossils, including what was then the smallest dinosaur fossil and some rare Trithelodont skulls, a reptile group closely related to mammals and previously found only in Africa. Of even more interest than the quantity of this impressive assemblage was what it told about the evolution of life on earth. It substantiated the theory of the catastrophic extinction of reptiles around 200 million years ago, a time when they dominated the planet. A huge meteor crater near Manicouagan, Québec, has been dated to this period, lending support to the extraterrestrial origin of these mass extinctions.

I often return to Five Islands, but not for gemstones, fossils or even mythical treasure. Rather, for the colours, textures and forms, the chameleon-like land/seascape. And also for the peaceful isolation in a tiny paradise all my own, one that even the errant clamdiggers cannot disturb.

The Bay of Fundy is a special challenge to the paddler, a region full of contrasts and unlike all other coastal waters on the eastern seaboard. During calm summer days it more nearly resembles a vast, tranquil lake than the sea. There is no swell, nor even the hint of a surf, especially around the Five Islands in the Minas Basin. The currents seem benign, and the action around

headlands and over shoals is modest. However, such calm is an often short-lived, and with the wind comes a seething cauldron of conflicting currents and standing waves. This, mixed with cold water (though the Minas Basin is often warmer than the coastline of Maine), creates a place best avoided, even by the experienced paddler.

Campsites are a tad scarce. Moose Island is no problem, but elsewhere you may be restricted to a beach that could disappear, along with you, following a full moon. Consider the provincial park on Economy Mountain (also a good launching point). From there, you can explore the islands on day-long outings.

This is also a novel realm where time seems to speed up. A casual lunch break demands constant alertness if you don't want to pursue your craft down the bay. Or, conversely, if the tide is ebbing, you might have to transport a fully laden canoe over glistening, ankle-straining seaweed and angular rock to a waterline that is receding hundreds of metres per hour. These extremes are difficult to internalize for someone accustomed to a more moderate range of the Atlantic, and even more so for the lake paddler. Experience tempered by caution is essential.

Nova Scotia Waterways
Confessions of a Know-It-All, or Why Take a Clinic?

Sheena Masson

It was a warm day in May, and a friend and I had just put in on the Waughs River near Tatamagouche. The upper Waughs is too stony to paddle in the summer, but in the spring it's a two-hour stretch of Class I and II rapids, ledges and standing waves. Nothing major — just a bit of spring tonic for a couple of intermediate canoeists.

Ahead of us we saw the main channel narrow, deepen and turn to the left around a gravel bar. More importantly, on the right side of the bend was a large tree in the water about 3 metres from shore. I steered the aluminum canoe to the left, away from this obstacle, which of course slammed us sideways into the tree. We half-tipped and took on water. The impact was hard enough to dent the Grumman and cause my friend, who was in the bow, to drop his paddle.

More seasoned canoeists will understand why this happened and that, in my situation, I should have actually been steering toward the tree. This became clear after I took a Level III whitewater course with Canoe Nova Scotia. But more on that in a minute.

I've heard similar stories from occasional canoeists like myself, out for a pleasant river trip, who suddenly find themselves literally in over their heads. This is very frightening. Canoes are destroyed, gear is lost, and lives are endangered. My experience was minor by comparison, but it was enough to shake me up.

Why does this happen? I'm sure there are lots of reasons. In my case it was lack of whitewater skills and, I must confess, an attitude that needed adjustment.

My canoeing background is probably quite similar to that of many other canoe enthusiasts in this province. Most of my paddling has been essentially flatwater, since whitewater time in Nova Scotia is short and sweet. I often go upstream and then down the gentle tidal sections of the river along the North Shore, where I live. Since we don't have much in the way of lakes around here, I also paddle on the ocean, usually in calm water.

Despite that experience on the Waughs River, I tempted the Fates and went on a few other river trips, including two more on the Waughs (we portaged around the tree by crossing the gravel bar). I was feeling pretty confident again. I thought I knew how to get down a river. I was something of a know-it-all, though in reality I knew very few strokes and little about reading a river.

Bad Habits

I began to see the error of my ways after my friend lent me a copy of *Path of the Paddle* by Bill Mason, and I realized there was much more to this white-water paddling than I had ever imagined. A little later I spent an afternoon on the Wallace River with Scott Maston, a skilled paddler and nephew of veteran paddler George Maston. As we ferried easily back and forth and turned into eddies, I saw the folly of my ways. My approach in fast water had been to use the paddle like a rudder and yell instructions at the muscle up in the bow (perhaps I picked this up from my coxing days with the Dalhousie rowing team). This is a limiting technique in a canoe.

That day on the Wallace we let the river do the work. I decided it was time to learn more about paddling. I knew that Canoe Nova Scotia offered clinics, so I attended a whitewater clinic on the LeHave River and learned more about current dynamics as we set the angle of the canoe and shot across the river. The clinic began with an evening talk about river hydrology (how water moves in a river) and manoeuvres such as pointing toward that tree on the Waughs River, which is admittedly against our natural instincts. The increased flow of water on the right side would have pushed the bow to the left and downstream, away from danger.

Over the weekend we practised braces, bow cuts, peel-outs and other strokes and manoeuvres, and then we applied all we had learned in a small hydraulic (an upstream rotating wave). We also spent a lot of time on what to do if you flip over, and the right way to float downstream in a current. For the grand finale, we all took turns rescuing each other. It will take a few more clinics and river trips before the moves come naturally, but I am definitely prepared for an emergency.

Like many other paddlers, my whitewater trips had always been bow-first, downstream all the way. I had never once thought about turning my canoe upstream and playing in the rapids! Not only did I learn more about canoe control, I discovered a new way to have fun. I'm still a downstream canoe-tripper at heart, but this new discovery is a great way to liven up a trip.

A final word about flatwater clinics. I got my Level I and II flatwater certification at a one-day clinic. I found it to be an excellent place to start,

even though I had been paddling for years. I relearned the basic strokes, and again there was an emphasis on safety and rescue techniques.

So what did I learn in a Level III flatwater clinic? The clinic I attended at Kejimkujik National Park was one day of tandem paddling with a review of the basic strokes followed by a day of solo strokes. Until that clinic, I thought solo paddling was something you did if you couldn't find anyone else to paddle with. I had never tried it. What are solo strokes, I thought?

This was another eye opener. Here were all these canoes with just one person in each, and they were sitting way over on one side in the middle of their canoes with the gunwales just about touching the water. Over the weekend I realized what a skilled solo paddler can do — move the canoe sideways, pirouette around the paddle, and turn gracefully with a little forward momentum. Meditation in motion. If whitewater paddling is slam-dancing, solo flatwater paddling is ballet. I had discovered another way to have fun instead of just crossing the lake.

The instructors showed us more strokes than I could learn in two days, and I didn't get my Level III flatwater certification. That's okay. Some people take the clinics two or three times before they pass. I'll be back.

P.S. Not long ago I went down the Waughs River again. This time it was with Gerry Oickle, a Canoe Nova Scotia instructor who teaches in the Kedgie area. Instead of steering to the left, we headed straight for the tree. It worked.

P.E.I.'s North Shore
Far from the Madding Crowd

Scott Cunningham

I ALMOST STEPPED INTO IT WITH MY BARE AND SUSCEPTIBLE FEET WHEN
the sudden warning came from behind: "Don't move!" With a start, I looked
down at the seemingly innocuous expanse of sand and scattered vegetation.
I had stopped just in time. Before me, reaching back to the dunes, were hundreds of short, woody shrubs that would have meant days of misery if I had
blundered only a few feet further. Poison ivy! Its shiny green trifoliate leaves
identified it immediately, once my attention was focused. But I never
expected to encounter it on a coastal paddling trip. Poison ivy is rare along
the rugged and rocky eastern shore of Nova Scotia, where my ramblings usually lead me. However, I was to come across much that was different during
this trip along Prince Edward Island's north shore.

I had often thought of making a trip to the island with canoe in tow, but
I never took the time. The region didn't strike me as particularly interesting
from a coastal paddler's perspective. It wasn't that I didn't know the
province. On the contrary, I knew it well. I had lived there once and, as a
kid, my summers were spent digging for clams and constructing sandcastles
on beaches that stretched well beyond the horizon. It was a great place to
bask in the sun, play a little beach volleyball or bury my reluctant pooch
neck-deep in the sand, but I recalled little that would maintain my interest
during an extended paddle. Or so I thought.

My childhood memories were selective. I didn't see, or have a chance to
appreciate, the variety of landforms and seascapes — the shallow bays and
salt marshes, the steep, stratified cliffs, or the large, deserted dune islands.
This all had to wait until potential stardom and a regional television network, looking for a novel theme for a program on the northern shore, enticed
me and my craft across the strait to Canada's garden province. It was to be a
memorable trip.

P.E.I. is a large, convoluted crescent nestled in the Gulf of St. Lawrence
only a few kilometres from the shores of Nova Scotia and New Brunswick. Its
characteristic red soil was deposited during the Permian era, over 250 million
years ago, before the dinosaurs dominated the planet. At that time the entire

gulf was a huge delta that served as a basin for the eroded material from the surrounding mountains. The climate was dryer than in earlier carboniferous periods, and the vegetation wasn't dense enough to produce the coal beds common in the older strata of the mainland. High temperatures and an arid environment oxidized the minerals, especially iron, and the result is the deep red sandstone that forms the bedrock of the island. The loosely cemented grains eroded away easily to create abrupt escarpments, beaches and sandbars, and the rich, colourful soil for which P.E.I. is famous.

The island's north shore is a popular tourist destination, and the national park draws vacationers from across North America. Each summer over a million people converge on this narrow strip of sand and warm water, filling campgrounds and cottages to capacity. But there is more than beaches on this coast, and the stretch from Cavendish to Alberton combines a variety of features that will satisfy even the most demanding paddler.

My week-long trip began at North Rustico, where the sheltered bay opens a safe passage through the surf, common on the gulf shore. Bobbing on the gentle swells just beyond the breakers, our small flotilla followed the low cliffs of layered sandstone, weaving toward the dune system at Cavendish. Here, minute waterfalls occasionally spill from the aquifer where it cuts the escarpment, a source of fresh drinking water. Guillemot roosts lie concealed in the crevices of the serrated cliff face. These black-and-white birds with narrow bills circle around to find out what is going on, their stubby, short wings beating rapidly to keep them just barely above the surface of the water.

Green Gables

At Cavendish the red-and-white striped lifeguard tower and supervised swimming area are less prominent when viewed from a canoe, 100 metres from shore. The crowds don't seem as significant, either, dwarfed as they are by the extensive coastline. Behind the sunbathers and swimmers, the village of Cavendish has changed considerably since the days of my youth, and commercialization has descended upon this once-quiet hamlet. A fantasyland-like world has developed, with Green Gables the centre attraction. The park, though, is well managed and the facilities are excellent. For those with a naturalist bent, wooden walkways guide visitors through the distinctive biological systems of the area, complete with interpretive panels. The park staff also offer films and slide shows that provide an insight into this dynamic coastline.

After the main beach we leave the other tourists to follow the dunes stretching westward to Blooming Point. This long, undulating mass of sand

and beach grass is, as with similar areas around the island, in a constant state of flux. Over the past 30 years it has migrated a few hundred metres into New London Bay. The beach has a brownish tinge, since the hematite, which binds the sand to form rock and is responsible for its intense colour, is washed away in the seawater. Here, the endangered piping plover can nest in relative safety, far from the wandering feet of beach lovers and their furry friends. But its unfortunate habit of setting up "home" in competition with blankets and towels may eventually prove to be its undoing.

The national park ends at Blooming Point, and across the narrow channel, which should be traversed with caution, the scenery changes radically. Gone are the seemingly endless sandy shores, and again we confront the cliffs, this time the highest in the province. We have arrived at Cape Tryon.

The Rockies this is not, but while paddling along the wave-cut base of the overhanging escarpment, one feels an eternity away from the crowds of Cavendish. The ledges, fashioned from the horizontally layered strata, provide an ideal site for the largest cormorant colony in the province, and the white excrement draping the rock gives the impression of snow-covered peaks. This rugged shoreline continues up Malpeque Bay, interrupted along the way by several broad coves. Towering flowerpot islands, sculpted caves and arches adorn the route, and the colours, contours and textures of the landscape are reminiscent of a desert, a patch of the Sahara sandwiched between the sea and a garden.

Malpeque Bay is a special place. The shallow waters are even warmer than in the gulf, and the barrier dunes protect the bay from the fury of storms. It is famous for the Malpeque oyster — the gourmet mollusk by which all others are judged. If you want to collect a few clams or mussels, pay attention to the tides or you could possibly find yourself sharing the bottom with them — a kilometre from firm ground. Take along a good chart.

Sand Dune Islands

Unique to this part of the coast are the long, narrow sand dune islands that form a bar across the entrance of Malpeque Bay and continue on to Alberton. This is where the coastline was situated not so long ago, when the sea level was lower. It is continually changing with the forces of erosion. The new coast-line will eventually disappear, as will all of P.E.I., under the waters of the gulf.

Hog Island, the largest of the barrier islands, is a mini-paradise. It has all the beach of Cavendish, but without the people. Sand dunes, standing 15 metres high and stretching over 15 kilometres, front a landscape of blowouts, salt marshes and heath barrens, and provide an excellent opportunity to study the active physical and biological processes that mould much of P.E.I.'s north-ern shore. The contrast with the rugged Atlantic coast of Nova Scotia is total. I spotted more shorebirds here in one day than I usually see in an entire sum-mer near my home in Nova Scotia: sandpipers, plovers, curlews, yellowlegs as well as the ubiquitous gull and cormorants flying back to the tryon colony. And, in among the beach grass, which keeps the sand in place, the trail of a red fox, king of the dunes, weaves back toward the patches of bearberry.

These mounds of sand opposing the gulf seem to go on forever, and it is a great place to play in the surf. If the going gets too tough, you don't have to worry about breaking up your boat or yourself while landing. Absent are the slippery, algae-covered rocks. It is also an easy portage over the Conway Nar-rows, which offers a sheltered route into Cascumpec Bay, a smaller version of Malpeque. The temperature of the saltwater, reputed to be the warmest north of the Carolinas, is a welcome treat for coastal paddlers (including those from the Great Lakes) who are always conscious of the dangers of an unexpected spill.

By the end of the week we had arrived at the picturesque village of Alber-ton, and the end of the voyage. But I plan to return soon. P.E.I. is the country's smallest province, a quarter the size of Vancouver Island. Its population of 125,000 inhabitants is less than that of a small city. But the hospitality of the people and its pastoral charm lend it a distinctive character. In addition to the northern shore, there are other places where you can savour the beauty of the isle in relative isolation, many of them ideally suited for the paddler.

Nepisiguit River
The River Strikes Back

"Miramichi" Bill Palmer

How Doug Shippey and I got together on this junket escapes my memory. He was very keen to experience some canoeing and had heard I was going and came aboard. I guess that must have been it. Well, we got together and started planning and getting gear together. The north end of Bathurst Lake, in northern New Brunswick, would be our put-in spot. The water would be high and fast, so any upriver travel would require a great deal of poling, portaging and a lot of time we didn't have.

We finally departed with a friend who would drive the wagon back to Fredericton. We eventually arrived at Bathurst Lake and put my old 16-foot Chestnut in the water. (I purchased the canoe from an outfitter on the Miramichi River; I tossed a coin to determine whether I would pay $30 or $40. I lost.) We loaded the canoe — as usual we had enough gear to open a hardware store and enough grub, or "stogins" as the woodsmen call it, to feed several canoeists. Doug's old Duluth pack looked about the size of a Volkswagen beetle. With Doug over six feet and pretty hefty and me weighing 140, we had a small problem with balance. Doug had not done much stern paddling, so it was decided that I stern. We shifted cargo until we were balanced, after a fashion. A bit nose heavy, but we were able to move.

We departed shore and were a bit dismayed to find that while the ice had broken up, it had not yet departed the lake. Fortunately, the ice was a bit scattered and the current had made a path to the outlet into Camp Lake, where we arrived and proceeded in good fashion.

The ice in Camp Lake (named after the log cabins belonging to an outfitter) was scattered in large rafts, some quite large. These were, mercifully, spread well out, so progress was okay. There were some people at the log cabins, and we waved a greeting. We were signalled by an elderly lady to come to a small dock, where she treated us to a cup of tea. A normal procedure here. We really appreciated this, as it was quite cold.

We moved along and got into Teneriffe Lake in about 20 minutes. Lots of ice but clear enough to be no problem. We worked our way down the lake to the dead waters of the Nepisiguit, a long, wide stretch of shallow water.

Alongside is a moose bog, a half-kilometre wide and very shallow. It can, however, be paddled by good mudslingers. As we worked our way along this bog we spied a dark mass ahead. It was a large, bloated moose floating amidst the ice pans, probably a casualty of the rotten spring ice. Regrettably, this is all too common here and on the Miramichi.

Doug did not seem very impressed. At the end of this stretch was the entrance to the Nepisiguit River. We stopped at a suitable place, unloaded and pulled the canoe up. We turned the canoe over, put one end between two trees, and our "table" was ready. We got a fire started. I gave Doug the "bilging" can to get water, but he flatly refused. The moose was still in sight. We compromised and went to a brook, fittingly called Moose Brook, about 15 metres away and flowing into the Nepisiguit. We had supper, cleaned up and decided to get some trout for breakfast. I fished Moose Brook while Doug cleaned the trout. We had a dozen in no time. We bagged them and hung them in a big maple, for varmint-proofing, for the night.

I have visited this place several times since this trip, and, unfortunately, it has been set up as a camp spot with a refuse barrel, table, etc. The bears regularly play soccer with the barrel. Meanwhile, campers leave all sorts of debris strewn about — the usual slop imprint on the environment. It takes about an hour to tidy up, and I'm always sure it will be littered again in a day or two.

We got up smartly at daybreak, had a panful of trout, cooked with bacon, and lots of tea. Thus, with the inner man at peace with the world, we packed up and resumed our journey. The water was high and fast, and fortunately the ice hadn't got into the river in any great quantity. We were able to paddle around most obstacles. The river smoothed out a bit and became clearer. It finally registered in my feeble mind that we were moving rapidly. I had talked to some old-timers about the bad rapids on this river and had been warned about Indian Falls, a series of cataracts especially threatening in high water. There is a 5-kilometre portage around it. I was somewhat less than happy about such a long portage.

An Accident Waiting to Happen

The next little while was fairly quiet and we were pooh-poohing the alleged difficulties when we heard turbulent water ahead. We pulled ashore and looked it over. The first hundred metres looked okay, so riding a crest of foolish invincibility, we picked the best route and paddled on. We made it through with only a few buckets of water sloshing around in the bottom of the canoe. In our false sense of security, we felt we had avoided the dreaded portage, even though the portage path was clearly visible ahead (it had been worn deep by thousands of feet over hundreds of years). Incredible as it seems now, we completely disregarded the obvious. We scouted the next stretch of river and blithely agreed to run it. Dead ahead was a sluice between huge, jagged rocks, and just beyond, a monster haystack. We were fools even to be looking at this stretch; we should have been portaging. Instead, our plan was to run through the middle of the sluice then haul hard left to avoid the haystack.

We climbed into our canoe — an accident going somewhere to happen — and started down the sluice. We completely lost control. Doug hit the dreaded haystack dead on and disappeared. I followed. We surfaced upright, but full of water. We both screamed "driver ashore" and paddled as hard and carefully as our scared and soaked carcasses could manage.

About 25 metres from shore we hit a ledge broadside. The canoe tipped upstream, as usual, and as Doug attempted to secure us, he was caught between the canoe and the ledge. The stern was projecting out into the current, and then I was thrown overboard. I tried to hang onto the canoe but lost my grip and sailed downstream. Fortunately, Doug was able to grab the painter and leap ashore, while I finally grabbed a rock and climbed on. We lost a lot of our gear, including cameras, even though some was tied in.

As I stood on the rock I realized I was vibrating. Man, it was cold! It appeared to be about 7 metres to shore, but in one leap I landed on half land and was scrambling up the riverbank. I took my clothes off and Doug wrung them out. As I had no dry gear I had to put the wet clothes on again. The canoe was banged up a bit, but not too bad. We scurried about to gather wood for a fire when a truck came along on the road that parallels the river. We were informed that there was a camp about a kilometre down the road. Away we went to the camp.

We were lucky. The camp was open and I knew the owner, my former army commander. Doug and I peeled off our clothes, were given blankets and treated to several libations of tomato juice spiced with life-saving tonic. Warmth returned at an astounding rate.

There was a phone so we called our contact at Bathurst. He came out immediately with a friend who he claimed was an expert canoeist. We agreed that the "expert" would bring the canoe down to the camp while Doug and I dried out. Our contact took the "expert" to the canoe and they gathered what was left of our gear, put it into the truck, and our contact returned to the camp.

Meanwhile, the "expert" lost the canoe in another set of rapids and it tumbled among the rocks. It was really trashed. I have never seen a canoe open up like a pea pod, bow and stern wide open. The remains are at my camp on the Miramichi. They stand as a monument to stupidity and mental unpreparedness for canoe-tripping.

L'Eau Claire River
Going with Nature

Story provided by Don Smith, Valley Ventures, Deep River, Ontario

AFTER TWO DAYS OF DRIVING AND A THREE-HOUR FLIGHT IN FROM Radison, we were happy to set up camp where we had landed. We could have paddled, but the magic of the land held us. No sound but for a gentle breeze in the trees, with clear blue skies overhead, hills and lakes all around. "Ah, if I could put into words the music which I hear," wrote Thoreau.

It was good to be back in Canada, and to be starting out on another trip with Sharon and Don, good friends from Valley Ventures, and joined this year by Alastair, who had flown out with me from England.

The L'Eau Claire is not a long river but descends rapidly through its 135-kilometre length, draining Lake L'Eau Claire into Lake Guillaume–Delisle in northern Québec. It is a region of subarctic and tundra. We were attracted by its remoteness, whitewater, and the possibility of seeing beluga whales and seals at the end of the trip.

Caribou could be seen against the skyline, and they drew us like a magnet. We climbed the hills and gazed down on a vast world of lakes and craggy outcrops. Antlers were found, but the caribou had moved on.

Next morning, we were up early to enjoy a breakfast feast — the original natural blueberry camp Pop Tart. To really enjoy this Canadian treat you must soak your pita bread overnight in dew, collected on an upturned canoe, before filling with fresh berries gathered from the hillside. A little frying is required to bring out the flavour.

Canoeing was postponed until we had searched again for caribou. From the campsite we had spotted a small herd grazing high up, but where had they gone? Armed with cameras, we hunted the hills, but not a sign of them. Then, suddenly, above us stood a caribou, its head of antlers in full splendour silhouetted against the skyline. We moved forward silently, but as soon as we got close he was off. We gave chase, but the animal proved illusive.

Time to leave and head downriver. Gentle paddling eased us into our journey. The water was clear and flowed swiftly. We approached the first set of rapids with caution, but they presented no problem. We relaxed and settled into an easy rhythm. Lunch was eaten as we glided along.

After 8 kilometres we encountered a more serious set of rapids. They required careful scouting. A route down the right, avoiding the holes and curling waves, was decided upon. Don and Sharon led the way. Alastair and I followed but lacked a little precision and left it too late to decide whether to go left or right of two large rocks that loomed ahead. The bow caught and we spun into the gap, kept on turning — and slid down the rest of the rapids backwards.

Sailing Along

The river opened into a lake and we took advantage of the wind by rigging the tarp as a sail. We sat back, soaked in the sun and enjoyed a gorp break as we sailed along, letting the wind do the work.

Ahead, the river narrowed and picked up speed as it dropped over a series of small ledges. The waves looked too large to run. As no easy portage trail could be found, we decided to float the canoes down a side stream, a simple solution that quickly had us wading and heaving the boats over rocks and branches that didn't want to bend.

That evening we stretched out beside the campfire, reflecting on the pleasures of the day. As we looked up at the stars, a curtain of light formed over us, parted and swirled away only to reform and gradually open the full panorama of the northern lights before us. The rugged hills made a perfect stage.

Fresh trout for breakfast. Who says fishing and canoeing don't go together? On the water by nine. The small rapids and swifts made paddling easy, but as the morning wore on, the hills began to close in and the river narrowed again. Ahead lay the first major set of rapids of the trip, the river dropping over three ledges — very spectacular and impossible to paddle through.

The portage trail led up over the rocks to the left. The ground was marshy and slippery in places. The temperature was close to 30 degrees Celsius, and we were glad for a lunch stop before running the tail of the rapids. Looking back upstream, the rapids were even more impressive, but that portage — it was hard going. A little taste of what was to come!

By midday the next day we were once again scrambling over the hills with canoes and kit on our backs. Granite rocks and caribou moss were a treacherous combination at times. At this point, the river splits as it flows around a large island, dropping over a series of falls. Fortunately, we were able to line down in a few places; the portaging was far more difficult than anticipated. Ahead, the river rejoined its other branch, falling in a cloud of spray. We landed below the falls and climbed high into the hills. Below, the L'Eau

Claire tumbled down among the rocks. All around was a magnificent vista of rugged hills and lakes. Unspoiled beauty and power.

That night we camped on an island overlooking the river as it dropped over a small falls. Alastair joined Sharon and Don in fishing for breakfast, and they quickly landed a good catch of succulent trout. The campfire blazed and we celebrated the L'Eau Claire with sparklers and watched the stars appear.

Mist shrouded the hills and trees as we emerged from our tents. The sound of the river was hushed and slowly the sun burned through as we made our way downriver. A peaceful start that was soon forgotten as once again we struggled along the portage trail. It was hot and getting hotter. The trail was not really there — just rock and moss interspersed with bog. We scrambled and slid to the bottom of each rapids, taking every opportunity to line or lift the canoes over ledges. Anything to avoid portaging, but the last rapids of the day left us with no choice.

By halfway we'd had enough and called a halt. Not an ideal spot, but we managed to pitch the tents on the moss-covered rocks. A quick meal of pasta and tuna was devoured and, after copious cups of tea and coffee, we turned in early.

Sleep came easily but didn't last long. Howling winds and crashing gear woke us. No one wanted to move, but as the tent began to lift, quick action was called for. Morning brought no relief from the weather. We pushed into strong winds and drifting rain. We planned to camp at the start of the first long portage, but a sheltered site among the trees changed our minds. The ground was level and dry. We put the tents up and slept, had something to eat, and then slept some more.

As we broke camp, two caribou approached through the bush. Hardly daring to move, we waited for them to get closer, but they must have sensed our presence because they turned toward the river and swam majestically to the far side. Heads held high and antlers aloft, they made an impressive sight as they moved effortlessly through the water. Ahead lay the most spectacular section of the L'Eau Claire — a 50-metre waterfall plunging into a narrow gorge 2.5 kilometres long. The river descended rapidly over a series of ledges and falls. Needless to say, it is necessary to portage the whole of its length.

Portage from Hell

The sky was overcast and a light drizzle fell as we heaved gear and canoes onto tired shoulders and started our slow ascent away from the river. By midday we had climbed through thick willow and alders, and were able to look

down on those falls. Great clouds of spray rose from below and drifted across the hills. The sun had eventually broken through and turned the mist into a rainbow of colour. At moments like these, where the wild places are at their best, pain is forgotten.

As the afternoon wore on, the air got hotter and the terrain more difficult. There was no trail to follow, just thick wood and scrub to climb over. At times it was easier to use the canoes as sledges and force a route through the alders. As soon as we rested, the blackflies descended and forced us to move on. By 5:00 P.M. we had only managed to cover half the distance. We'd done enough, so we camped on a ledge with the ridge towering above us.

Woke up and began portaging. Below, the river could be seen winding through the gorge to run out into a sandy bay. At the end of the ridge, we loaded the canoes with all the gear and fitted the drag ropes. With a good heave, we descended quickly through the trees. It seemed to take forever to reach the river, but what a relief to be back in the canoes and be taken by the flow.

Eight kilometres to paddle before the final obstacle on the river. A 2.5-kilometre portage over the tundra hills. The forest is dense along each side of the river, and the portage necessary to avoid 3 kilometres of rapids that flow into Lake Guillaume–Delisle. All we had to do was climb the vertical rise on the right and down into the lake's sandy bay. If we had found somewhere to land where it had been possible to climb the vertical rise carrying the canoes and equipment, it might have gone according to plan. We gave up the struggle after two hours of wasted effort and opted to line down the left bank.

No textbook lining here. We waded, nearly swam, scrambled, and slipped our way down the river. Running out of daylight, we camped as best we could among the alders, perched on a narrow ledge with the river rushing below. The rest of the rapid was lined without mishap, but the river constantly threatened to take control and wash us from our precarious foothold on the bank and riverbed.

That night we relaxed in an idyllic spot overlooking the lake. A waterfall sparkled in the evening sun and, as it set, the sky turned a rich red and gold. After two really hard days, it was a pleasure to head out across the lake through crystal-clear water. We wanted to reach the far shore so that we could hike across the headland and look out on Hudson Bay, but a strong headwind blew up and forced us to seek shelter in a bay. Time was against us. We were due to fly out the next day. Still, spirits were high and we could get up early and hike to the top of the cliffs and possibly spot belugas.

Where's the Plane?

We spent the day searching the lake for seals and whales, and the sky for a plane. Late in the afternoon a plane flew over but didn't land and we resigned ourselves to another night camping on the lakeshore. Next morning, we decided to break camp and head back along the south shore and make use of the delay to explore an old Hudson Bay trading post.

The morning calm gave way to high winds and breaking waves. Keeping close to the shore, we crept toward the trading post. Rain began to fall and the waves threatened to swamp the canoes. A black bear watched our progress from the beach before wandering off into the bush, a rare sight that gave us a lift as we surfed through the waves to land on the beach below the old settlement. There were half a dozen buildings in varying states of disrepair. Fortunately, the old church was reasonably sound and dry. We moved in. This was to be home for three days.

We occupied ourselves as best we could by searching the old buildings and surrounding terraces while we waited for the weather to clear. Saturday was calm, and we sat on the beach waiting for a plane to fly in. Fires were lit and the emergency transmitter triggered. Time dragged, everybody was restless, but there was no elation when the plane flew in just after 4:00 P.M.

On the way back to Deep River, we talked about returning to the L'Eau Claire — a land of wild beauty waiting to be explored.

George River
Fear and Loathing from Shefferville to Ungava Bay

Gino Bergeron
Translated from French by Gaye Wadham

I WAKE UP, NUMB WITH COLD. THE TARP, STRETCHED FROM THE CANOE TO the ground, isn't enough to protect us from the torrents of rain. My sleeping bag hasn't been dry for four days. Why did I decide that we could live without a tent? Who knows why we make these decisions? Running down from the land of the Montagnais and the Naskapis to the seas of the Inuit, the George River represents, for me, the road to the Far North. A trip that flows over 600 kilometres allows me to visit the meanders and undertows of my fears.

In mid-August 1988, three of us — Alain, 27, from Nice, France; Monfreid, 19, from Paris; and me, 24, from Lac St-Jean, Québec — are crammed into my old Renault. We are already exhausted after driving 1,000 kilometres from Montréal to Sept-Îles, on the lower north shore of the St. Lawrence River. A 12-hour train ride the next day takes us to Shefferville, 600 kilometres further north.

Just four days into the trip, and not yet even on the George River, Monfreid abandons us and joins another group we have met.

We are two.

After 200 kilometres on the DePas River, we are thrown onto the George River. From this point there are 400 kilometres of river to Kangiqsualujjuaq, on Ungava Bay. Everything is bigger here — the landscape, the rapids, the wind. On Lac de la Hutte Sauvage the wind blows in gusts up to 70 kilometres per hour. Towards noon, hugging the shore and shaken by the waves, our arm muscles are so tired. We have paddled like frenzied demons for an hour and only covered 500 metres. We stop and rest. Waiting under the shelter of the hastily erected tarp, morale is at its lowest. The George doesn't seem to want us. We discuss abandoning the expedition at the next *pourvoirie* (a series of hunting-fishing camps or stations throughout northern Québec). We have not yet acquired patience. We wait until 4:00 P.M., when the wind lets up slightly. We set off again into a still very strong wind.

We are hurting.

At 8:00 P.M., still on the river and anxious to cover more kilometres, we move away from shore in order to make a direct line to Point Wedge as quickly as possible. The uneven topography of the river valley creates a strong, localized wind that causes deep, choppy waves to slam the side of our canoe. Two kilometres from shore, our impatience turns to anger and our paddle strokes become frantic. The canoe takes on water with each wave. I'm really frightened. The water is 7 degrees Celsius, but I don't want to think about getting swamped in such a wind. My muscles hurt, and the darkness is complete.

We finally get to a point of land where the waves are less alarming. Somewhat protected, we bail the canoe. My fear and guilt bring to mind a single phrase: "Thank God." But because I'm so tense and I'm not thinking rationally, we decide to round the point.

Madness.

The point, which is abrupt and about 30 metres high, forms a barrier from the huge waves coming out of the north. We round the point and the waves lift us up 2 metres before breaking on the rocks behind us. We try to paddle eastward into the wind. Alain, who is over 200 pounds, is in the bow, and he is being tossed up and down like a rag doll. The canoe fills up a little bit more with each wave until we are half full; a final wave fills the canoe completely. We are swamped. Four or five more waves push us near shore. Fortunately, we are able to stand in the shallow water. We scream in anger but are able to get the canoe out of the water by sliding and bumping it up the rocks. We climb the rocky 45-degree slope and haul the canoe up to safety. It is completely black. Without a fire, I fall asleep, in my sleeping bag, huddled between two rocks. My bag provides no warmth, so I pull on a large green plastic bag in a desperate effort to get warm. Alain, who is just as wretchedly uncomfortable, is under the tarp further up the slope. The night is very long.

Around 4:00 A.M. everything is calm. Without a bite to eat, we are back on the water to find a site where we can rest and dry out. We do. The following 40 kilometres are calmer, and we begin to appreciate the spectacular landscape. The peace and quiet don't last long, however. We are surprised by the first set of rapids on the George. What seems, from far away, to be a few ripples without a lot of rocks are in fact titanic waves. Incredibly, we stay upright and survive the 3 kilometres of powerful whitewater. We should have heeded the advice of the guides we met earlier — we should have lined the rapids. We are arrogant and stupid.

Below magnificent Helen Falls, we encounter Ungava Bay's infamous tidal zone. As the river gets wider, the sea rushes in and creates a whole new set of water dynamics. Used to a running river, we scramble to understand an oscillating river with over 12 metres of tide as well as sandbars that stretch for more than a kilometre. The tension, which had dissipated during the last few days, reaches new heights. The trees are too small and the wind is too strong. We feel the sting of the cold, humid air from Ungava Bay. Vigilance is in order.

The world of the Inuit — this new geography — welcomes us, insisting that we learn and understand it quickly. Everything is too fast; everything is wonderful. It's August 31, and Kangiqsualujjuaq is only two short hours away. The current and ebbing tide take us there quickly. A real feeling of accomplishment has grown in us.

French River
A Short River with a Long History

Toni Harting

It is a relatively short river, only about 100 kilometres long, but in many aspects a major one. Located some 320 road kilometres north of Toronto, in Ontario's Near North region, the French River connects Lake Nipissing to Georgian Bay, dropping its waters a modest 19 metres through several attractive rapids and small falls separated by long stretches of quiet water.

But this is by no means your typical river confined to a single stream bed. The French is much more complicated, a true waterway system of delightful intricacy that should warm the hearts of all lovers of recreational canoeing. There is no other river system anywhere that offers such rich diversity of streams, channels, lakes, ponds, bays, gorges, falls, rapids, chutes, flat- and whitewater, forest, bush, islands, swamps, wetlands, beaches and Canadian Shield rock. The French River and the surrounding region present enterprising paddlers — canoeists as well as kayakers and sea kayakers — with a wealth of possibilities for adventure and discovery in an area of exceptional natural beauty, filled with fascinating flora and fauna.

The usefulness of the river as an efficient trade route was discovered many centuries ago by the Aboriginal inhabitants, long before men from Europe crossed its waters. They had invented and developed the highly adaptable birchbark canoe and used this superb craft for countless years to travel the continent's waterways, including the one we now call the French River.

When the first European — probably Étienne Brûlé, who was sent over by the Governor of New France, Samuel de Champlain, to learn the lay of the land and the ways of the Aboriginal peoples — travelled down these waters in 1610 (in the company of Aboriginals, of course, who guided him every step of the way), he could not have imagined in his wildest dreams that his actions would one day contribute to the creation of a vast nation called Canada.

In the centuries following this first tentative encounter with an alien world, thousands upon thousands of adventurous people followed in his path. First there were the explorers and missionaries, then the growing tide of fur traders, who gradually created the economic basis of this country. They all traversed the French River, which was an integral part of the most direct water-based link between Montréal and Georgian Bay, and further south and west, enabling them to penetrate deep into the North American continent. And every one of those travellers used the magnificent birchbark canoe — some more than 36 feet long and 5 feet wide — to transport themselves and their goods up and down the river in the relentless quest for knowledge, souls and profit. These were the glory years of the voyageurs, the tough French-Canadian canoemen who paddled the fur trade canoes on countless North American rivers and lakes.

By the middle of the nineteenth century, the face of the fur trade had changed considerably and canoe traffic along the French River had slowed down. Settlement of the French River region had begun. It was based upon the exploitation of natural resources. Logging became the main industry until its decline in the first decades of the twentieth century.

The use of birchbark canoes for purposes of trade diminished, and recreational canoes, made from canvas-covered wood and other materials, gradually took over the French River, as well as everywhere else. Since then, canoeing on the French River system has become purely recreational, and boats of many sizes, designs, construction and materials are now used by paddlers, from novice to expert.

Canadian Heritage River

To help protect this delicate river system from overdevelopment and misuse, the French River was designated as a Canadian Heritage River in 1986, and in 1989 a major part of the river was made a Provincial Waterway Park. In certain areas there is considerable cottage, resort and residential development. To a large extent, however, especially in the intricate delta where the river empties into Georgian Bay via several outlets, the landscape is virtually unchanged since the times long ago when first the Aboriginal peoples paddled these waters, and later the men from Montréal who frequented the river for more than 200 years.

Significant archaeological and historical evidence of previous use and occupation has been discovered in many places along the river. Paddling these waters gives the modern canoeist a magical feeling of history, as if the fur trade voyageurs are still there, just around the next bend, coming down the river with their huge *canots du maître* loaded with trade goods and people. And one can easily imagine the fast express canoes with their relatively light cargo of mail and messages cutting through the waves, powered to great speed by the 60-strokes-per-minute cadence of the voyageurs. It is a thrilling experience to be able to relive history and touch the country's past so directly by canoeing the same streams and lakes, walking the same portage trails, and camping on the same shores as the fur brigades did so long ago.

For the present-day paddler, getting to the river is quite simple. There are many convenient access points that enable canoeists to visit the whole river system or any part of it for as long as desired. Leisurely trips, from one

hour to one or two weeks or more, can be undertaken to please the tastes of trippers of all levels of experience. Car shuttles are simple to organize but can be avoided by doing a loop trip, several of which are possible. Numerous campsites are located along the length of the river, ranging from primitive to quite comfortable.

Most of the rapids can be run by experienced whitewater paddlers, but all the rapids and falls have relatively short, easy portages around them for those who prefer not to take unnecessary risks. Canoeists who really want to take it easy and still wish to enjoy the magic of the river can make use of a number of lodges, resorts and fishing camps that are available along the spread of the river system.

Trying to describe the extensive and complicated river in the context of this small article is, of course, not feasible. A good way to find out about the paddling possibilities is by talking with knowledgeable people and studying maps, such as the standard 1:50,000-scale topographical maps and especially the French River Provincial Park map distributed in the area by the Friends of the French River Heritage Park.

The following suggestions represent only a few of the longer paddling trips that can be undertaken on the French River system:

⇆ *Starting from one of the marinas at Dokis village, paddle on the island-studded part of the river that is in fact the southwest arm of Lake Nipissing. All flatwater and easy going.*

⇆ *From Dokis, go counter-clockwise around Okikendawt Island, down the Little French River, and up the Main Channel to the historic portage in the Chaudière dam area.*

⇆ *From Dokis, go down the Main Channel all the way to Georgian Bay via one of the several mouths of the river. Take-out at Key River on Highway 69.*

⇆ *From Wolseley Bay to the Five Miles Rapids area, begin with Little Pine Rapid and end at Crooked Rapid; return upriver to Wolseley Bay.*

⇆ *From Wolseley Bay, go around Eighteen Mile Island, down the Main Channel, up the North Channel, and back to Wolseley Bay.*

⇆ *From French River village access points near Highway 69, go around Eighteen Mile Island either clockwise or counter-clockwise.*

⇆ *From French River village access points to Georgian Bay via one of several outlets.*

⇆ *From access points on the Pickerell River near Highway 69 to Georgian Bay via the Pickerell River outlet or other routes.*

⇆ *From Key River on Highway 69 to Georgian Bay islands (a perfect trip for sea kayaks).*

There are many possibilities for exploration of the French River system by canoe or kayak. It is up to each paddler to select the one that is right for his or her aspirations and abilities. The French River is a paddler's dream come true. It is not only a priceless and irreplaceable part of Canada's natural and cultural heritage, but also one of the most scenic and diverse recreational areas in the country. Love and enjoy it with care.

Ottawa River

Moonlight Madness

Paul Mason

THE OTTAWA RIVER HAS MANY MOODS: SERENE FLATWATER SECTIONS that can be whipped into a wind-blown seascape; stretches that pass through urban centres; and whitewater that is equal to the Colorado River for huge mountainous waves. Each year the renowned whitewater near Beachburg, Ontario, attracts boaters from all over eastern North America. Every summer they come with kayaks, rafts, canoes, catarafts, duckies and boogie boards. As well, approximately 40,000 thrill-seeking novices sign on to river trips with six commercial rafting companies.

At the spectacular Beachburg section, the river drops about 30 metres over a distance of approximately 7 kilometres. Here, boaters have a choice of either the Main Channel, consisting of five big rapids and four smaller ones, or the Middle Channel, which has one falls, three major rapids and three riffles. The Middle Channel is the route of choice if the gauge, located on the rock below McCoy Rapids, reads over 8 feet. It is not that the Main Channel is unrunnable above 8 feet — indeed, one of my most memorable trips on the Main Channel occurred when the water completely covered the gauge, indicating a level of at least 25 feet!

On this day the gauge reading was a moderate 1 foot, so we chose to do the Main Channel. A good pre-run warm-up is essential to loosen up your paddling muscles, and it's also a great way to avoid dealing with the upcoming rapids. So there I was, at dusk, sitting in my open canoe above McCoy preoccupied with one of the aforementioned activities. As I contemplated McCoy, two kayakers emerged at the head of the portage trail, on their way back to the put-in after an evening of surfing. They expressed concern that I was paddling alone, but I assured them that my buddy Mark Scriver was around the corner surfing above Phil's Hole. We exchanged comments on the water level, then I waved goodbye and headed off downstream.

(Although this article is not to be taken as a guide to the Ottawa River, a brief account of some notable features may be of interest. Phil's Hole is certainly a notable feature. The preferred route is to surf across a wave in front of the Hole, and technically it's not really a hard move, but the consequences

of missing the surf wreaks havoc on your concentration, hence the nickname "the scary ferry." After passing Phil's, you must work quickly toward the centre "V" through Sandra's Hole, which stretches river-wide at the bottom of McCoy. Riding through on this "V" is definitely the preferred route, if you aren't too fond of big juicy holes.)

Mark and I regrouped below McCoy for the short paddle to Black's Chute (The Lornes). This is usually a good time to take a break, drift along, and perhaps munch on a snack. Not today, though, or more accurately, not this evening. When we put on the river at 7:00 P.M. I expected that we would be doing a little paddling in the dark. In fact, I suppose, if pressed, I would have to admit that this was our unspoken intention. As dusk set in, it was now just a question of how many rapids we would have to run in the dark. I knew it would be truly dark by the time we hit the last two biggies, which even in daylight are impressive enough to keep your attention!

White Knuckle Light

I didn't think they would be any harder at night, as I expected we would be able to see them okay by the light from our white knuckles. By now we had arrived at the second rapid, Black's Chute, which consists of a large "V" that ends in a wave called the Garberator. After blasting through that wave, there is time to roll up and gather your wits before catching a right-hand channel through the second drop. At water levels above 2 feet on the gauge, this second drop is where you'll find a real juicy surfing wave called WA-KI-KI. But for the ultimate surfing experience, I suggest spending some time trying to catch a surf on the Garberator wave itself. Eventually Mark and I were able to draw ourselves away from the Black's Chute playground, knowing that we would soon return. The shoreline was by now a deep black shadow with no definition, so we hustled through the next few riffles to a major rapid called Butcher's Knife. This is a fairly straightforward rapid, provided you take the sneak route on the left side.

This night run was something Mark and I had been discussing for a year or two. While several friends had made evening descents before, they were usually paddling kayaks. I had immediately dismissed them as waterlogged, the paddlers not the kayaks. However, our familiarity with the river had increased over the past two seasons and, having made one or two trips on the river per week for the last month, we felt we were as ready as ever for a night run. The water level was low and there were no nasty obstacles such as sweepers or drift piles. One of the attractions of this section of the Ottawa is that it is relatively free of pinning rocks, undercuts and other captivating geological features, with the exception of the right side of Butcher's Knife. So experienced paddlers consider the Ottawa to be a friendly river. Familiarity is no substitute for common sense, which was disregarded on this occasion. Mark and I realized that by leaving Ottawa after work we could be on the water before dark, squeeze in a night run and then, after catching some shut-eye at the put-in, paddle the river a second time at dawn. That way we could make it to work by noon, only missing half a day of work but getting in two days' worth of paddling. Perfect!

So it was that I now found myself above Hair Rapid, also known as The Normans, squinting against the bright moonlight to pick out Mark's white helmet in the eddy at the bottom. I splashed my face, a ritual that acclimatizes me to the water temperature, I hope. Then I lined up on the downstream "V" and began picking up speed. A few power strokes later, and after lots of bracing, I cruised into the eddy beside Mark. We smiled. The next rapid, Coliseum, is well named; it is the last big one. Running this rapid involves cutting through several diagonal waves to line up a "V" that is messy at best. It twists and plunges under boils and small whirlpools before either pushing your canoe downstream past a hole, or pushing it left into a strong eddy that will carry you around for another dose of the swirlies.

It was now 10:30 P.M. and we were becoming quite adept at sensing the different waves and currents, and reading the rapids by moonlight. I watched Mark run through Coliseum, prepared to offer assistance if necessary, but he "floated" through the usual route with practised ease. Encouraged, I peeled out and started to punch the first diagonal waves in my quest for the "V." But where was it? I blinked then closed my eyes, there wasn't much difference. The moon! It was gone, squelched by a big black cloud. Fortunately, whitewater is aptly named. Spotting a pile of white foam, I quickly pivoted and punched through it to the dark water "V," which carried me directly into the boils. But boils are not white and definitely not friendly. I was not having a good time, and I was now having second thoughts about paddling at night. But once again the old low brace paid off, and I eventually ended up in the calm water with Mark. I could have sworn that I could hear someone giggling in the dark, but as the moon reappeared he had a remarkably straight face.

Our last stop was at Farmer Black's Hole, a small ender spot just before the take-out. I pulled out my camera and we took turns doing enders and pirouettes by moonlight, punctuated by the strobe of the camera flash. Finally satisfied, we headed for shore and shuttled back to the put-in to catch some sleep. As I snuggled down in my sleeping bag, I reflected on the thought that we only had to wait five hours until our next paddling fix.

Whenever you choose to paddle the Ottawa — spring, summer or fall, during the day or at night — expect adrenaline-pumping whitewater and more fun than is currently legal!

Algonquin Park
Where It All Began

David F. Pelly

ALGONQUIN PARK. JUST THE NAME CONJURES UP IMAGES AND EMOTIONS that resonate deep within the soul of many thousands, maybe millions, of Canadians. The impact may be most apparent in our response to the howl of a timber wolf on a moonlit night. But not everyone understands the language this landscape speaks, only because they haven't been there, and it's not obvious from afar. Algonquin is not a place of spectacular scenery, with tow-ering mountains or cascading waterfalls, forbidding coastlines or endless vis-tas. "What is it about Algonquin?" asks an outsider. The question very nearly defies response.

On a bright, crisp autumn day, with my vintage 1928 Peterborough cedar-canvas 15-footer on my shoulders — the old way, with two paddles lashed down to the centre thwart to bear the weight — I wend my way along the forest path, stepping blithely on fallen leaves that have laid out a thick carpet of crimson, gold, orange, scarlet, damson and butter yellow on what was once an Aboriginal portage. The sun's rays penetrate through the upper canopy and down to the forest floor for the first time in months, and a thick, rich aroma of the deep woods rises to my nostrils. I move slowly, all my senses overactive. For me, the portage here is part of the pleasure; it's not like my trips on some of the Far North's wild rivers, where a carry around an unshootable set of rapids seems a nuisance and a chore, often a heavy toil, little more than a delay before getting back into the current. Walking through this woods is a vital part of understanding Algonquin.

Autumn is the best time, in my mind, to go to Algonquin: no bugs, very few people, and only a little rain. In any case, the routes I choose to follow in the park are away from the crowds even in midsummer — the ones that do not lead you to anywhere, really. The park map offers a smorgasbord of tiny "back" lakes where you can be alone, in a world of your own.

One time, paddling up a small creek with only just enough water to float the loaded canoe, we rounded a bend to face a gloriously content cow moose standing knee-deep in mud and water. There was no way around her. She looked straight at us, as if to say, "What are you doing here?" and simply refused to budge. We approached cautiously, respectfully, but nonetheless hoping she would eventually yield us the right of passage. We could easily have prodded her with the bow of our canoe. Instead we waited patiently, observing the detail of her powerful body and rich chocolate coat, until at last she slowly moved to one side, all the while apparently aware that she was in full control of the encounter. She, the denizen, let us, the interlopers, pass — after due inspection — to venture further into her domain. Camped on a lake at the head of that creek, shared only with the natural inhabitants, we found the reasons for going.

Canoeing Algonquin takes me back to my roots. As a young lad growing up in Toronto in the 1950s and '60s, we went "north" in the summer. I think my parents took me to Algonquin for the first time when I was only two. Though I don't actually remember it, I went for my first ride in a canoe on one of Algonquin's lakes. My mother knew them well; she had paddled here as a young girl in the 1930s. As did my grandfather — the original owner of my treasured old Peterborough — before her. It's like that for a lot of my generation in Ontario. So when we began to take canoe trips of our own, it was only natural to go to "The Park," as we called it, for in our minds there was none equal. Algonquin, for us, was the beginning of an important part of our lives.

Today, sitting in camp as the setting sun sheds its golden light across the mirror surface of our private lake at the head of a moose creek, with the loons gathered in anticipation of the coming migration and filling the air with their haunting wails, I can look across the water and renew my connection to

those beginnings. And every time, it is a renewal. It is with spirits braced that I paddle home after a week in the backwaters of Algonquin.

Beyond Their Dreams

One time, I took some friends from Scotland — absolute novices to the joys of the Canadian canoe trip — on a 12-day "expedition" (their word) through a corner of Algonquin. We managed a stretch of seven days without seeing another human being. It proved to be a wilderness experience beyond their dreams, with all the benefits of a new beginning. Writing an epilogue in her journal three weeks after returning home to Scotland, 60-year-old Rosemary said: "I remember sitting by the campfire and saying to David, 'I wonder what the wilderness experience will do to me?' and, privately, I did not really feel it would teach me a lot, except to overcome physical discomforts with a ready smile! But, how wrong I was! We carry the memory of it constantly, and it gives us strength. We feel invigorated, mentally refreshed, physically stronger, and 15 years younger."

Rosemary left Algonquin with her spirit revived, as do nearly a million visitors every year.

It was, arguably, the Group of Seven who first put expression to this power of Algonquin. It is no accident that several lakes in the park bear names commemorating some of these famous painters. Even before they became known through exhibitions in Toronto, Lawren Harris, Arthur Lismer, A.Y. Jackson and Fred Varley were paddling and painting in the park with their guide, Tom Thomson, who drowned there under mysterious circumstances in 1917. But by then the roots of this famous group of painters were firmly planted in the Canadian wilderness landscape, revealing what Lawren Harris called "the rugged and unspoiled character of this country." Decades after the Group of Seven was at its peak, Harris lamented that "the Canadian landscape is much the same today, but our sense of environment has changed, and with it our values; we no longer think of the northland as remote and inaccessible . . . the canoe has become largely a pleasure craft, rarely a vital necessity," as it was for these painters in the early part of the 1900s.

Algonquin nonetheless represents our link with that past, and our hope that that part of our souls may not perish, that at least part of our wilderness may somehow be preserved.

Some Algonquin paintings by the Group of Seven have become Canadian icons. Thomson first sketched *The West Wind* in April 1916 on the first documented canoe trip in the northeast corner of the park, with Harris. It became one of his most famous paintings, which Arthur Lismer described as "the spirit of Canada made manifest in a picture."

Prints of *The West Wind* hung above the blackboard in hundreds of Ontario schoolrooms for many years. I remember gazing at that lonely windswept pine on the rocky shore of a lake, lost to the teacher's words, travelling north in my imagination.

In the decades since those daydreamed trips, I have been to Algonquin countless times, not unlike most Ontario paddlers. It is our collective favourite, though for each of us it offers something different. The Petawawa River has its devotees, including George Drought, who knows it well enough to have written a guidebook. His praise is unequivocal: "For beauty and quality of rapids, the Petawawa outshines everything else in Ontario." For others, it is the traditional routes that loop north from the Highway 60 corridor: Canoe Lake, Big Trout, the Otterslides, Opeongo, all the oh-so-familiar names. There are 2,500 lakes in all, with 1,600 kilometres of canoe routes and 3,000 prepared campsites.

You don't have to work hard or travel far in order for Algonquin to bestow its gifts. It was Pierre Trudeau who wrote: "Travel a thousand miles by train and you are a brute; pedal five hundred on a bicycle and you remain basically a bourgeois; paddle a hundred in a canoe and you are already a child of nature." In Algonquin, you don't even need to go that far. That's why it remains the smaller, less-travelled lakes that draw me back. That's where I find peace. That's where I see an old-growth white pine so large that it takes four of us to link hands around its girth. That's where I feel the bond to wild places that stirs deep within us all.

For those who know it, the park provides that primeval connection. It is a steady, reliable friend — a place that is always there waiting for your next visit, a place that never disappoints. Ralph Bice, in his nineties, the last of the park's old-time guides and trappers, summed it up nicely: "Anyone who knows Algonquin Park will be disappointed when they get to heaven."

With thoughts like that in mind I reach the end of the portage through the autumnal forest, swing the canoe gently down from my shoulders to straddle the border between water and land, and stand there in the refreshingly cool air coming off the lake, taking in the view. It is a tiny, picturesque lake — like a painting by Lawren Harris — with only one campsite, on a rocky point, and it looks empty. I'll be alone, as I'd hoped. An unseen loon's tremulous call adds his welcome from across the way. I feel at home . . . in Algonquin . . . where it all began.

The Kawarthas
Going Alone

Gwyneth Hoyle

Fall had arrived, but still the sun poured down with the languidness of mid-August. Each perfect afternoon reminded me that the summer had gone and I had not been on a canoe trip. All previous canoe trips had been in the company of my now grown-up sons, or with organized groups of adults. Once it was with my husband, who enjoyed it enough to suggest that I was thereafter free to go as long as he was equally free to stay at home. So it came about that on a Friday at the end of September, with the promise of one more fine day, I decided the moment was right to try a 24-hour solo trip in the tame wilds north of Peterborough, Ontario.

At noon, my always co-operative husband arrived, helped load the canoe, and drove us north for an hour to familiar Long Lake. The drive gave me time to mentally check my brief packing and to consider whether I really wanted to go off alone, knowing that when we reached the lake I was free to call the venture off. The sight of the lake, long and narrow, framed by wooded rocky slopes, the water very blue and still, removed any doubts.

Quickly the canoe was lowered into the water and the gear stowed. We agreed to meet at the dock at the same time next day, and I pushed off. With a slight pang I turned for a last look as our car climbed a little rise and disappeared around a corner, heading home. The adventure was beginning.

In September there is a density to the atmosphere that magnifies sounds, so that even city traffic has a disturbing roar. The same heavy atmosphere magnified the stillness on the lake. The first paddle strokes were embarrassingly loud as the shaft of the paddle knocked against the wooden gunwale. I adjusted my stroke and soon the only noises were from the swirling eddies that followed each stroke with a sucking sound. Even they were loud.

The day was magnificent and hot. About an hour after starting, I pulled in to the shaded shore, ate a sandwich, peered about with binoculars, and marvelled at the complete freedom and the lack of compulsion to do anything. Finding a campsite before dark was the only requirement. Farther up the lake I pulled in to a campsite and climbed the high granite ridge behind it to look north, where more granite ridges march on into the empty distance.

The lake is very narrow at this point, but the campsite would give no view to the west and no sunset. I pushed on.

Around the next bend some cottagers were having an alfresco lunch. I slipped by unnoticed under the lee shore. When I was almost out of earshot, there was a sudden loud hissing sound as though a powerful gas jet for the barbecue had been turned on, and I looked back expecting to see flames. Instead, I saw that the lake, perfectly calm around me, was ruffled in the distance, and the tops of the trees were stirring in a puff of breeze blowing toward me through the gap. So pervasive was the stillness that a great blue heron, startled into flight, passed low over the canoe with a faint aerodynamic whistle from its wings, like the sound of a distant jet.

The lake narrowed and became a stream, then, rounding a curve, opened into oval-shaped Loucks Lake. A few cottages on the far shore gave no signs of life. Following the near shore I came to a campsite seen on a previous visit to this lake. It was in a tiny crescent guarded by high sentinel rocks. The cleared ground was shaded by clumps of white birch interspersed with tall pines, sloping away from the shore so that a tent would not be obvious to anyone passing on the lake. Two granite ridges formed sheltering arms to the north and the east — a perfect site.

Time, which had dawdled, now began to race along. So much needed to be done. In a few moments a fire was blazing in the fireplace and water was boiling for tea. Thirst quenched, I explored the path leading back from the water up a rocky rise, but found that it led to a swampy area and petered out. Setting up the tent came next and gave the campsite a comfortable, occupied feeling. With a collapsible saw I set about replenishing the stock of firewood, planning for a companionable campfire later.

The blissful silence was shattered by the drone of a motorboat as cottagers arrived for the weekend at the far end of the lake. Another group opened up the cottage on the opposite shore, but no one appeared to notice me.

Crescendo of Colour

The sun was dropping and I hurried to cook dinner so I would be free to sit on the sentinel rocks and watch the sunset while I ate. As the sun dipped toward the horizon it was obscured by hazy cloud and the promise of a spec-

tacular sunset faded. The sun disappeared without fanfare, but slowly an apricot glow began and steadily rose to a crescendo of colour, orange and gold, then crimson and purple. The colours increased, spread across the sky changing continually, and gradually faded. For two hours I was totally occupied, moving from one vantage point to another to experience the panorama from every angle.

Next came the stars. First the familiar bright ones became visible, followed imperceptibly by infinite numbers of tiny ones. Brightest of all, the Big Dipper hung straight above the lake, making a perfect reflection in the water.

By eight o'clock it was fully dark. I was determined not to go to bed for at least an hour, knowing that even with company, night in a tent can be very long. That next hour crawled by as I built up the campfire and restlessly sought a way to be comfortable. First I sat looking into the fire until the woods closed in around me, dark and forbidding in contrast to the flames. Next I would stand with my back to the fire and look about, my eyes becoming accustomed to the dark but my body casting an eerie giant shadow up into the trees. Then I would move away from the fire to the rocks and watch the stars above the lake. That was the least disquieting alternative until there was a commotion at the cottage across the lake. Raised voices at the cottage dock caused concern that I was about to have unwanted visitors. The flurry subsided and I returned to the fire to start my restless wanderings over again.

At last it was nine o'clock and I could decently retire. In the absence of mosquitoes the tent had stood open all day, but closing the zippered screens now gave a feeling of security, though the night was warm enough to leave the flaps wide open. Air mattress inflated, sleeping bag arranged, I blew out the candle and snuggled in. The fish jumping in the lake and the odd twig landing on the tent with a loud report were the only sounds. After the exertions of the day, I was soon asleep.

At precisely three o'clock my back signalled that it was time to get up and change positions. I stumbled out of the tent and looked around. The half-moon was caught in the trees behind the tent, as bright as if a light had been switched on in the woods. The Big Dipper had moved on and a new constellation was reflecting in the lake. The night was warm, still and silent. I went back to bed filled with a sense of wonder and ecstasy at the beauty of the night, and relief that it was going so well.

Nighttime Visitors

Sleep had not yet returned when I heard footsteps coming through the woods. With all senses alert I lay very still and listened. The footsteps stopped nearby and gave way to scratching sounds on the pack, lying tightly closed near the fireplace. I sat up, clapped my hands and said "Shoo" in my bravest voice. There was a satisfying sound of scurrying, receding feet — then silence. But not for long. The pack was too inviting and the scratching began again. Remembering the flashlight, I shone it in the direction of the pack. A black-masked face looked up and a large raccoon jumped guiltily away. The pack contained very little, so I broke the rules and fetched it into the tent. Moments later more footsteps were followed by the sound of cup and spoon being knocked over; I shone the flashlight again. The big raccoon was undaunted, but a small one approaching the tent leapt nervously away.

For the next hour footsteps and undefined rustlings seemed to be everywhere and to belong to a myriad of unseen creatures. By five o'clock I was tired of listening and felt ready to sleep again. With more air in the air mattress, I rolled over and fell into a sleep filled with dreams. After a good nap, my senses became aware of steady, precise steps getting louder as they approached. This was no raccoon. The sounds were quite different. I strained to listen as the steady thump, thump, thump grew louder and closer. Could it be a deer? No, bigger! A moose? There was no rustle of leaves, no breaking of twigs. Gradually it dawned on me that the steady footfall was the sound of my own heartbeat amplified through the pillow of the air mattress! I opened my eyes — daylight — seven o'clock — a good time to get up.

It was as joyful to sit and watch the morning breaking as it had been to watch the previous evening's sunset. Reluctantly, I began to dismantle the tent, taking time to brush it out thoroughly, packing carefully and slowly to delay the inevitable moment of departure. Returning to the campsite after loading the canoe, I startled a partridge standing where the tent had been. The red squirrel, chipmunks and chickadees had accepted me without comment.

The morning was so deliciously perfect that I wondered why I was leaving when suddenly seven canoes full of Boy Scouts and their leaders came shouting onto the lake, passing near me but quite oblivious of any other presence. It was the right time to go. The return trip could be made with leisure.

It was Saturday morning and Long Lake was now humming with activity. Clouds were spreading across the sky from the east and a headwind began to blow. Within sight of the dock, our car suddenly appeared and flashed its headlights. I signalled back joyously with an overhead sweep of the paddle. The rendezvous was complete.

On the drive home I was quietly content. In the past 24 hours I had been alive in every fibre of my body, all senses fully alert, even while I slept. I had been dependent on no one but myself, and had experienced a freedom not possible with companions. It had been an exhilarating and totally satisfying trip.

Rideau Waterway
Paddle Back to the Nineteenth Century

Max Finkelstein

THE RIDEAU WATERWAY IS ONE OF THE BEST-KEPT CANOEING SECRETS IN Canada. Here, you can find the best mix of wildlife, city life, and country life; pastoral scenery, fine restaurants, great fishing, quaint hotels, museums and living history sites, scenic backwaters. Along the Rideau, the past and present, nature and culture, all come together in a unique melding — just the recipe for an unforgettable canoe experience. Here, you can glimpse history and heritage, and find tranquillity, beauty and charm. All along the way, the canoeist can learn about the past and present of this part of Ontario at numerous museums and exhibits set up at the 24 lock stations. Many of them remain virtually as they were when they were built over 150 years ago — peaceful and secluded havens that take you back to the nineteenth century. Today, there's paddling, swimming, fishing, candlelight lock-side dining, a soft bed at night — hey, this is canoe-tripping!

Built in 1832, the Rideau Waterway is the oldest continuously operating

canal in North America. The Waterway is like a series of giant beaver ponds. Dams control the water levels; locks and canals link the ponds. It was built to provide Upper Canada (now Ontario) with a safe transportation route from Montréal to Kingston (then Upper Canada's largest settlement) on Lake Ontario, bypassing the St. Lawrence and out of range of canons, in case of war with our neighbours to the south. The Waterway was never used for defence, but it has served as an immigration route and an artery of commerce. Today, the log rafts, barges and steamers have given way to recreational power boats and a few canoes. Much of the wilderness has also given way to roads, towns and farms, but I am always amazed at the abundance of wildlife and fish along the Waterway. Otters, deer, beavers, muskrats, mink, foxes, loons, ducks, Canada geese, great blue herons, osprey, marsh hawks, black rat snakes, choruses of bullfrogs — these are just some of the species that have kept me company during my many journeys along the Rideau.

Canal Works

Nominated to the Canadian Heritage Rivers System in 1999, the Rideau Waterway is considered one of the great engineering feats of the nineteenth century, and, even in this age of computers and space-age technology, you can only marvel at the engineering ingenuity of its builders. Thirty-one locks raise boats from the Ottawa River to Newboro Lake, the highest point on the route; fourteen locks lower boats to Lake Ontario. Locks link the Rideau with the historic town of Perth via the Tay Canal. Canoeists, of course, can portage around the locks. It's a lot faster, especially around the major lock stations, but it's fun to lock through with the big boats. The original locks and canals are still there, and, except for three hydraulic locks, all are still operated by the muscle power of lock staff who crank the distinctive "crab" winches. Even some of the swing bridges over the canal are rotated by hand-operated cranks to let boats pass.

The massive doors that open and close the locks are built just like the original gates. The first gates were made from oak. Now Douglas fir is used, as the large oaks needed to make the massive beams can no longer be found in Rideau forests, or anywhere in Canada. The lock chambers are filled by tunnels passing around the lock gates. Tunnel valves are operated by winches and chains. When you portage around the locks, you will notice manholes covered with black grates. These are necessary to let air out as water rushes through the tunnels, like punching two holes in the top of a juice can for easy pouring.

The walls of locks are built like a pyramid, almost 3 metres thick at the bottom and 2 metres at the top. It's an interesting process, locking through in a canoe — an intimate look at the stone walls, algae clinging to them, water spurting and seeping between the limestone blocks and through the massive wooden gates. It's also interesting locking through with large power boats, being rafted between a cabin cruiser and a houseboat gives you a feeling of power, knowing that your canoe will take you anywhere these large, expensive motorized craft can go, and many places they cannot.

When to Go

The best time to go, as an old adage states, is whenever you can get away. But my favourite times are in the spring and fall. At these times you have the Waterway to yourself. In spring, the lilacs are in bloom, colouring the old farmsteads purple and perfuming the air. Birds are everywhere, filling the forest with colour and song.

In late September, the maples are in full resplendent colour. Wild grapes festoon the banks of the Waterway, and the bright orange berries of bittersweet add a fiery dash of colour. But canoeists beware, though summer has its charms, some sections of the canal are like a freeway at rush hour, and the paddler must be prepared to ride out wakes that look like tidal waves.

I've paddled the Rideau more times than I care to remember, from a 22-hour sprint to a leisurely 7-day sojourn. At least five days should be budgeted for a relaxing trip from end to end (202 kilometres), but the combinations are endless. With road access at every lock station, car shuttles can be set up for one-way trips of any length. The Rideau also links up with other canoe routes, including Frontenac and Charleston Lake provincial parks.

Drinking water, toilet facilities, picnic tables and fireplaces are available at all the lock stations except the Ottawa Locks. The lock stations are also ideal campsites. All have a special charm and are peaceful havens, even those within towns. Of course, if you don't want to camp, there are many fine hotels and bed-and-breakfasts along the route.

The Rideau Waterway is anchored at either end by a large city, Ottawa at the north and Kingston at the Lake Ontario terminus. Because I live in Ottawa, most of my trips start there. However, the chances of tailwinds are better if you start at Kingston. The prevailing southwest winds seem to blow straight out of Kingston and get stronger the closer you get to Lake Ontario. Don't be surprised to find yourself windbound on some of the larger lakes. Those winds, those winds, those damn southwest winds . . .

Many times I've paddled down the Ottawa River to the Ottawa Locks, to start my trip in the shadow of the Parliament Buildings, where giant steps lift and lower boats 24 metres from the Ottawa River to the canal that winds through the city. Halfway up is the oldest building in Ottawa, converted now to the Bytown Museum, the first of many museums housing much of the memorabilia of the canal and the people who built it.

It's a hefty portage for the paddler, but ice cream stands, french fries and the best pizzas in Ottawa await the weary paddler along the concrete banks of the canal. Ten kilometres and two lock stations later, you reach Hog's Back, where the canal merges with the Rideau River.

A Few of My Favourite Places

After leaving Ottawa, the first town you reach is Manotick. The name of this historic town is derived from an Algonquin word meaning "Long Island," the name of the lock station close to the town. On the river in the centre of town is Watson's Mill, built in 1860 and restored in 1979. It still grinds wheat into flour using huge grindstones and water power. Across the street from the mill is a tearoom staffed by seniors, where you can replace some of those calories you burned off with the best pie on the Rideau.

Heading south from Manotick, you paddle through the "Long Reach," 39 kilometres to the next lock station — Burritts Rapids. This is one of the most picturesque sites on the system. A human-made canal bypasses the rapids, lined by cut limestone blocks and cedar trees. A hiking trail runs alongside the river through shaded cedar forests. A few kilometres further is the historic town of Merrickville, home of the Canadian Recreational Canoeing Association. Don't miss the bakery as you paddle by. The town is worth exploring, with its historic buildings, the ruins of a woollen mill and a blockhouse turned into a museum.

The Rideau cuts through rich marshes on the way to the next town, Smiths Falls. In the centre of Smiths Falls is one of the three lock stations on the system operated by hydraulics. A pleasant saunter through the park from the Combined Lock is the Rideau Canal Museum. A trip to the Hershey's chocolate factory to stock up is also a required side trip in Smiths Falls — a short portage from Old Sly's Lock.

A narrow canal lined with limestone blocks and winding through cedar forests and wetlands links Smiths Falls to Lower Rideau Lake, a shallow lake noted for great bass fishing. An interesting side trip leads from Lower Rideau Lake up the Tay Branch to the historic town of Perth. Along the way, the

canal passes through the Tay Marsh, now a wildlife reserve where nesting and feeding areas have been established for Canada geese and wood ducks. A few kilometres further and the skyline of Perth comes into view, with its water tower and the graceful rooflines of its stately homes. Here, the best butter tarts and date squares in Lanark County (and perhaps in the world) can be found at the local bakery.

For many, the most scenic section of the Rideau Waterway is between The Narrows at the waist between Big Rideau Lake and Upper Rideau Lake, and the hamlet of Morton. A short detour takes you to the village of Westport. Climb Foley Mountain to Spy Rock for a view of Upper Rideau Lake that will stay with you for a lifetime. The view takes in high cliffs, wooded hills, and blue lakes upon lakes upon lakes.

Jones Falls is the unique site on the Rideau. The keystone arch dam was the highest in North America when it was built in 1830. At that time, this was deep in the wilderness. In summer, the smooth waters of the lock basins echo to the sounds of a hammer striking hot iron on an anvil. You can watch the smithy working in the blacksmith shop, reconstructed to 1843. The hilltop lockmaster's house has been restored and furnished to give you a glimpse of the life of a lockmaster in the nineteenth century. But what I remember most are the huge maple trees that frame the bottom lock and blaze red and orange in late September.

We head now to Kingston through a series of long, shallow lakes. The River Styx, a shallow, stump-strewn reach of the Rideau Waterway, leads to Kingston Mills, the last lock station on your way to Kingston and Lake Ontario, and a place time seems to have overlooked. There is a visitor's centre, with films and exhibits, and a restored blockhouse. The granite cliffs framing the deep gorge below the locks make you ponder the immensity of Colonel By's undertaking, his men armed with hammers and wedges and gunpowder.

My Rideau Dream

It is hard to imagine what the river was like before the construction. The locks and dams have slowed the rivers, drowning rapids to create long, narrow lakes and vast wetlands. Many of the lakes were once swamps. Despite, and in some cases because of, the changes, the Waterway is still a vital water ecosystem, filled with life. However, the Rideau ecosystem is fragile and it's beginning to show its age. The work of Colonel By has accelerated the natural aging process by clogging up the flow of water. Cottagers and permanent residents have built retaining walls and cleared away shoreline vegetation to make beaches and expansive lawns. The most common activity of residents along the Rideau seems to be cutting grass! Destroying the fragile ribbon of shoreline decreases the ability of the Rideau to absorb nutrients and pollutants. At the same time, increasing use of pesticides, herbicides and fertilizers, along with a growing population and heavier boat traffic, have all contributed to the rampant aquatic weed growth. But steps are being taken to reverse this trend. I have hope that our children, and their children, will still be able to paddle this route and find it as beautiful as I do today. I also wish that they will be able to eat the fish without worrying about contaminants, swim anywhere, and even drink the water. This is my dream for the Rideau.

Lady Evelyn River
Where White Falls Roar

Bruce W. Hodgins

In haunting memory, the landscape of the Lady Evelyn keeps drawing me back for canoe voyages of both the imagination and the physical. Often more appropriately called the Trout Streams, its waters are as close to mountain flows as the Canadian Shield in Ontario can deliver. The Lady Evelyn has so many small, often unnavigable rapids, so many captivating high-yet-small falls, rugged Precambrian shorelines and heights, white and red pine stands, cedars, lily pads, shallows and depths, sunsets and portages, I simply must recanoe it and reimagine its mysteries.

It was back in 1956 that I first tripped its lower reaches, up to Divide (Katherine) — that is, "up the South and down the North" channels — in late August of my first year with Wanapitei, leading staff and older campers. The next year, Carol (my wife) and I led a teen youth group up to the Forks and back, and in 1958 up to the Grays and over and down the Makobe. Then, in 1959, it was up past the Forks to Gamble and over the great carry to Sunnywater and Smoothwater, and down the East Montreal, past Gowganda and over the Arctic Divide to the Grassy–Matagami. In the sixties there were more youth trips, short and long. In 1965 to Florence and over to the Sturgeon River at Ghoul Lake. In 1969 it was all the way up to the source of the North Branch, past Elizabeth Falls to Isobel (Beauty) Lake, and beyond. In the seventies and eighties we often led downstream adult Trout Stream trips, flying in to the Gamble Strip or Florence, sometimes involving the Makobe and Sturgeon, sometimes climbing Maple Mountain.

We took our imagination of the Trout Streams to the successful politics of establishing the Lady Evelyn–Smoothwater Wilderness Park, and the harder battle of stopping the hookup of the Red Squirrel Road Extension with the southeastward building of the Liskeard Road — right through the park and Wakimika, a battle that was only won (in 1989-90) because of the Teme-Augama Anishnabai leadership, resolution and calm persistence. With Maple Mountain and Wendaban, the area is the spiritual heart of their N'daki Menan, their homeland. In 1987, even our trip itself was very politi-cal, escorting high-profile sponsors of the Temagami Wilderness Society —

Margaret Atwood, M.T. Kelly, Judy Erola, etc. — through its taxing mysteries, and followed the same year by a nostalgic trip with ex-staff of a previous generation. In 1989 the Lady Evelyn was my first trip after an illness that almost ended my canoeing along with my life.

I anticipate many more trips on the Lady Evelyn, trips of the imagination and hopefully a few of the corporal. We have paddled so many diverse and mighty rivers of the Far North and the Arctic. We have experienced the landscape and challenge of tundra, taiga or black spruce, hundreds of rapids, great weather variables, easy, hard, memorable and forgotten portages. Yet it is always back, again and in between, to the Lady Evelyn.

Trout Streams

In 1888 Robert Bell of the Geological Survey inappropriately named the river (and lake) for an obscure young beauty of Scottish aristocracy, Evelyn Catherine Campbell, eighth child of the Duke of Argyle. She had earlier visited her brother the Governor General, the Marquis of Lorne, at Rideau Hall. Yet locally the river was still called by the Anishnabai name *Majamaygas*, "the Trout Streams," which was approached by Namabinnagasheshingue, Sucker Gut Lake, when in 1903 James Edmond Jones wrote about it so glowingly in *Camping and Canoeing*. In 1918 Jones wrote, with slight misrepresentation, for the YMCA's Tuxis Boys: "Some day you may have the glorious experience of climbing Maple Mountain, above Lady Eve-lyn Lake, Temagami, up the River Namabinnagasheshingue. In the joy of your youth and vigor you will revel not only in the beauties of that tiny trail, but will even glory in the portages, more than a score, which take from stretch to stretch, past falls and ledges varying from one foot to over one hundred feet in height, your camera ever busy to record the succession of scenes in unforgettable beauty."

No single canoe trip can readily "do" the Lady Evelyn, the system with its two branches and two channels, its Grays and Florence tributaries, and its very upper reaches. While each trip is separately remembered for the fellow-ship, the moods and adventures, the repeated visual impact of each glorious scene on the streams blurs together as a permanent, water-centred landscape and *nastawgan*, or route of the imagination. It is so clear that the exploration of the images almost exist apart from their so-called geographic reality.

A Lady Evelyn trip is not for the faint of heart or muscle. The portages are numerous, short but often steep, both up and down, about 17 up the North Channel and South Branch to Florence, and perhaps 23 from Isobel all the way down to Franks Falls and the Lady Evelyn Lake. For portages, there are the memorable Seven Little Sisters, from the Forks down to Macpherson, then about three portages to Divide. From there down, each channel has about five carries: the North, with its three spectacular falls (Helens, Centre and Franks); the South with its Golden Staircase, its Bridal Veil, and its Fat Man's climb or descent. Great campsites are numerous, and only around the civic weekend does the landscape appear to be heavily pop-ulated. Quiet nooks, crannies and natural grottos can always be found. In the South Channel, before August, there are two stretches of excellent Class II whitewater (which can be easily portaged); with the same calendar con-straints, crossing over from the Grays to the Makobe delivers a small stream of demanding and challenging runnable rapids.

Ideal Trip

In my trip of the imagination, we arrive by van with kevlar and wood-canvas canoes at Isobel, near the source of the North Branch. Along the lakeshore and downstream at least up to the skyline, there has been little logging. Then, after Elizabeth Falls, we enter the more pristine forest of the park. We stop to camp on the peninsula campsite in Gamble Lake, fishing pike that evening, from the canoe, using daredevils. Then it's down to the area of the Forks, just a very short paddle, for the next night. Two glorious pine sites to choose from. The first looks up from its low clay banks, its jack pine and its blueberries into the meanders of the North Branch. We take the second site this time, by the first carry, on river-right. The spectacular sunset glows yellow and mauve through the pines, a Temagami campfire, reflector-oven prepared, individually baked wilderness pizza. The next day it's the Seven Sisters. We run the first without gear; we try shooting one or two others, empty for sure, perhaps solo. We stand at the carrying spot, where you can look back to the last portage and forward to the next. We camp at the north end Macpherson site, high amid the Killarney-type quartzite hills, cliffs and crevices, everywhere the craggy, dark great white pines, against a clear blue sky, glancing down to blue ponds. After dinner, we bake bannock into cinnamon rolls. Then we talk vehemently about the meaning of the Near North and the future of the Teme-Augama Anishnabai, whose homeland this still is, the lived in, used and modified wilderness, the old-growth forest.

The year is 1993, and fire damage, or is it renewal, exists downstream for a spell. But, after pushing off in the morning, we dream of the Grays, claustrophobic Gray Mud Lake, and the Makobe beyond, the Grays entering the Macpherson as a little trickle off to the left in a wetland — not this time, maybe next.

Then at Shangri-la (Stonehenge), we curse the landing and the big, uneven rocks that must be jumped across or crawled over, with either a teetering canoe bouncing and creaking on the head tump and thwart or the tumped wanagan off-balancing you from left to right and back. We camp away from the main trail at one of the sites that, all together, could accommodate three or four large groups, each with a sense of privacy and remoteness. We shower under the falls by the flat main campsite.

It is only a very short hop down to Divide Lake, so part way down — there are two good sets of light rapids here — we take a side trip, without gear, portaging up into Dry Lake and climbing the glorious Dry Lake Ridge, looking out across the top of northern Ontario, with Maple Mountain to the east and Ispatina Ridge (Ontario's highest place) to the west, ancient old-growth pine valleys and slopes, ridge after ridge, indentations suggesting the many hidden lakes. Only in glimpses to the southwest (outside the park) is there evidence of the horrific, destructive clearcut practices of the seventies and eighties. Then, back in the canoes, we try without success to catch (and throw back) one of the famed speckled trout that has survived the former acid-rain scourge from Sudbury, not so far away, or one of the young ones hatched during the slow comeback.

Now it is on to Divide, where we unload at the narrows, set up camp, cook, ladle out a dram or two of Scotch to each. That evening and other evenings we argue over the meaning of life and the proper role of the state. Nothing is resolved, but our own conceptions have been tested and modified. Then we listen for the truth from the call of the loon and song of the whip-poor-will as we see the moon rise big through the trees. It's off to our tents for the deep sleep that only the Lady Evelyn and other great tripping rivers can bring.

Next day, with great wistfulness, we opt for the greater mysteries of the South Channel. The intriguing falls of the North will have to wait. We take the hard first carry and then struggle down the Golden Staircase. At

the halfway point, we cross the pond to the right bank briefly to visit Hap Wilson's "allowable non-conforming" cabin, which is open. There we see above a view of white and yellow water rushing through banks of burnt sienna rock, by foliage of diverse greens, against a bright blue sky. We reread the cabin's historic logbook, with its entries of humour, insight and pathos. We eat a cold lunch outside, again admiring the view. Then it is on to the split-rock Bridal Falls, perhaps the system's most beautiful, but one with the task of a 45-degree angled carry that runs down diagonally from the top, a carry that concentrates the mind away from the landscape. Now we move slowly through the gorge, with its high clay banks and black spruce — a site more in tune with the James Bay uplands than the Temagami country. We carry the gear around a kilometre of rapids and run the canoes through the three pitches of these great, narrow, rocky, yet deep enough sets. Then it's on to Fat Man's, the portage, and after a huge and complex dinner, we ease the canoes down the steep carry and fish before dark, with modest success. In the morning we fry the catch using lots of flour, oil, pepper and lemon.

Then it's through and around the lower rapids and reaches. By the bottom of the river-right, we find again the last remains of the old Murphy lumber camp, with its tumbled-down buildings and rusting vehicles, including the 1944 right-hand-drive Chev truck built in Oshawa for British lend-lease. Rotting, it's all part of our cultural heritage, incongruous but wonderful, nestling in a wilderness park. We lunch at the barn campsite, where memories of many glorious nights spent sleeping on the deep hay are clear, though barn and hay are now gone. We paddle on, passing on the right the unlamented "two miler," a carry direct to Diamond. Instead, we go up north and around, in and out of the pond, onto the south bay of Lady Evelyn Lake, and stop for the night at the high Dewdrop Island site. In the morning we paddle the bay and channel, enter Diamond Lake, paddle past the fading but haunting pictographs, portage into Sharp Rock Inlet of Lake Temagami, carry on over the Napoleon Portage to Sandy Inlet, and finally, as always, to the peopled walking bridge over the Red Squirrel River at Wanapitei. But surely we'll be back again soon, to the Lady Evelyn.

This trip of the imagination had ten people on it. Carol and I were not really leaders, more gentle mentors and facilitators. We were all adults; half were women and the other half men. Some had long been friends; others were new to us. Now we are all bonded together. We are all friends who do not see or remember the same essential landscape of the Trout Streams, nor do we agree on the truth and the essence of the Canadian experience. Yet, with George Marsh and his old canoe, we all still ask, "Do the white falls roar as they did of yore on the Lady Evelyn/ and the square-tails leap from the black pool deep where the pictured rocks begin?"

Steel River
A Remarkable Canoe Loop

Toni Harting

"A LOOP, A CANOE LOOP — WHY AREN'T THERE ANY INTERESTING CANOE-trip loops?" is the often-heard cry of frustration among many wilderness canoeing aficionados. A fair question. Who doesn't prefer to begin and end a trip in the same location, thereby avoiding the dreaded and time-wasting car shuttle?

The Steel River offers a remarkable 170-kilometre adventure just north of Lake Superior, all in one loop, beginning and ending on Santoy Lake. In many respects, this is a superb wilderness tripping river: remote, clear, lots of flatwater and manageable whitewater, between 15 and 20 portages, ranging from the killer 1,000-metre Diablo Portage to an easy 5-metre liftover, excellent to bad campsites, several scenic waterfalls, few people, bugs, rain, sunshine, wind, hard work, easy days — you name it, it's all there. A marvellous river indeed, but not a trip for novices without sufficient whitewater and portaging experience.

There are two access points to this river, which is the main attraction of the Steel River Provincial Park. The put-in point that forms part of the loop is at a government dock at the end of a gravel road leading from Highway 17, a few kilometres east of Terrace Bay on the north shore of Lake Superior, to the southern end of Santoy Lake. The other access point is located near the far northern end of the river, but more about that later.

If you paddle north for about 8 kilometres on Santoy Lake, a depression or saddle between the hills on the west shore appears. This is the location of the very difficult Diablo Portage between Santoy and Diablo lakes, a vertical climb of about 100 metres over a trail 1,000 metres long. The first few hundred metres are by far the steepest: the trail goes straight up the 30- to 40-degree slope, climbing about 70 metres, then it enters a steep-walled ravine, levelling off a bit but becoming extremely dangerous because of the countless slippery rocks, with deep, foliage-hidden trip holes between them that can easily break your leg if it gets caught. Indeed, a portage trail worthy of respect, the toughest one of the lot, one you unfortunately have to do at the very beginning of the trip, with all the food packs still at maximum weight and your body not yet accustomed to hard work.

At Diablo Lake, the highest point of the trip has almost been reached; there are still about 10 metres to be climbed to the first big lake, Cairngorm Lake, via three more portages. None of these portages is simple or short, and it's easy to lose your way at the end of the last one, having to manoeuvre through bush and marsh to find a put-in point.

Then, at the far southern tip of splendid 16-kilometre-long Cairngorm Lake, the good part begins — from now on, the rest of the 170 kilometres is all downhill via lakes and moving water, a drop of 110 metres back to Santoy Lake.

The narrow stream that connects Cairngorm Lake to Steel Lake is the first indication of the Steel River's flowing waters. The upper part of this stream is not canoeable and ends tumbling over a waterfall, First Falls, into a pool partly filled with logs and deadfall.

Undulating Carpet

This unnavigable stretch of the Steel River is bypassed via a 400-metre portage that begins at the end of a narrow bay at the northeast tip of Cairngorm Lake. The easy trail leads to a good campsite overlooking the pool below First Falls. Just before you get to the campsite, the forest floor becomes a thick, richly green, undulating carpet of moss and ferns, accentuated here and there by dark red bunchberries and cream-coloured mushrooms — a perfect spot to just sit on a log and do nothing, just absorb nature's beauty.

Below the First Fall's pool, the narrow river is very shallow and in places obstructed by fallen trees. Wading the canoe is necessary until the river becomes deeper before it enters Moose Lake, a quiet and unremarkable body of water about 1.5 kilometres long. Two portages and several beaver dam liftovers later, the southern tip of Steel Lake is reached.

This lake presents the longest stretch of flatwater on the trip — 30 kilometres of easy paddling down a typical Canadian Shield lake. Both shores are often quite irregular, with several deep bays and granite rock faces interrupting the line of trees. There are some islands, and a few sand beaches offer good camping spots.

The last section of Steel Lake turns to the northeast and ends in a shallow bay. Here, the river proper continues its run, dropping via three rather rough but scenic rapids (portages with some hard work available on river-right) into Aster Lake, the most northerly point of this loop trip.

At Aster Lake the Little Steel River comes in from the north. The second access point mentioned above is located on Kawabatongog Lake, which is

part of this tributary, just east of the north–south road between Terrace Bay, on Highway 17, and Longlac, on Highway 11. This is a nice point to start a trip down the whole length of the river to Santoy Lake, but not the loop discussed here.

Just below Aster Lake, the real fun starts. Until now the trip has consisted of flatwater paddling, portaging and some wading. The rest of the river, however, provides lots of moving water, including many runnable rapids and riffles, as well as long runs of fast current. In places there are lake-like wider stretches without discernible current, requiring pool-and-drop paddling. An occasional short portage can be made to avoid some nasty spots, but there are no really dangerous or unexpected surprises, just a tremendous ride down a fast, diverse river. The water level has, of course, a big influence on the safety of the runs, so scout when necessary.

This river-lake paddling ends at Rainbow Falls, the second of the Steel River falls, which has a total drop of about 20 metres. It is a scenic spot with a nice campsite that provides ample space for several tents; a good place to spend a day of rest.

A few kilometres downstream from Rainbow Falls, the river takes on a completely different look. It leaves most of the Shield rock behind and starts to meander lazily back and forth through a long plain filled with sand and rock flour (extremely finely ground rock that clings to everything it touches), all the way to the northern end of Santoy, where it empties into the lake. In many places the banks of the river consist of "beaches" of sand and rock flour, ideal highways for moose, as evidenced by the numerous tracks.

This meandering part of the river has no rapids but is partially or completely obstructed in about eight places by huge logjams. These consist of thousands upon thousands of logs that have been carried down over many years of high spring water levels and pushed together into massive walls that somehow still allow water to seep through. The towering constructions are most impressive, some of them being hundreds of metres long. The bigger

ones are stationary, not moving from their established spots on the river, most often at a sharp bend. But smaller ones are sometimes taken apart by the current, the logs then drifting downstream until they are absorbed by the next jam. Or they may form a new barrier themselves further downstream. When planning this trip, take into account the time involved in negotiating these logjams by portaging around them.

When the river finally flows into Santoy Lake, it carries with it an enormous amount of rock flour and sand, much of which settles in the quiet waters of the lake to form a huge sandbank that almost blocks the river's outflow.

There is one more sight to enjoy before the end of the trip. Just south of a 100-metre vertical rockface called Windigo Wigwam Point on the east shore, the river flows out of Santoy Lake. The water tumbles down a most impressive series of cliffs and rapids, known locally as Staircase Falls, with a total drop of more than 40 metres into a deep valley with fast current and several rapids. A portage trail on river-right gives access to some nice lookout points that offer a good view of the falls. The trail continues down to the river, for those planning to explore the river to its end, where it flows into the cold waters of Lake Superior. However, if doing the loop trip, stay on Santoy Lake and paddle back to the original access point.

Quetico
Quintessential Canoe Country

John Stradiotto and Martha Morris

THERE IS ONE WAY TO EXPERIENCE THE ESSENCE OF QUETICO. BY CANOE.

Glide out onto the waters of Quetico and you drift into a timeless world of ancient Canadian Shield, northern boreal forests, and clean, cold water. It is the region's most remarkable aspect, this water. Within the bounds of this park, this water flows boundless, following age-old contours and drawing an intricate pattern of over 330 lakes and rivers, which, viewed from the air, clearly dominates the landscape. Planes permit only an overview, though; travel by canoe makes you an inseparable part of your surroundings.

Quetico Provincial Park, in northwestern Ontario, is renowned as a canoeists' mecca, and deservedly so. Spanning over 4,600 square kilometres, the park offers approximately 1,500 kilometres of canoe routes from which to choose. In recognition of these and other unusual merits, the government of Ontario has classified Quetico as a wilderness park and prohibits general use of motorboats and other motorized vehicles within its borders. Further to this, logging has been banned, and any roads that may have witnessed the passage of hauling trucks are now overgrown. These human-made regulations, together with nature's gracious handiwork, make Quetico ideal for the canoeist seeking a wilderness experience.

John and I are fortunate to have Quetico quite near our doorstep. And though we are able to enjoy it year-round, our exuberance peaks when the ice makes its final break in May. After more than five months of winter, the arrival of spring is wondrous, as Quetico is suddenly alive with movement, sound and colour. The longer days and greater warmth cause the ice to "candle," to form groups of independent shafts that twinkle gently, continuously, as each breaks from its neighbour to return to its companion water. Above, the call of Canada geese, the awkward, welcome cry of the herring gull, and the lonely laugh of the loon. And all around, birch and poplar burst forth in vivid green.

For our first trip of the season, we choose to begin at French Lake, in the northeastern corner of the park, and make a loop down Baptism Creek, along the Cache River, and up through Pickerel Lake and River. It is a route that will take us through remote, unknown territory, as well as sections well-known to us. We are intrigued by John's previous introduction to it from the air: having seen the serpentine Cache River, he wants to paddle its waters.

Paddling up Baptism Creek, I am reminded of Shirley Peruniak's comment, "In Quetico you can imagine you are the first person travelling in the area." Shirley, a retired naturalist and historian for the park, knows whereof she speaks. Her strong devotion to Quetico was sparked in 1957 when she made her inaugural canoe trip into the region. Today, her doorstep verges on French Lake.

Indeed, we will travel for three days before seeing another person. Quetico is like that. It is a happy compromise between the familiar and the unexpected, between accessibility and remoteness. This combination, as one station ranger pointed out, attracts "a wide variety of people — people who are expert canoeists and have been on canoe trips across North America, and people for whom this is their first trip. Families with young kids, too. People of all ages." Anyone entering Quetico must purchase a permit at one of the six ranger stations located on the periphery of the park. Entry station attendants greet visitors, offer advice and information, and answer questions.

As we paddle up to an island for dinner, we glimpse a dark, amorphous shape hidden by jack pine. A cow moose makes her presence known by moving heavily over the underbrush, then splashing as she takes to the water. Swimming easily through the green water, the only sound is that of her deep breathing, and the only visible part of her body is her majestic head held high.

Portent Portage

While we eat, we ponder our next move. Ahead is a 3,700-metre portage, the longest in the Park and an anomaly among portages that average only 400 metres in length. Having made the decision, we find it marked by a stick stuck upright in the mud, impaling a battered tennis shoe. It is prophetic, for customarily portages are signified by only a blaze in a tree by the shore. Similarly, there are no fire grills, no established latrines, no tent poles at campsites; nothing but a canopy of red pines and a carpet of needles in keeping with the park's wilderness classification. As Shirley explains, "Quetico can provide the opportunity for us to appreciate the way the country was for our ancestors."

A country in which waterways formed the highways and byways. We are keenly aware of this as the Cache River bends and turns; all around, there is bog and black spruce, no man's land. There are often contradictions in this modern world and we are aware of these too as we come across a bridge fallen into decay after many years, and are startled by the intrusion of a passing helicopter.

It is a fragile region, as attested to by the delicate, pink bog laurel, the bog rosemary, and the cotton grass. Fragile perhaps, but testing as it cuts through rock and the quiet water foams into whitewater. The shallowness necessitates that I carry packs across the portages while John navigates the lightened boat over the rapids. For the most part, rapids in Quetico are unsuitable for running, due to abrupt and rocky drops in water levels between lakes. Portages around these sections are always available and for good reason.

Coming across the entrance to a portage from Cache River to a lake, we opt to leave the river, despite the warning conveyed by two battered tennis shoes impaled by two crossed sticks. Hard work is often rewarded, or that is the premise, and we are treated to the brilliant colours of the marsh marigold after tramping knee-deep through a pond. Seeing the expanse of lake and hearing the familiar welcome of the loon, we relax. This is home.

"Home" always evokes a flood of memories. Sailing with the wind down McKenzie Lake, we pass an island where John once met a middle-aged man, paddling alone and in a reflective mood. He recalls a pearl of wisdom offered by the older man: "Come while you can. I've been coming for twenty years, and each year it is harder to pull away from external demands."

Further on, we paddle beneath intimidating cliffs composed of the granite that dominates the park, complemented by metasediments and greenstone. To the Aboriginal peoples, the rock was a canvas, and sketched upon its face are red ochre paintings that describe the Aboriginals' physical and spiritual life. The canoes that supported their nomadic lifestyle are also represented in these pictographs. There are more than 30 such pictographs in Quetico.

"It is a place of natural and cultural history that is still being discovered. I remember finding a stone knife at French Lake and thinking about the person who shaped it thousands of years ago," Shirley remarks wistfully.

Another discovery, by a favourite naturalist, was the inland rush. This plant is a prairie species and exemplifies one of Quetico's unusual characteristics. It is a meeting ground, a place where east meets west and north meets south; where mountain club moss and inland rush grow; where black spruce dwells with red ash; and where the great blue heron shares the skies with the gray jay.

Quetico is also a confluence of weather systems, a battleground of western and northern opposition as the continental dry air mass collides with the continental polar air mass. During the spring, summer and autumn, the sky wars can last throughout the day as the foes vie for supremacy.

On Sturgeon Lake, we awake to an arctic chill and a strong, steady wind fortified by terrific gusts. Riding the waves, we make the sanctuary of Deux Rivières, a restful, shallow and unpredictable waterway. Each year, resident beavers raise the dams as quickly as canoeists lower them while pushing and pulling their crafts over the mud and sticks. Last autumn, the route had been impassable; this spring, the unusually high water levels submerge the dams. Nature has provided a lovely solution.

Deux Rivières, with its rich aquatic plant life and forested shore, is an ideal region in which to see wildlife. Migrating ducks are flushed at every bend in autumn, and animal paths indicate the passage of boreal creatures. Later in spring, we would unwittingly startle a bull moose, then, rounding another turn in the river, come across a cow and her calf feeding leisurely on plants pulled from beneath the water's surface, water streaming through their lips.

The hardy, boisterous voyageurs followed the Ojibwa's paddle through Quetico and wove their way down Deux Rivières on this shuttle between the northwest region and Montréal. During the fur trade era, two routes were plied by the voyageurs: the southern route left Lake Superior at Grand Portage and traced the border lakes that now separate Ontario's Quetico Provincial Park from Minnesota's adjoining Boundary Waters Canoe Area; the northern route led up the Kaministiquia River from Fort William and entered Quetico at the French Portage.

The names of the waterways within Quetico reflect the canoeists who have passed over them. Some appelations that trip up the unaccustomed tongue belong to the Ojibwa language: Kahshahpiwi, Saganagons and

Kasakokwog. "Quetico" itself, also the name of a lake in the park, is believed to have been derived from the name of a generous Ojibwa spirit who inhabited areas of great beauty.

As we approach the portage, we are greeted by a party of men. They watch us land, then one of them states, "We just wanted to make sure you were okay." Their concern is appreciated and reciprocated when, an hour later another group relates the unfortunate story of their canoe being lifted by the wind and dashed upon a rock. The canoe's cut is clean and can be temporarily fixed. To make sure, we accompany them, watching warily while taking pleasure in the waves that propel us along Pickerel Lake.

We part company upon reaching the river leading to French Lake and are joined momentarily by a muskrat at our side and a bald eagle above. It is a world apart, or as William Keating expressed it in 1823: "The scene was such as a painter might have selected to depict a perfect calm of nature...." Professor Keating, a geologist and journalist for the Major Long expedition, was forcibly impressed by the Pickerel River and described it in his journal as a "highly romantic stream." Away from the blustery winds and rolling waves, this river is romantic and sensuous, as the sweet smells of the forest surround us and a gentle breeze greets us at every bend.

Finding Re-Creation

Once on French Lake, we pass the island where, as Shirley has told us, bald eagles have nested since 1937, right at her doorstep. Every March, these magnificent birds have returned to their home. They are not alone. On our trips we have met a retired executive paddling in Quetico for the fourteenth time; two brothers from distant locations who meet here year after year; a woman from west of Chicago and her German shepherd, for whom Quetico is a summer home.

When I mention this to Shirley, she nods her head. "So many people that come to Quetico have been here before. They must find 're-creation.'"

We will return. In the summer, when the heat is intense but the water cool, when loons and their chicks explore the waterways. And in the autumn, when the forest is ablaze with the gold of birch and filigreed tamarack, when the young mergansers try their wings, and double-crested cormorants fly silently overhead.

Maybe the "re-creation" people find in the quiet of Quetico is a balance to the tightly scheduled hustle of today's citified world. An elixir.

Come try the waters.

Hudson Bay
From the Seal River to Churchill

Stephan Kesting

A MAP LIBRARY IS A DANGEROUS PLACE TO BE IF YOU HAVE THE URGE TO jump into your canoe and go for a paddle. It only took one September afternoon in the University of Toronto map library to connect enough lakes, streams and rivers to get me from Jasper, Alberta, in the Rocky Mountain foothills, to the coast of Hudson Bay. This was a trip that would take me halfway across Canada, most of it far beyond the reach of roads and civilization. It took another eight months of preparation and almost three months of paddling to complete this trip of a lifetime.

From the beginning I knew this would be a solo trip. All my paddling partners were firmly entrenched in their jobs or studies, so a three-month trip was out of the question. Partners would have made the going easier and safer, but I was going to have to rely on meticulous planning and cautious canoeing to provide a safety net. As my friend, longtime arctic trekker Gino Bergeron, once told me: "It's okay to go on a solo trip, but you need to make sure that you always stay at least one notch below your limits."

The Athabasca, Fond du Lac, Cochrane and Seal rivers carried me 2,700 kilometres across Canada, but it was the last 60 kilometres — from the Seal River delta along the coast of Hudson Bay to Churchill, Manitoba — that caused me the most hardship. I feel a real danger in glorifying canoeing on Hudson Bay. This was the only part of the whole trip that I would hesitate about repeating on my own or recommending to other paddlers. The threat of sudden storms, extremely swift tides, and the ever-present danger of polar bears should not be underestimated: Hudson Bay is the most potentially dangerous and unforgiving body of water I have ever paddled. It was also beautiful, unforgettable and, in retrospect, the perfect ending to my journey.

As the Seal River spills into the cold water of Hudson Bay, it divides into a huge delta — islands and channels form such a complex mosaic that even with a compass and a detailed 1:50,000 topographic map you soon give up trying to keep track of your exact position. Most river deltas deliver a slow and tired waterway to its resting place in a lake or ocean, not so with the Seal. This delta seethes and churns with whitewater all along its 15-kilometre

length. After several hours of careful manoeuvring in the delta, I was finally able to spot the vast expanse of Hudson Bay. One enormous rapid later, I was able to taste salt in the water.

I pulled my 16-foot Kevlar Prospector through the intertidal mud and climbed to the promontory where paddlers meet their pick-up boats from Churchill. There was no boat waiting for me. The trip had been so long and had involved so many variables that I hadn't been able to arrange an exact pick-up date. My plan, for better or worse, had been to paddle the Bay itself. Failing this, my backup plan was to hitch a ride with some of the canoe groups I thought I was likely to meet along the river. I had, in fact, met two such groups in the last few days, including a group of 18 teenagers and two adults. Although they were amenable to my request to come along on their chartered fishing boat, I was hesitant to take them up on it. I love canoeing with people, but I didn't want to spend the final three days of a spectacular solo trip in the company of any group.

I filled all available containers with fresh river water, checked my EPIRB (Emergency Position Indicator Location Transmitter) and tide table, buckled down my spray deck and took paddle in hand once more. It is difficult to explain now, but at the time there was a feeling of doing the right thing. An acute awareness — almost a hypersensitivity — of the wind and waves came over me. This red-alert mode stayed with me the whole time I spent on the windswept and tide-torn coast.

Beluga Whales

I pulled out toward navigable waters, but my heart sank when I saw white-caps on the waves. Looking more closely, however, I realized that the whitecaps were the white backs of surfacing beluga whales. In a matter of min-utes there were hundreds of these great mammals all around my fragile craft.

I was transfixed by the sights and the sounds. There were squeaks, moans, whispers and a hundred other whale noises. Once I swung around, trying to locate the crying baby, only to realize that the keening had come from a beluga surfacing only 3 metres behind me. Although full of respect for the power of these magnificent creatures, I never felt that I was in danger; they never came close to touching me.

This dance continued as I paddled south along the coast. Paddling away from the belugas, I felt I had made the right decision in venturing onto the waters of the Bay. Even if I was stormbound for a week, paddling with whales was so exhilarating and worthwhile.

Late that evening, about 10:00, I decided to get some rest. Unfortunately, the tide had gone so far out that making it all the way to shore was impossible, so "camp" for the night was established on a small elevated mud plateau in the intertidal zone, about 2 kilometres from shore. I dozed fitfully for a few hours, not wanting to sleep for fear of polar bears and the returning tide.

At this latitude the sun rises at about 3:00 A.M. during the summer

months, and as it rose I started dragging and portaging my gear toward the approaching tide. With the wind so calm, I wasn't content to stay put and await the return of the water; I wanted to get in as many hours of paddling as possible before the afternoon winds picked up. It was hard work, and I became absolutely ruthless with my heavily laden canoe. I dragged her through puddles that barely covered the toes of my boots.

Eventually I was afloat again, and in the early hours of July 22, I paddled past the Knife River Delta. I was now halfway to Churchill. But in order to find water deep enough to paddle I had to be far offshore. The low relief of the land and its tundra vegetation meant the shore was barely visible, often just a thin line across my right-hand horizon; I had to follow compass bearings while trying to compensate for the effect of wind and tide. The consequence of getting washed out to sea in 5-metre tides was constantly on my mind.

To avoid the steadily rising offshore winds, I decided to make camp in the early evening. The site was on a sandbar parallel to the coast. The presence of plants and a high waterline were reassuring: they told me it was unlikely that I would be washed away during the night. While eating dinner I studied the far-off grain elevators of Churchill. Suspicious clouds in the distance convinced me to use several boulders from the tidal flats to secure my tent. That night, despite the ferocity of a tundra rainstorm, I fell into a most delicious sleep. The adrenaline had worn off after 32 hours of almost constant paddling and travelling.

Offshore Tide

During the third and final day of paddling, I decided for the first time to try to paddle with an offshore tide. To be safe, I stayed between the shore and last exposed boulders of the intertide. If the tidal current overpowered me and started washing me out to sea, my plan was to paddle over to one of the tiny rock islands and hang on for dear life until the tide went down. I also resisted the temptation to leave the shore and cut across the final large bay between me and my destination. Although this shortcut might have saved me about 10 kilometres of paddling, I had heard too many horror stories about storms coming in as paddlers set out to cross the expanse of Button Bay.

But hugging the shore had its own inherent difficulties. The 3-metre tide made it necessary to set the canoe at an angle and ferry across the swift offshore current just as if I were crossing a river. There were times when it was easiest to use the paddle as a pole, shoving myself along the sand and gravel seabed. Just as my arms were ready to fall off, I reached the base of the thin peninsula separating me from the outflow of the Churchill River and the port of Churchill. The 2-kilometre portage across the base of the peninsula was easy when compared to the prospect of having to paddle around the tip in ever-more-turbulent seas.

As I prepared my final dinner of the trip and waited for the winds to die down enough to cross the Churchill River, I reflected on the past months and realized that arriving at my goal created conflicting and discordant feelings. On the one hand, I was elated at having arrived; the grail was within my grasp, the goal I had striven for in eight months of planning and paddling was finally before me. On the other, I knew this was the end of the process. Every bit as important as achieving the goal had been the action of travelling and living in the bush. These would be the last few hours of that process.

Nonetheless, I was ready for ice cream, warm showers, music and train travel. I wanted to see what was on my 15 rolls of film, and I wanted to spend time with friends and family. I also felt slightly guilty about wanting these things, so seemingly antithetical to the experience of the whole summer.

On the three-day train ride from Churchill to Toronto, I started to make peace with those conflicting feelings. I mourned the close of the adventure. But nothing could take away or diminish my memories. And because I still had two weeks of food left, every time the train crossed another mysterious and inviting river, I wanted to stop, get off and start all over again.

Souris River
One-Sided Canyons

Bob Waldon

From a boater's perspective, rivers flowing through the southern Canadian prairies frequently suffer one serious flaw — no water. The Souris River is no exception.

In the pre-railway days of settlement in southwest Manitoba, a coal deposit near the Turtle Mountains attracted enough eager speculators to actually get some coal dug out. But the scheme called for it to be barged down the Souris River. In short order, the poor quality of both the coal and the navigability of the Souris combined to kill the scheme. One assumes the investors, having learned something of the vagaries of the prairie rivers, put what was left of their money into rail stock.

Better adapted entrepreneurs had previously done quite well on prairie river-based commerce. The Assiniboine River, as prone to swing from flood to trickle as any dry-land stream, nevertheless served commercial purposes well in the days when the birchbark freight canoe was king of the waterways. The fur-laden brigades swept downstream on the spring freshet. After a short break for debauchery at The Forks, those voyageurs who were fit to travel took their heavy heads and injuries back to their canoes for the return trip. If water was low, the canoes, being the amphibious craft they are, could always be lined around or carried over the sandbars and rocky bits.

The Souris River no doubt served as a minor fur feeder route to the Fort Garry trading posts. It would also have been a source of pemmican when its sheltered, well-watered meadows drew bison from the parched autumn uplands of southwest Manitoba and the adjacent Dakota territory. In the days before trains and trucks, this concentrated food was the equivalent of modern-day gasoline and diesel fuel. Run through the calorie-ravenous guts of the voyageurs, pemmican powered the paddles on the routes west of the Red River. It was essential, and it was consumed in huge amounts. Supplying it to the fur companies was a prosperous undertaking for the buffalo hunters, traders and wholesalers of Red River.

A River by Another Name

The bison have long since been replaced by Herefords, the grasslands by checkerboard fields, the winding cart tracks by a road grid. Neither has the Souris that winds its way through this transmogrified landscape escaped alteration. Dams have been put in to slow it down, ditches and canals dug to speed it up. Most of these modifications have been done along the portion of the river that loops far down into North Dakota, where, the folks there being blissfully unbilingual, it is called the Mouse. When it eventually finds its way over the dams and diversions back into Manitoba, south of Melita, the Mouse once more becomes the Souris.

To the wayfaring paddler, the Manitoba section of the Souris reveals a split personality. From the American border to the town of Souris, a good four-hour drive west of Winnipeg, it is a quiet stream, looping through a gentle valley of pastures and fields. Not to be outdone by the Americans in the business of riverine manipulation, townspeople and farmers along the way have added several dams and weirs. If you don't mind an occasional portage or pullover, this section of the river affords the opportunity to float and photograph. Bird and mammal life are surprisingly plentiful, and this section of the river does have its pastoral charm.

The river's other personality begins below the dam at Souris. This half is rambunctious, assertive, energized by a steeper gradient that shows itself as soon as you put in below the dam. From there to its confluence with the Assiniboine, less than 80 valley kilometres east, the river drops 90 metres, and only the Wawanesa Dam interrupts its hurried flow. As a result, the river is not only much more interesting water to paddle, it retains vestiges of its original appearance and spirit. Amidst some of the province's most astonishing and delightful scenery you can still imagine Aboriginal encampments, herds of elk and bison, lurking buffalo wolves, and perhaps even the menacing presence of the plains grizzly.

For the first few kilometres below Souris, you won't pay much attention to the cuts on the outer sides of each bend. At first they are modest gravel or clay banks, their steep sides rutted by cattle paths. But as you go further the river seems to gain momentum, biting ever deeper into its valley walls with each sweep. The banks become higher and steeper. At their most spectacular they are near-vertical cliffs rising 30 metres straight from the water's edge. In most places these awesome one-sided canyons are carved in an even, sweeping crescent, placing the paddler on the river below in a succession of magnificent natural amphitheatres.

The cliffs themselves are composed of alternating strata of shale and clay. Where layers of water-absorbing bentonite clay are exposed, miniature poplars and hardy shrubs trace straight horizontal lines of lacy green.

This kind of scenery is hard on a roll of film; the effect is especially arresting if the paddler has any eye for lighting, takes time to frame the shots, and has a choice of wide-angle and telephoto lenses. Though you have to keep an alert eye to find really good ones, campsites can be equally captivating. My own memories go back to grassy swards among stout sheltering maples and ash on the inside of a bend, with the rolling river and a towering canyon wall for a backdrop.

The river course itself boasts more rapids and riffles that any other stream of similar size in southern Manitoba. On some stretches, especially below the Big Bend, there is an interesting disturbance every couple of hundred metres. In high water these can vary from slightly wavy passages to rapids well worth a pull-out and a reconnoitre.

Elbow of Capture

The Big Bend is not labelled on maps, but its location is obvious. Called by geographers an "elbow of capture," it marks the place where the river, in a great flood long ago, blocked off the normal channel, charged the wrong way up a tributary, broke through its top end and joined the Assiniboine.

One of the variations to be particularly wary of is debris. With the banks being repeatedly undercut with each flood, trees collapse into the water to become "sweepers" that can catch and swamp the unwary. Eventually the sweepers wash out; a sprawling cottonwood hung up in the middle of a rapid can be a deadly trap, especially in ice-cold spring water.

Now, what about those water levels? The seasonal fluctuations can be moderated or exaggerated by the timing of precipitation as well as its amount, and by whoever is fiddling with the controls on the American stretches of the river. If snowmelt is early and light, and spring rains delayed, the break-up flood can be so fleeting that it comes and goes before even local paddlers can set up a trip.

Even a half-decent interval of high water can abruptly end. I vividly recall a trip that I led for the Manitoba Naturalists' Society in the late 1970s. As any conscientious leader must do, I had checked the river at the Big Bend the previous weekend, and it had been in prime condition. But when we arrived there to leave a couple of vehicles for transportation at trip's end, I was dismayed to find that someone had turned off the water! What had once been a pair of lovely, noisy rapids above and below a charming pond had shrunk to a matched set of rock piles with a stagnant slough between. I managed to stave off active mutiny by relocating the trip to the stretch between Melita and Hartney, where, thanks to the dams, there was at least enough water to float our convoy of disgruntled paddlers and their thoroughly discredited leader.

As measured by the Water Survey of Canada, the flow can vary between a dribble too meagre to measure and a high flood level of over 349 cubic metres per second (85 cubic metres per second makes for a very pleasurable and interesting canoe trip). Daily discharge limits can be obtained from the Inland Waters Branch of the Water Survey of Canada, Department of the Environment offices in Winnipeg. Other sources of information include the town offices of Souris and Wawanesa.

The scenic Souris–Wawanesa stretch can be done with ease in two weekends or three consecutive days. The two-weekend recommendation is for the traveller who is within reasonable distance of the river, and who wants to allow some time to explore. There is some hiking and scrambling to be done amid the oak- and aspen-clad ridges of the Big Bend Wildlife Management Area. And you should make at least one excursion to the top of one of the bluffs for a look around.

The run between Souris and Wawanesa can be divided into two roughly equal halves by ending the first run either at Highway 10 or at Provincial

Road 346 north of the village of Margaret, which is on Provincial Trunk Highway 23. Number 10 is a better choice if the second run is to end at Wawanesa. But if you want to extend the trip and go on to the bridge south of the site of the village of Treesbank, two or three hours' time below Wawanesa, the better dividing point is Highway 346. Don't confuse the village site with the former ferry site of the same name, which is on the Assiniboine several kilometres east of the old town.

You can, of course, use the Souris as the starting leg of a trip that includes the scenic stretch of the Assiniboine that flows through Spruce Woods Provincial Park.

Public amenities along the lower Souris are minimal. Both Wawanesa and Souris maintain acceptable public campgrounds adjacent to the river. There is a small picnic site several hours below Souris where the village of Bunclody used to be, and where a branch of the Great Northern Railway, abandoned in 1936, crossed the valley on its way between Brandon and Grand Forks, North Dakota. At the Big Bend, the province put in a picnic site with tables, privies, garbage cans. Apart from these public camp spots, you're on your own.

By all means take plenty of water. Thanks to cities and towns upstream, the untreated water of the Souris is, regrettably, unfit for modern-day voyageurs.

Drinking River
Canoe Trip Guides Find Magic — Eventually

Ric Driediger

PLEASE NOTE: The names of the participants on this canoe trip have been left unchanged in order to protect the innocent.

WE WERE A GROUP OF SIX CANOE-TRIP GUIDES. AFTER A SUMMER OF taking teenagers on canoe trips, we were ready to get away without all the responsibilities of looking after a bunch of people. After studying the maps, we decided on the Drinking River. It looked like a river where we might not see other people and it had all the characteristics that would keep other people away: too far from a road for easy access, a few runnable rapids, and enough portages to scare off the weak. Now, finally, here we were on a canoe trip with good friends and no responsibilities — the right ingredients for a perfect canoe trip.

Since we had more time than money, we chose to start our trip at McLennon Lake, about 50 kilometres by road from our base in Missinipe, Saskatchewan (the other option was to fly in to the headwaters of the river at Robertson Lake). The first three days would be spent getting to the Drinking River by working our way through a connection of lakes and portages. The next three would be on the Drinking River. The last three days would be on the Churchill River paddling back to Missinipe.

DAY 1 ⌐ The first day of paddling went beautifully. We all congratulated one another on how light we were able to pack. Kevin suggested this was a fine example of how much extra stuff teenagers often take. Gerald said this showed our experience as guides. "Take all that is necessary, but only what is necessary," was one of his favourite lines. Nata noted how peaceful it was without having a group of teens yelling back and forth. On the portage, Lois commented on how relaxing it was not to have to organize the group to get everything across. Paul mentioned again how good this trip was going to be for all of us.

There was a lot of discussion about where on Davis Lake we would camp that night. The problem was that there are two great camping spots on the lake — Kevin's favourite and Gerald's favourite. It was decided by taking a vote. Kevin's won. It was closer.

It was assumed that Nata would cook supper. She always talks about how much she enjoys cooking over an open fire. She refused. "This is my holiday," she explained. After a lot of helpful suggestions on how to properly cook this meal, Paul kicked everyone out of the kitchen.

Gerald set out to put up his tent. After searching through all the packs it was discovered that someone had forgotten all the tents. Nata was sure that Kevin was going to pack them. Kevin was sure he had seen Lois carrying a tent, so he assumed she had packed them. Lois told Kevin that what he thought was a tent was actually her laundry. Gerald set up the large tarp we use as a cooking shelter in bad weather.

Later that evening, while sitting around the campfire, Lois mentioned how fortunate it was that we use a checklist when packing a canoe trip for a group of kids. Paul said that with a group of such experienced guides, a checklist wasn't necessary. Someone would remember to bring what the others forgot. Except the tents.

DAY 2 ∾ The next morning Paul was up first, so he cooked breakfast. At the smell of coffee the rest of us got up, except Kevin. "This is my holiday and I'm sleeping in," he said. After getting syrup on his sleeping bag from having breakfast in bed, he finally got up.

Later that morning we had a long argument about whether it was quicker to paddle 2 kilometres or portage about 300 metres. After stopping on an island to switch paddling partners, Paul and Nata went to portage while the other canoes paddled the extra 2 kilometres. After meeting on the other side at almost exactly the same time, we continued on our way.

We stopped for lunch on Colin Lake. Lois asked how many packs we were supposed to have. We were one pack short. Paul and Gerald, the two strongest paddlers, paddled back to look for it. They were back in an hour. The pack had been left on the upper end of the last portage. Nata asked who had been the last person across the portage. Kevin said on our regular canoe trips one of the guides is always the last across, to make sure everything is taken. Paul asked whose responsibility it was to make sure all was taken across the portage on this leaderless trip. No one had an answer.

Even though it was nearly 6:00 P.M., Paul, Lois and Gerald wanted to push on for another hour and a half to get to the gorgeous camping spot on Solymos Lake. The rest wanted to camp on Settee Lake near the diving cliffs. Since the weather wasn't warm enough for diving, we pushed on.

At the evening campfire, Gerald said the unthinkable: "We need a leader." Lois agreed that it might be more relaxing if we had one. After a lot of negotiating we came up with a plan. We pulled out the maps and decided approximately where we would camp each night. And we decided we would take turns being the "leader of the day."

DAY 3 ⌒ Life on this canoe trip seemed to settle down to some semblance of normalcy. The "leader of the day" worked fairly well. The only problem seemed to centre around those who weren't the leader. They were too much like the teens we were trying to get away from.

The next day we portaged off the main route (we called it the main route because we had all done it several times before with groups of teens). The portage led us into Robertson Lake, the headwaters of the Drinking River. When we paddled out onto the lake we all felt a bit let down. There was nothing wrong with Robertson Lake. It had clear blue water, rocky shores and lots of islands. The problem was that we had the Drinking River built up so high in our minds, we expected magic.

We found a beautiful camping spot at the far end of Robertson Lake. Paul came back from roaming around to announce that there was no trace of anyone ever having been here before. The magic was beginning. Even the loons' calls that evening seemed more plaintive than before.

DAY 4 ⇌ The following morning we portaged in to Wapassini Lake. At the end of the portage Nata commented that it seemed no one had walked the trail that summer and the moss on the trial had not been disturbed. Yet, she had noticed that all the fallen trees and branches had been cut away. Paul complained that all the branches and trees over 5 and a half feet had been left (he is 6 feet 2 inches tall). Nata, who stands just under 5 feet tall, hadn't noticed this. Gerald suggested the reason for this mystery was that maybe the trail is only used in winter by a trapper riding his snowmobile.

This day was one of those days that you wish would never end. Wapassini Lake was so calm you could see the shore perfectly by looking into the water. The only clouds in the sky were little marshmallows. Much of the lake had high, rocky shores covered in black spruce and jack pine. The group hardly spoke all day, but when someone did, it was in whispers. Whenever possible, we paddled next to shore and watched the rock and forest drift by. No one was in a hurry.

Later in the day, a family of loons guided us to our camping spot. They serenaded us while we set up camp and ate supper. We didn't even bother to set up our cooking-sleeping shelter that night. We lay in our sleeping bags not wanting to close our eyes, while the northern lights danced overhead. This was a magical spot.

DAY 5 ⇌ Even though the day was bright and sunny, the portage out of Wapassini Lake seemed quite dark. At the rest stop Lois also noted the same thing. Paul pointed out that we were in a grove of very large white spruce, which only grows in very old forests in this part of the North. We marvelled at their size. Gerald called this portage Dark Portage.

After setting down our gear on the shore of Dirks Lake, we noticed a small trapper's cabin. We went to take a look. It was only about 8 by 10 feet, about 5 feet high at the walls, and 5 and a half feet high in the centre. But what was truly amazing was that it was only three logs high.

We paddled through Dirks Lake and portaged into the next lake. Gerald, who always needed to know where we were, asked Nata, the "leader of the day," what lake we were on. Nata said this lake and the next two did not have names. Paul, who has guided in the Boundary Waters of Minnesota, said when lakes in the Boundary Waters had no names they just called them Lake One, Lake Two and Lake Three. So that is what these lakes became.

We paddled through Lakes One, Two and Three and camped on a point near the start of Irving Lake. A southeast wind had been picking up all day, so Paul and Gerald set the tarp in such a way that we would all stay dry during the night. It started to rain toward morning. Later Kevin, the new "leader of the day," suggested it was a perfect day to stay put. The only response was the sound of a few sleeping bags shuffling as people rolled over.

DAY 6 ᔕ Around noon we started to wake up to the smell of wood smoke and coffee. Kevin, who was taking his role as "leader of the day" very seriously, had gotten up and was in the process of making pancakes. When he noticed eyes from sleeping bags watching him, he asked if anyone else wanted coffee.

We lay in our sleeping bags under the tarp most of the day. The light rain continued. We talked of many things. We laughed about the many adventures and misadventures of the summer. One example was when Nata and Gerald were just beginning a canoe trip with a group of eight teens. During the night Paul and Kevin quietly paddled to their campsite and moved all their canoes, except one, to the other side of the lake. Another example was when Lois and Kevin were nearing the end of a canoe trip, Paul and Nata made a large "M" out of foam and set it up on a nearby point. They had french fries, hamburgers and coke waiting for Lois and Kevin's group when they rounded the point. The stories went on and on.

Later we began talking about what we would be doing after the trip was over. Lois was going back to nurse's training. Nata and Gerald were getting

married (not to each other). Kevin was heading to Mexico for a holiday, and then to the B.C. mountains to instruct downhill and telemark skiing. Paul said he was just going to hang around until he found something to do that he liked. We began to realize this would be the last time we would all be together.

DAY 7 ⌒ The rain continued all night and into the morning. We packed up and left. We would always remember Irving Lake by the good time we had talking under the tarp in the rain. There was only a narrows between Irving and Soroski lakes. When we reached the outlet of Soroski we noticed the river had grown considerably. Gerald, Day 7's "leader of the day," noted that there were many feeder streams flowing into the two lakes. There was now enough water to float the canoes down the river connecting Soroski and Rink lakes. We had to lift over several ledges but arrived on Rink Lake without incident. We attempted to do the same thing going into Malchow Lake, but we had to carry our canoes around Hepburn Falls, a drop of about 25 metres.

From our campsite on Malchow Lake, we couldn't see the falls, but we could certainly hear them. The rain had stopped around noon and now the sky showed some blue. Later we sat drinking tea next to the evening fire while we watched a spectacular sunset.

DAY 8 ⌒ Lois woke us up early with the banging and rattling of pots. Gerald commented that Lois never could do anything quietly. Soon we were all up, except Kevin. He wanted coffee in bed as a payment for two days ago. Lois refused, so he got up.

We were able to walk our canoes through the rapids most of the way from Malchow Lake to Pitching Lake. At the south end of Pitching we came upon the last portage of the Drinking River, where there were some wooden structures. We found out later that years ago someone had attempted to mine gold from the riverbed here. He soon gave up.

That night we camped on Drinking Lake on the Churchill River. The Drinking River had lived up to our expectations. We had enjoyed a very relaxing trip. We had ended our summer the way we wanted to. And we had appropriately said goodbye to our fellow guides. Even though we still had two and a half days of paddling left to get to Missinipe, we felt the trip was over. These two-plus days were through very familiar water. Soon everyone would go their separate ways and this summer would become a memory.

Churchill River
Call of the Wild

Sheila Archer

EVERY SUMMER THE CHURCHILL RIVER IS MY DESTINATION. I COME TO renew something.

If you drive 80 kilometres north of the town of La Ronge, which lies four hours north of Saskatoon, you will come to a place called Missinipe. It is a hamlet on the section of the Churchill known as Otter Lake, about halfway down the Saskatchewan section of the Churchill River.

Otter Lake is a destination for canoe-trippers from all over the world. Some paddle in from upstream, others start from Missinipe to head downstream, perhaps as far as Sandy Bay, eleven days to the east. The Churchill is a place where many come to paddle in the wilderness, drink the river's living water, and breathe in the rich smell of this special place. The original name of the river means "big water." A canoe trip on the Churchill is unforgettable, and its memory will not release you. You will come back.

I first came here on a canoe trip when I was 17, and for seven years following I had recurring dreams of flying above channels of rapids. At 24, I returned to paddle the Churchill again, married my paddling partner, and now, nine years later, our nearly complete house is waiting ahead on Walker Bay. It is June, and I am driving north on Highway 2, passing the Stanley Mission turnoff, repeating the names of the signs again, "Lynx, McKay, Lussier . . ."

My memory has fed me in the dark winters . . . I am lying back in the boat, legs spread over the gunwales, the sun showing red inside my closed eyes as it sucks water beads off my skin. A walleye jingles the fish chain. In the stillness a raven calls. Then I am walking out of the boreal darkness, late on a September night, the roar of the distant rapids blowing over the lake. The island I'm on is surrounded by brilliant northern lights, a sky so beautiful I cannot stand up. Now it is the morning and eagles circle over the channels downstream. The early sun begins to heat the black slope of rock that slants down into the bay. I walk down from the tent and plunge into the river.

The Churchill is a river without banks, only endless lakeshore that joins one basin to the next. Where two lakes meet the river, it roars through rocks caught in a losing battle to hold back the water. Each lake in the drop pool system is a variation on the Precambrian tree-and-rock theme that all Canadian Shield lakes follow, some with many islands, some with few. Paddling down from Sandfly Lake, leading a group of five women along the very old highway through the Shield, I miss a heading in the Black Bear Island maze. I lose us for an hour and finally determine our position by getting up on a high rock to draw what I think an aerial view of our position would look like, then find the shapes on the map.

The rapids and falls that join the lakes are unique, each with its own form and character. At the end of every lake you will find new beauty and challenge. Some drops allow shoot-ing with canoes, others with cameras only. There is always an old and well-used portage trail. The water volume is normally large, highest in early July, when it peaks at 24,000 cubic feet per second. By then the water is warm, 20 degrees Celsius on the sur-face, delicious for a swim. It is a big river, but sweet.

Necklace of Lakes

If you cannot see the whole Churchill, you may be sure that it is all this beau-tiful — a blue-beaded necklace of lakes flowing along the 56th Parallel. To start, you can drive as far west as Ile-à-La-Crosse and begin there, pad-dling down through Shagwenaw, Dip-per, Primeau, Knee, Dreger, Sandy, Pinehouse, Sandfly, Black Bear Island, Trout, around Wanahichewan Island via Stack and Mountney or Crew and Torranee, then Nipew, Hayman, Barker, and Devil to Otter Lake. You can start at Missinipe and go east, down through Mountain, Nistowiak, Drink-ing, Keg, Trade, Uskik, Iskwatam, Wintego, Pita, Pikoo, and Sokatisewin to the dam at Island Falls, and end your trip at Sandy Bay.

You can fly. The view from the air is a stunning extra for all who can afford to go by plane, either to reach the upper lakes of the Churchill or to paddle the river's small tributaries that have no access. In a Twin Otter,

heading west over the rapids above Devil Lake, I swoop across the place where Murray Channel meets Murray Falls, looking down into the eye of the huge whirlpool formed by their joining. Some of my friends have been down in there. It is a very deep place.

To the women in my group, the endless landscape of lakes and islands is all unknown. After we pass over Black Bear Island Lake, I too am looking at water I have never seen. Circling over Sandfly, the pilot warns us that he is going down for a closer look. The power turn is unbelievably sharp, the plane's wings nearly perpendicular to the water's surface. In this wind, the lake is rolling pretty good, and with the river level at a record low, rocky shoals are everywhere. "I'm putting her down in the middle," says Frank. "It's too dangerous to get near a shore. You'll just have to paddle."

As though they have always done this, the women unload the canoes into the waves and fill them with gear. I split them into pairs, taking Wendy with me. Turning north to the nearest land, we head into the wind. Wendy tells me she has never flown in a plane before. They will love this place.

In the lee of a rock point, we rest together after the first leg of our journey. I tell them we will find a good campsite. There will be a big granite rock, a shoulder curving up from the water, flesh-pink in the late-day sun. The site will have a fire pit and several tent spots. It has always been there. All along the river are these places.

There are other creatures here. Our first day on the river we spot a yearling black bear searching along the shore for lunch. A resting moose crashes off into the forest when I step into his grove of trees, checking tent spots. Each day white pelicans, fishing in the eddies, glide away at our approach. Our last night out, seven loons dance in the sheltered bay at sunset.

I show our group the sacred places: red rock paintings on the cliff faces of Kinosaskimaw and Black Bear Island Lake. There are also images at water level along the route, symbols we cannot read but which remain from a time even before the Cree were here. My unofficial second, Lynn, knows a story about the beings painted on the rocks, learned from an Aboriginal story-teller. It is very quiet while she tells us about the People of the Stone Canoe.

On the wide-open water of Crew Lake, the air is hot and the wind calm. Lynn sings a song of the voyageurs, which I know too, so we join voices. She is a historian and a musician, and we all listen to her stories and songs, imagining another time. We do not travel like the voyageurs, nor wish for that day, but we know they must have loved this place as we do. The river gives us everything it has, just as it did them, and the Aboriginal people who came before them and who remain.

The women learn to paddle whitewater, to manoeuvre with confidence along routes they are taught to find and follow. We have one novice in each boat. Gail and Lynn have some prior experience in rapids, but Allison, Susan and Wendy are starting green. There is a golden moment, running the last set of rapids from Torranee into Nipew, when the newly trained crews come through with sun flashing on their paddles and smiling faces. I remember that feeling, and now they know it, too.

On the last day of the trip, I am step carefully on the rain-slick trail, carrying Wendy with her sprained ankle down the 1.2-kilometre Great Devil Portage. It is a long way, still, so I ask her about her family, hoping to cheer her, to help her forget her thoughts of being a burden, while distracting myself from the physical task. We keep each other's spirits up. She has been my paddling partner for the trip. We are a team.

Back in Missinipe that night, we recollect together, passing around the little glass mug of brandy. We have been fortunate, having had mostly clear weather in the midst of the wettest summer on record. There are toasts to the river, to the guide, to the group. Everyone is warm but sad, for trips always end.

Next morning, I wave goodbye as the women drive home to the rainy south. It will be later, in September, when I paddle here for the last time this year. The sky will be blue on that perfect day, because that day I will have to go south, and this will be here, and I will not. But I will come back.

William River
River of Golden Sands, River Beyond Dreams
Cliff Speer

I KNEW I WAS ON HOME TERRITORY, BUT I FELT LIKE I'D BEEN TRANSPORTED into an alien land. Such was my encounter with the exotic landscape of the William River. This "otherworldly" impression was created mainly by the immense sand dunes bordering the final quarter of the river's 200-kilometre navigable reach. "Marvellous is the word for the great sand dunes of northern Saskatchewan and adjacent Alberta. Viewed in the dazzling light of long summer days, they seem an enchanted landscape — a portion of Arabia magically transported to the boreal forest and displayed along the south shore of blue Lake Athabasca," says Canadian ecologist Stan Rowe in his book, *Home Place: Essays on Ecology*.

The Athabasca Sand Dunes Provincial Wilderness Park contains the world's largest northerly sand dunes, some of which are 30 metres high. The park is situated on the south shore of Lake Athabasca, in the northwest corner of Saskatchewan, not too far from the Northwest Territories border. The William River, which flows through the western portion of the park and empties into Lake Athabasca, takes in the Athabasca region's largest dune field (about 17,000 hectares), about half the active sand surface in the park.

For wilderness canoeists, the seemingly contradictory elements of water, desert and forest are pleasantly bewildering. But the surreal experience of the William River is more than gigantic sand dunes. A unique ecosystem has developed in the windblown sediments of the former glacial lake that covered the region about 9,000 years ago. Sixty species of plants that inhabit the dunes are considered rare; ten species are so rare that they exist nowhere else in the world. They're called endemics. They gave me the feeling that I was travelling in a very special place — treading on hallowed ground.

Our party of six Saskatchewan paddlers launched into the supernatural world of the William River via Hale Lake, about 60 kilometres downstream of the river's headwaters. La Loche Airways provided float-plane transport from its base in the Aboriginal community 650 kilometres northwest of Saskatoon. Apart from a few blackflies and a relocation to avoid disturbing a nest of bald eagles, our camping time on Hale Lake was uneventful.

At the outlet of Hale Lake, the William River is a small, winding, willow-bordered stream with an easy-going gradient and a few riffles here and there. Beautiful pink and mauve blossoms of bog laurel line the banks. By midday the streambed had flattened and presented us with a major boulder garden. A quick scouting from shore revealed a narrow passage through the obstruction.

Moving on, we wound our way through more "gardens." Most of the rapids in the upper reaches demand precise manoeuvring. It seemed like a mythical ice-age stonethrower had peppered the river bottom with an impressive rock arsenal. Our group paddled Kevlar and ABS canoes, which withstood the bump and grind of the Athabasca sandstone fairly well. Very few of the numerous rapids are marked on the topo maps, so we had to keep our eyes and ears well tuned to the river's signals.

The William is wild and remote, with very little evidence of other travellers. But there were a couple of exceptions. On the third day we stopped at a nice beach where, in mid-June at 59 degrees north latitude, we swam without shivering. Backed by a sandy, pine-clad ridge with a view of distant boulder-strewn eskers, this beach had attracted others long ago. There were remains of rusted pails and domestic utensils at a very old cabin site. A few kilometres downstream we came across more recent evidence of an abandoned

diamond-drill camp. This blotch on the pristine landscape is a relic of the uranium exploration industry and is to be rehabilitated, according to Saskatchewan Environment and Resource management.

Campsites abound along the river. Riverbank sandstone ledges are backed by sand lichen-covered ridges, while open jack pine stands create a naturally groomed, park-like atmosphere. One such site could be described as northern savannah, complete with low ground cover and widely spaced groupings of pine trees. Such were our campsites before reaching the dunes. After that, camping on the dunes was always an option, but one that we avoided, since we would get sandblasted if the wind got rowdy.

By day four, we were close to the junction of the William and Carswell rivers. En route we passed a federal water surveys monitoring station. Important data from this little building determines whether you canoe the river, or push, pull or drag it. Because of its shallow, bouldery bottom, most "official" reports conclude that the William is not canoeable. A lot of the time it isn't. Fortunately for us, the flow was almost double the 14-year average. Even with that margin of comfort, a few inches less would have made progress much more complicated.

Dunes Await

The Carswell River junction marks a demanding stretch of whitewater. After the Carswell rapids, we make our way toward the giant William dunes. Expectations rise. So far, apart from sandy shoreline ridges and golden beaches here and there, the William hasn't revealed what awaits downstream. But as we round a bend, suddenly, smack in front of us stands a 15-metre-high wall of fine, golden Athabasca sand, blocking off the river and transcending the surrounding landscape. Climbing to the top of our first sand dune, we are treated to a strange, unearthly scene — expansive, undulating fields of sand and gravel, with huge dunes beckoning in the distance. We will be treated to many variations of this theme for the next three days.

After running a few more rapids and lifting over a major ledge spanning the entire river, we reach the highest dunes — rising about 30 to 40 metres from the river. We climb up the closest one to view the surroundings. Another fabulous view, with immense dune fields stretching to the northwest. To the east, the river cuts off the marching sands. Then, on the other side of the river, a spruce and pine forest extends to the horizon. The contrast is stunning. Endless fields of golden sand, a winding band of blue and white water, a carpet of green foliage — the juxtaposition is unearthly.

The overall sensory impact of the river dunes is overpowering. But certain parts of this desert environment are vulnerable to heedless visitors, especially the desert pavements. These fragile gravel plains exist between major dunes. They are formed when the wind lifts the lighter surface material, leaving a thin layer of closely spaced, sandblasted pebbles covering the remaining sand. Disturbances to the delicate sand-gravel balance can apparently take years for nature to restore.

As we moved downriver the dunes got bigger, and so did the sandstone ledges and the boulders on the river bottom. The river picks up groundwater discharged from the dunes, and the increased flow makes the rapids more pushy. A major obstacle loomed on the river horizon. An extended series of falls is marked on the map, but it is actually several ledges on an S-bend, forcing our first portage of the trip. Scouting this section involves climbing up to a high point on the sand dunes to get a bird's-eye view downstream. The sight is awesome. A half-kilometre of whitewater stretches to the next bend, with giant dunes sitting on the horizon.

Our scramble over the dunes brought us to a spot where an encroaching dune face was slowly, relentlessly burying the living forest. It looked devastating, but it is part of a process that occurs throughout the active "sandscape." On the flip side, exhumation may occur eventually. As the sand moves on, buried trees are unearthed and left standing like forlorn phantoms in the desert.

On our last day on the river we saw fresh bear, moose and wolf tracks crisscrossing the beach where we landed. We expected an evening visitor, but no one appeared. The next morning I photographed a moose in the river.

We had seen bear and moose earlier, on the upper stretches of the river, and the black bear is the most abundant large mammal inhabiting the dune region. We were fortunate not to have had any close encounters, but others have reported being charged by bears. Protection and/or precaution against such occurrences is a good idea.

Bird life on the dunes is not prolific. Bald eagles are evident occasionally. I have a photo of an osprey touching down on her nest and, in the braided section of the river, I captured a sandhill crane lifting off a sandbar.

Spotting Endemic Plants

I spent our last evening on the William River dunes searching for as many of the endemic plants as possible. This was a fascinating task. The most abundant species seems to be the felt-leaved willow. No problem finding this one

— the furry leaves are unmistakable. Not so for the other three varieties of willow, whose similar features make them difficult to discern. In spite of identification challenges, I was able to spot eight of the ten endemics inhabiting the Athabasca sand dunes

Other rare plants also inject spurts of colour into the monochrome sandscape. We found moss campion, a small, purple-petalled alpine cushion plant, on a expansive gravel plain. Here the little pimples of purple perched on the plain were slowly building up their "pincushion" mounds by trapping wind-blown sand.

About 20 kilometres from the mouth of the William, after a rush through a maze of gigantic boulders, the river flattens out and turns into a braided stream with intertwining channels and shifting sandbars. At water level, this final portion of the river is not spectacular, but from the air it is absolutely dazzling. The rust-tinted water reflects hues of gold and copper of varying intensity off the changing sand bottom. Saskatoon photographer Courtney Milne eloquently records his impression of this aerial abstraction in his photoessay "Witness to the William," in the March 1993 issue of *Photo Digest*: "When I did witness the William from above, the evergreens that bordered the water were still identifiable, yet the sand pattern took on the quality of another world. The trees . . . acted as a taunting reminder that what one saw was in fact the real world, allowing the viewer to immerse into a dream world — just for an instant — then to be plucked back into the reality of the moment. The result was the outrageous condition of simultaneous belief and disbelief, while gazing at the best of nature's art."

We skirted the broad, expansive delta at the mouth of the William where the river drops its load of 3,000 tons of sand a day into Lake Athabasca. We were able to slip down a side stream that quickly shot us out to the lake. Our trip continued for 100 kilometres eastward along the south shore of Lake Athabasca to the mouth of the MacFarlane River. Upstream, the river opens into a picturesque lake. We camped here to await our float-plane pickup.

The William is a special place whose attractions can't be duplicated anywhere else in the world. It deserves special respect from visitors: respect for its wild and remote character; respect for its unparalleled beauty; respect for its unique, surreal charm; and above all, a deep respect for its fragile environment.

MacFarlane River
Down to the Kingdom of Sand

Dave Bober

Bill had it all figured out, but being slightly claustrophobic I wasn't all that enthused about squeezing my anatomy through the narrow crevice in the canyon wall of the MacFarlane River's awesome Middle Canyon.

"You mean we have to squeeze through that little crack?" I shuddered.

"No sweat," Bill quipped. "If Roger can make it, a little guy like you should have no problem. Or you can portage an extra kilometre."

The possibility of reducing a 3-kilometre bushwhack portage convinced me to go for it, and soon the four of us — Bill Jeffery, Roger Devine, Daryl Sexsmith and I — were standing on top of the 15-metre-high canyon rim, exclaiming, "Wow! It's hard to believe this is Saskatchewan."

This is where our topo maps came alive as the river plunged down across nine contour lines in 5 kilometres of rugged, pristine beauty. Sheer canyon walls rose 12 to 18 metres high, and the 80-metre drop pounded itself out in countless ledges and four sets of falls up to 12 metres high. In some places, huge pieces of cliff had fallen or detached themselves from the main canyon wall, creating all sorts of weird crevices and bizarre overhangs.

While this was just a scouting trip, the next morning was the real thing as we descended into the ominous canyon, hugging the west side, all eyes peeled for the exact spot, our escape crevice, where we would take out just above the first impassable ledge. Adrenaline assisted us in manhandling the canoes and packs up the canyon wall with a rope, and then it was the final squeeze through the gloomy escape hatch.

Seldom does reality meet expectations, but when it comes to wilderness canoeing, our June 1991 MacFarlane River trip had it all — remoteness, lengthy runnable rapids, ideal campsites, abundant wildlife, spectacular whitewater canyons, and a benevolent "Ol Sol" that shone brilliantly for almost two weeks.

The MacFarlane rises about 50 kilometres north of Cree Lake, running 300 kilometres almost due north through the Athabasca sandstone geological formation. Just before emptying into Lake Athabasca, the river cuts through the east side of the unique Athabasca sand dunes, a world unto themselves. The entire region is uninhabited and virtually untravelled today, offering the wilderness seeker some of the most isolated canoe country to be found south of the 60th Parallel.

The 170-kilometre flight into the headwaters was a turbulent ride and our stomachs played "the butterfly boogie." The pilot handed us each a doggie bag, but we managed to hold our own by trying to concentrate on the jigsaw puzzle of small lakes and interconnected streams below. After circling for 15 minutes, our pilot finally figured it out, landing at the northeast end of Lisgar Lake. While the Cessna returned for our other two crew members, Daryl and I set up our first camp on a carpet of reindeer moss, and by 10:00 P.M. the plane had returned and left again, leaving the four of us alone with the summer solstice.

The weather pattern for the next 11 days was set when a bright blue sky greeted us the next morning, with a majestic bull caribou crossing from island to island as a good omen.

There was something exhilarating about paddling a river without a written record from previous travellers, and sometimes I found myself engrossed in a voyageur fantasy of peril and adventure. But I do take offence at those who claim a first, or whatever, descent of a river, as the Aboriginal people did .them all long before there were any white men around. George Bihun, a friendly conservation officer from Uranium City, shared a Geological Survey Map dated 1932, indicating old Aboriginal routes that included some phenomenally long portages. Bill has personally talked to several Dene hunters, now elderly, who endured portages of 10 to 25 kilometres to access this area many years ago. It's a shame their exploits have never been recorded.

Our days on the river passed all too quickly as the MacFarlane grew from a shallow stream to a formidable opponent with long, bouldery Class II and III rapids that could usually be scouted from the river and then eddy-hopped down with caution.

While we paddled across the mirror surface of Brudell Lake, my mind wandered to trapping tales from the 1930s. I recalled a fascinating read, *North to Cree Lake*, by A. L. Karras. Something glittering in the sunshine on the far side of a small lake caught our attention and speculation as we investigated the bleached skeleton of an old homemade canoe hanging up in a jack pine, and two very short, handcarved spruce paddles leaning against the trunk. A few rusted stovepipes, some beaver hoops of willow, and several axe-cut poles gave evidence that this had been a trapper's camp. The temptation

to carry the paddles out as souvenirs seemed inappropriate, and there they will remain until consumed by forest fire or time.

Aboriginal Pictographs

Another surprise — and one much older — was spotted by Bill between two rapids and below an overhanging rock face. Three Aboriginal pictographs, red-line figures in the shape of a triangle, may have indicated a travel itinerary between Lake Athabasca and the Churchill River. The discovery of this artwork of antiquity was particularly rewarding in that there appears to be no written record of pictographs existing this far north.

With hills rising to over 100 metres above the river, it hardly seemed possible that we were cruising through so-called "flat" Saskatchewan. A favourite activity after supper was an evening climb up a high hill for a sunset panorama of sky, river and endless pine-covered hills in every direction. This brought on a feeling of minuteness, and yet a closeness to the Creator of it all.

One of the most charming places on the river was an exquisite three-split falls, an open-sky cathedral of primeval beauty where wild lady's-slippers grew in profusion. With warm sunshine on our backs, a gentle breeze and hardly an insect to disturb the tranquillity, it was as if we had already arrived.

At another location, the ever-curious Bill actually checked out an abandoned eagle nest and found that a man could comfortably curl up inside of it.

Campsites got a triple "A" rating as we tried to outdo each other in the quest for the perfect spot on flat jack-pine benches. When you start considering the scenic backdrop for a campsite, you know you're spoiled.

One evening we had some unexpected excitement around camp when a large bear decided to check out the lingering aroma of pasta. Although the animal did not charge right in for dessert, his determined pace put a little fear into us, and suddenly Daryl and I were blowing our whistles and ordering him to go elsewhere. He was a really big fella! All our hubbub did nothing to deter him, and as he approached to within 30 metres in the thin jack pines, Bill, our fearless leader, grabbed a large stick and lunged at the intruder. But Mr. Bear just stood his ground. When Bill laid down his feeble weapon and said, "We're outta here," we did not argue. In ten minutes flat we evacuated camp, rolling sleeping bags and clothing up inside the tents, just throwing everything into the boats. All the while the bear kept a silent watch from less than 30 metres, and when we had gained the safety of the river, we stopped to look back over our shoulders. Sure enough, that bear was sitting on the riverbank where we had been reclining only minutes before, finishing Bill's cup of tea (the only item we forgot), and if I'm not mistaken, he had a grin on his face.

Sand Everywhere

If any single word sums up the entire MacFarlane watershed, it is the word "sand." There was sand in the pancakes, sand in the sleeping bags, and sand in our shorts.

The three canyons were an exception to the sand rule as we neared river's end in the great drop to Athabasca. The 5-kilometre Lower Canyon was runnable but demanded constant manoeuvring. Taking a small side channel on river-right, we were able to avoid some of the bigger stuff but narrowly missed running over a busy beaver and colliding with a yearling bear. At last the whitewater was behind us and we glided across a small, roundish lake, bordered on two sides by high, almost barren dunes that marked the eastern limits of the Great Athabasca Sand Dunes. Camping at a superb site on the north end of this unnamed lake — which offers an ideal pick-up spot for a float plane, as opposed to the delta of the MacFarlane on the wind-tossed shore of Lake Athabasca, 5 kilometres to the north — we relaxed completely in the lingering calm of twilight, the muffled roar of the lower canyons lulling us to sleep.

We should have allowed more time to explore the Kingdom of Sand. A single day was pitifully inadequate. It was amazing how fast the dunes warmed up in the early summer heat, and our hike over the dune fields was like a trek on an alien planet. We thoroughly enjoyed the vistas from the most northerly dunes in the world. They are also some of the largest individual dunes in North America, reaching lengths of 1,500 metres and heights of 30 metres. Fortunately, the Saskatchewan government has set aside this entire area as a wilderness reserve, recognizing its geological and biological uniqueness as a habitat for a number of plants that exist nowhere else on our planet. The dune fields in our immediate vicinity were interspersed with spruce- and pine-covered ridges, an eerie and exotic land where the ever-shifting sands are either smothering plants and trees by burying them or building up solid formations firm enough to support new plant growth.

On our last evening we celebrated our fortune of health, comradeship and adventure. The MacFarlane had given each of us indelible memories, which were capped by a grand finale — these fragile and remarkable dune lands. The Cessna arrived on cue for the 320-kilometre flight south, and as our pilot dipped low over the Middle Canyon, I couldn't help but think we had, by travelling via canoe, gone down to the Kingdom of Sand in style.

Highwood River
Paddling Loony Lane

David Finch

A WILD LITTLE RIVER DRAINS "LOONY LANE." AT LEAST THAT'S WHAT Raymond Patterson called the upper stretch of the Highwood River, south-west of Calgary. The further west he went, the stranger the people he met.

Craziness comes easily along the Highwood. Perhaps that explains why I poled upriver from Longview one August afternoon. At the bottom of the canyon, camped on a gravel bar, I thought back on the river's other users.

Mackenize and Mann, railway contractors, ran logs down the Highwood from Cataract Creek in the early 1890s. They built the Calgary & Edmonton Railway on ties taken from these trees. In the early 1900s, the Lineham Lumber Company floated logs from the mountains to its mills in High River. Probably the first craft on the river was the company's lapstrake boat, which accompanied the log drive and helped free the logjams. Two men, without the aid of helmets, lifejackets or other safety gear, worked that boat. Just their corked boots and lightning-fast reflexes kept them alive.

Legendary people inhabited this river valley. Raymond (R. S.) Patterson had a ranch far up the valley and tells of his encounters in his book *The*

Buffalo Head. (Patterson is also author of *Dangerous River*, about his adventures on the South Nahanni River in the 1920s.) Guy Weadick, who instigated the Calgary Stampede in 1912, owned the Stampede Ranch and entertained rodeo fans around the world with his riding and roping tricks. George Pocaterra, an influential rancher, used his Highwood ranch as base camp for his explorations into the Kananaskis Valley and the eastern ranges of the British Columbia Rockies. Others rode horses through the Longview Bar. All entertained the British and American dudes who flocked to the picturesque foothills. Patterson's adventures made him the stuff of legends. In the summer of 1936 he took a trusting female dude down a stretch of the Highwood in a classic cedar-canvas Prospector. Unable to scout from shore, they ran it blind, capsizing, breaking some canoe ribs, and treating spectators to an entertaining display.

The ranches along the Highwood still raise cattle much as they did a century ago. Every summer, cattle drives take the cows and their new calves up the creeks into the forestry reserve. There, they feast on grass in the alpine meadows. In the fall, roundups bring them back to feed on the home pastures.

Mike Schintz remembers growing up across the river from the Buffalo Head. His father tied each of his three sons to a long pole and dunked them in a hole in the river to teach them how to swim. Life by the river called for strange initiation rites.

Around this same time, Father Bowlen of High River tried to pay a clerical visit to the Schintz family. After parking his car across the river from their home, he began wading the swift channel. Ted Schintz, Mike's father, suggested that the priest step only on small rocks. Believing in divine guidance instead, the father slipped and fell. Scrambling to his feet, he heard Ted yell, "See, I told you not to step on those big flat stones. If you'd listened to me instead of the Lord, you would have got over here safe."

There have been other kinds of visitors to this canyon. In 1936 Turner Valley Royalties No. 1 struck oil near the Highwood River. For decades, rigs punctured the surface looking for black gold. Even today, geology students clamber down into the Highwood Canyon to read the rocks and see the formations that trapped oil here so many thousands of years ago.

The reach above where I camped that night is reserved for expert paddlers. They check their brains at home when they take on the upper stretches of this creek-like stream. Kayakers, rafters and skilled canoeists must squeeze into wet- or drysuits, tug on their helmets, stow an extra indestructible paddle and check their throw bags. Self-rescue techniques are mandatory here. Highwood Falls, the Toilet Bowl, Dances with Fish, and many unnamed perils await the paddler above Longview, which is just a two-hour drive from Calgary.

Those not deemed clinically insane put in at Longview. The reach from Longview to High River includes many ledges, a few rock gardens and some holes. Best suited to the intermediate paddler, it can ruin a novice's day. The keen eye will spot wildlife around every bend. Eagles, hawks, deer, muskrats, mergansers and many other majestic beings call this place home. Cattle, too, since this is ranching country.

April Heronry

Just before the town of High River, the cliffs end and flood-plain cotton-woods reach far into the prairie sky. In April a heronry, consisting of dozens of heron nests, fills the upper branches of cottonwoods. The sharp-eyed great blue herons spied us from afar and launched into the air to divert us from their nesting mates. Normally a solitary bird, they gather here for a few weeks each spring. Approach carefully, watch respectfully, and you will be rewarded with an amazing peek into the nursery of the largest herons on earth.

Below High River, the lazy Highwood River parallels Highway 2 north to the confluence with the Bow River. Although calm most of the way, the river drops through one last canyon between secondary highways 547 and 552. A rock garden and some ledges thrill the intermediate paddler. The final stretch reverts to a wide, meandering bed. Inner tubes and laughing children abound in summer as vacationing families lounge at the private campground near the confluence. From here it's only about a half-hour drive to Calgary.

A cairn, almost invisible, is located near the confluence and marks the Oxbow Industrial School. It is a memorial to a time when white men tried to make the Aboriginal peoples in their own image. The school closed many years ago. Its memory reminds us that we must find sensible and sensitive ways to live together.

Harmony is not a trademark of life along the Highwood. Early European immigrant ranchers and settlers drove out the Aboriginals, then threatened each other with physical and psychological violence. The oil industry and people who lived off the land also saw reality through different lenses. Even today, conflicts over water use pits urbanites against the ranchers who draw moisture from the river to irrigate their land.

At the Buffalo Head in the 1940s, the Pattersons fenced off a piece of land by the Highwood for tourists. Unfortunately, inconsiderate visitors annoyed their reluctant hosts. Mrs. Marigold Patterson recalls: "Once my husband found a car and a really super mess there. He picked it all up and stuffed it under the car's hood. Well, something had to be done."

A Link to the Past and Future

If Loony Lane attracts you, don't forget the locals. Longview restaurants provide good country cooking, and the bar is a unique experience unto itself. Even if Ian Tyson is not in there playing guitar with the house band, you can use the truck wash next door, which he claims is the best in the west.

Provincial and private campgrounds along the river offer minimal facilities. Once on the water, however, a gravel bar can make a pleasant camp. Access points at bridges and campgrounds make any stretch of the river a comfortable day trip. The lower stretches also have their hazards, so treat this little river with respect.

While we camped on a gravel bar that August night, a full moon rose over the eastern horizon. As I poked at my little bedtime fire with a stick, I felt far from the city in space and time. The sun settled into the mountains west up the canyon. Peace lay on the land. Suddenly, silently, with majestic wings spread wide, a heron soared down the river valley, just over the top of my camp. Time seemed irrelevant. It could have been 1890 or 2090.

For me, the Highwood River represents a link to the past and the future. Paddling it gives me a chance to sweat, play, dream and relax. It is not Canada's biggest river, nor its wildest, most spectacular, most scenic, nor most remote. But it is a crazy little place. Welcome to Loony Lane.

Sheep River
Paddling Outside of Time

Sheila Archer

MAYBE THIS IS LIKE THAT BEND WITH THE TRICKY LEDGES," I SHOUT TO Craig, whose solo canoe is about 10 metres ahead of me, disappearing around a hairpin turn. Suddenly he drops out of sight, then reappears downstream in a cloud of spray. A jagged ledge stretches across the whole channel in front of me; I correct my position with one adrenaline-boosted stroke and propel my bow straight at what I hope is a good spot. I have lots of speed and fly through the drop. Craig, with a big grin on his face, is bailing in an eddy below. "That was pretty fun," he says, "but I think this should be called the 'Not for Sheep River.' Any idea where we are?"

My husband and I were looking for a little adventure, something to finish off the unusually cool and rainy summer of '93. Hearing that the mountain rivers were running way above normal for the time of year, we headed west from Regina to southern Alberta in search of some excitement, and perhaps a little sun.

Having no maps or any clear idea of where we actually want to paddle, our first goal is a rendezvous with Randy Clement, a paddling friend and instructor with the Rocky Mountain Paddling Centre. We arrive in Exshaw, Alberta, and find Randy preparing a foundation for a boat shed. That evening, while helping him shovel gravel, we ask him to recommend some day trips

Randy listens to our list of possibilities, then says, "Rivers you wouldn't normally paddle at this time of year should be running pretty good right now. You could try a warm-up on the Elbow, the Class III section from Canyon Creek to the Ranger Creek bridge. It has a few exciting spots and some good places to try a little surfing." He turns back to his shovel and says, "After that, the Sheep River is a fun little run. Yes, the Sheep is very nice." Of course Randy has no maps either, but we are not worried, as he seems to feel they are not necessary for what we plan to do.

The Elbow and Sheep rivers are located in the beautiful recreation area east of the Rockies called Kananaskis Country. Access to these rivers is easy and campgrounds are plentiful, though some fill quickly, as this is a popular destination for all kinds of recreationalists — from hikers to mountain bikers. One reason for this is the area's climate, which is usually warmer and drier than Banff and Jasper.

Heading east from Exshaw the next morning on Highway 1, we reach the junction with Highway 22 and turn south, passing through Bragg Creek Provincial Park before reaching the Kananaskis boundary. We spend our first day tuning-up on the always frigid Elbow River. Randy, who knows what warm-water prairie chickens we can be, has sent us to the ideal river to get back into mountain paddling.

Back at camp we agree we are ready for the Sheep, but the next day presents weather we don't want to paddle in. It's cold and the windshield wipers are slapping as we peer out at the highway road signs, looking for the turnoff to Route 546. At the Sheep River Visitor Information Centre, we get a little green photocopy of the park map. It shows contours, that's good, but even the park ranger can't tell us much. "Kayaks have run the falls and on down to the Sandy McNabb campground," he states, eying our open canoes with obvious skepticism. "There's a big logjam on the route that blocks the river." That sounds awful, nothing like what Randy described. "Must be the upper section, above the put-in Randy told us about," Craig says as we jump in the Jeep.

Not for Sheep River

We drive to the lookout at Sheep Falls, spectacular even on a dark day. We walk down to the shore next to the Class II+ rapids below and discover a trail. We are beginning to consider the possibility of putting in below Sheep Falls and decide to scout. Our mothers would have thought otherwise, but Craig and I are very cautious, with a great deal of respect for rivers. We have paddled by the "when in doubt — scout" rule for many years. Of course, this is perfectly natural on the Canadian Shield rivers so familiar to us. In the case of mountain rivers, with continuous rapids and difficult scouting conditions, this rule becomes truly challenging to follow.

Walking downstream from the falls, we scramble along the left bank for several kilometres. The river is beautiful, blue-clear and quite small in volume. About a kilometre downstream, where the Indian Oils Trail crosses the river by a wooden bridge, our hopes for running this section are dashed. There are more falls, and the river cuts swiftly deeper and deeper into the rock. Dropping fast through a series of tortuous turns, the rapids at this point are an obvious Class IV to IV+, certainly more than we're looking for, especially as just two solo boaters in a canyon without a map.

Back in our vehicle, we drive to the Gorge Creek put-in Randy described, a place where a creek passes under the road through a huge culvert. Paddlers can navigate the several hundred metres of rocky channel and pass through the culvert to emerge at the confluence with the Sheep River. There are no canyon walls, just steep, forested banks.

At Gorge Creek, we can see the river leaping beside the highway, grey and cold under the heavily overcast sky. It is still drizzling. The poor weather, our recent view of difficult rapids upstream, and lack of a good map or river report leave us uninspired to paddle. But our curiosity has been piqued, so we decide to spend the rest of the day scouting upstream from the put-in. We know Randy described the section he told us to paddle as best he could. "A nice little run," meaning there are no exceptional dangers, and we will just read as we run. What Craig and I are doing is research.

Upstream, the canyon walls are incredible. Composed of an easily eroded flaking rock, they drop at a steep angle and are obviously too unstable in most places for plants to grow. Rapids are visible far below, but the scale is a real problem. At one point we decide to risk climbing down for a closer look, a hair-raising experience. Each drop in the river turns out to be runnable, moderate IIs and IIIs, and as we work our way upstream we become more and more excited. It's a glorious day of adventure in the rain.

About 2.5 kilometres upstream from the creek, we come to a place where the forest has slid down the canyon wall. Far below, the river is pounding through very difficult rapids between steep rock walls. Right below us, the river smashes into an enormous tree that blocks the route completely and spells death for any paddler so unlucky as to run upon it. Upstream from there the drops are fast and furious Class IVs. A wipeout at this point could happen easily, with little time remaining to get out before the tree jam.

Closer inspection reveals where paddlers have carried around the tree on river-left, but getting out to do this would be a challenge in the turbulent water. We gaze upstream for some time, measuring the danger, and then turn back, believing we have walked to within 2 kilometres of the point we had stopped at on our walk down from Sheep Falls.

Before going back to camp and a hot supper, we drive to the Sandy McNabb campground and walk down to the shore. Determined not to miss the takeout, we fix the view in our memories for the next day. Tomorrow we will go to the Gorge Creek put-in and see what it's like downstream.

Committed to the River

The next day dawns clear, blue and beautiful for paddling. With gear ready for the day, we quickly eat breakfast, pack a lunch and race off to Gorge Creek. We drive down to the creekside, our bellies full of oatmeal and white-water butterflies, and don dry suits and stow lunch, first-aid kit and camera case before pushing off. Emerging from the black mouth of the culvert, we blink at the dazzling brilliance of the rising sun framed between the canyon walls that quickly close in. We are committed to the river.

The experience of paddling the Sheep River canyon is unbelievable. The river twists and turns a countless number of times below canyon walls that loom 100 to 300 metres above us. The river is narrow, less than 3 metres wide in one spot. Though the rapids are not exceptionally difficult at any given point, they are continuous and are so often hidden around corners of rock that we have to be constantly vigilant, giving the section an overall Class III rating.

Randy has not steered us wrong. The Sheep is a very nice run indeed. Soon we are in day-tripping ecstasy. The rapids are just right, and the view! Streams cascade down the textured walls, transforming into lacy veils of white spray. The rock walls change constantly in angle and appearance, endless variations of colour and form. High above us, there is another world, but we have forgotten it, paddling outside of time.

Every turn reveals new challenges, but the river is never too pushy or steep. We know we are there at ideal water levels, paddling in read-as-you-run heaven. The biggest standing waves are never more than a metre high. Twice we pull out to scout, once at a drop over a jagged broken ledge high enough that the best line isn't obvious from upstream, and then at a corner where a large hole on the outside of the bend leaves only a narrow route between it and sharp rocks on river-right.

We dine at noon on a rocky "beach" about halfway down the 12 kilometres of our route. After lunch the rapids continue. It is too fun, too beautiful, and will be over far too soon. At the 10-kilometre mark, the river broadens a little and the canyon walls are gone, having gradually disappeared over the last few kilometres, with only the occasional recurrence of a high wall. As we approach the takeout, we meet two flyfishermen angling in the shallows near the picnic area where we must leave the river. We are glowing. We don't mind the long walk to the road or the prospect of hitching a ride to our vehicle, for now, like Randy, we too have sparkling memories of the perfect trip for two down the "Not for Sheep River."

Bowron Lakes
A Gentle Wilderness Adventure

Lawrence Buser

OUTSIDE MAGAZINE CALLS THE BOWRON LAKE CANOE CIRCUIT "ONE OF the top ten canoe trips in the world." Laid down along valleys, the lakes form a sloping rectangle in the Cariboo Mountains west of the Rockies. The Bowron Lake circuit consists of six major lakes and several smaller ones, all connected by short portages or small rivers. Some shores rise abruptly to magnificent snowcapped peaks with hanging glaciers nestled between. Other shores are mostly conifer forest sprinkled with aspen or birch trees that provide brilliant autumn colours. A few flat areas are covered with willows, where we observed moose feeding and beavers gathering branches. A great number of birds brighten this paradise with their melodious songs and flashes of colour.

The circuit can be done by any active adult, and the guides are especially interested in making the trip available to people over the age of 40.

It is an ideal example of how adults, middle-aged and over, can enjoy a gentle wilderness experience while leaving trip organization and provision of equipment and meals to qualified guides. Our group of ten, plus two guides, met in Wells, which is about midway between the U.S. and Yukon borders and as far east as the road will go. Everyone was over 40, except two women in their twenties. The oldest participant was 79 and had learned to canoe only the year before. Two women were in their early seventies.

Among us were a nurse who had worked in Asia, housewives, an electrician who had panned for gold during the Depression, and an engineer from South America. Some came as couples, others were single or had left their spouses at home. There were almost twice as many women as men, and most of us had little experience paddling a canoe.

The Joys of a Guided Trip

Most doubts we had about our ability to handle the trip faded the first day. We began with the longest portage of the circuit. Two-wheeled canoe carriers made it quite easy. The heavier group gear was piled inside the canoes, which we then pulled along the trail. Our light backpacks with just personal gear were taken on a second trip.

The guides gave us a lesson and we paddled down the first lake with only a few zigzags. Once on shore, we were shown how to set up the tents, and then the rest of the afternoon, like every day to follow, was free time. We could fish, take photos, read, swim, write in our journals, or practice paddling a canoe to a nearby scenic spot. Meanwhile, the guides chopped wood, made tea for us and prepared dinner — a great advantage to a tour. At night, we sat around the traditional fire, sharing stories.

Chris Harris, our guide, started Pathways Canada Tours in 1984. His idea was to provide small groups of adults, particularly those middle-aged and older, the chance to enjoy wilderness areas such as this in a relaxed manner. With an assistant guide, Chris provides a very personal service.

Chris is an innovative outdoor educator and one of Canada's better-known guides, with about 20 years' experience. Jenny Wright, our assistant guide, has considerable outdoors skills and is a marvellous cook. The meals she prepared over a wood fire were amazing. Breakfast might be pancakes and bacon or seven-grain cereal with nuts and dried fruit, always with endless cups of coffee. Dinner might be a tasty vegetable-bean stew with pumpernickel bread or an Indian curry dish with papadoms. She even baked a pineapple upside-down cake for dessert. Lunch was served as a picnic, with a variety of cheese, meat, fish, antipasto and crackers, dessert and juice.

All equipment was provided, except for sleeping bags and backpacks, but anyone without these can rent them from Pathways at a low cost. New three-person tents for every two people made sleeping comfortable.

Pathways has its own special campsites, each with a distinctive and spectacular backdrop. While beaches were small in the spring, and the water usually cold, we went for frequent swims. This was also an opportunity to have a quick wash using biodegradable soap.

As we paddled, Chris would tell us about the history of the sites we were passing. Among the early settlers was Frank Kibbee, an American who claimed he fought with Custer against Sitting Bull in 1876. He later became the first warden of Bowron Lakes Park.

Two of the most interesting settlers were Thomas and Eleanor McCabe. He was an English major and she was a New England lady used to the finer luxuries in life. They built a home in the park, complete with a stone fireplace, French doors, shelves lined with volumes of books, and chairs imported from New England. They made scientific studies of the area, banding birds and making detailed maps using a wheeled measuring device. As Major McCabe put it many years ago, "We stay here, not because we have to, but because there is no place like it."

After just three days spent canoeing and portaging the northern edge of the park, I already understood his feelings. Yet ahead of us lay even more spectacular country. For the next two days we paddled under a warm sun down the eastern arm of Isaac Lake, enthralled with the vista ahead: ice-age glaciers draped over the peaks of the Cariboo Mountains, their dancing images reflected in the lake.

Isaac Lake flows into a fast river with rapids. I could see why Chris and Jenny had emphasized not only lake paddling techniques but also river manoeuvres. The river begins with a fast, funnelled current called The Chute, followed by a sharp bend and a series of standing waves called Roller Coaster. Anyone who wanted had the option of portaging around this section of river. It is a testimony to our instructors that all of us ran the river.

A couple of short portages and another section of river-running brought us to one of the most memorable lakes I have ever seen. It is small, caught between 11-metre-high falls on one end and the influx of the Cariboo River on the other, with mountains on the remaining two sides. But there is a mood to this lake that cannot be described just in its setting. Perhaps, as I am a person who loves the sea, it is that the lake rises and falls too, moved in this case not by tides caused by the moon but by the daily cycle of the sun melting glaciers at the headwaters of the Cariboo River.

We paddled down this river with caution, checking for sweepers and sandbars. Inexperienced paddlers can easily get into trouble here without a guide to show them how to reconnoitre the dangers and the best way to handle them. We stopped several times to walk ahead and examine the river. This was time well spent, for we all safely made it to the mouth of the river and the southern section of the park.

This is the land of giant mountains. Some still bear the names given them by the original settlers, the Takulli people, also known as the Carriers. Here are Kaza and Ishpa mountains, names whose sounds alone convey a feeling of ageless power.

We felt very small in our canoes, but with improving skills and endurance, we soon reached the last leg of our trip, the western lakes leading back to where our trip began. The mountains gave way to rolling hills. In one day we lined our canoes up a shallow creek, crossed several small lakes, made a couple of portages, and paddled through a marsh to reach our final campsite on the Bowron River.

That night we shared memories of the trip. Everyone had his or her personal peak moments, but we all shared one thing: our original nervousness had turned into confidence. We had become seasoned canoeists. The guides selected our final campsite, expecting to find a moose nearby in the morning. They did not disappoint us. Rounding a bend in the river, we came upon a mother and her calf grazing on the bank. We approached very quietly and watched closely for several minutes before they slowly walked away.

Kicking Horse River
Just for Kicks

Laurel Archer

Brad and I will get back in the saddle and ride the Kicking Horse River again. It's one of the best solo trips we know. Next time, however, I hope the stampede has a couple more open boats in the herd, as hitchin' up with three rafts and two kayaks on a commercial trip didn't allow for much stopping to scout rapids. I would enjoy seeing fellow canoeists kicking up their heels on this prized animal.

On a sunny, hot day in the third week of May, my husband, Brad, and I pull up to the Hydra River Guide base on the Kicking Horse. It isn't hard to find. Going west on the Trans-Canada Highway to Golden, we take the first left, on Beaverfoot Road, after the Yoho National Park boundary. After crossing Cozier Bridge, where there is a public access put-in, we turn west onto a small private road looking for Hydra. Roy Fraser, the owner and an experienced river-rafting guide, meets us with a beaming "Let's go paddle!" smile.

We first met Roy in Banff, and he convinced us that the Kicking Horse was ideal for christening our brand-new Whitesells. The spring runoff was late and we could join his trip for raft support. He was guiding one of three rafts, so we could jump on if things got too rough. There would also be two rescue kayaks. It sounded like the perfect opportunity to ride the "bronco." Brad and I took a couple of days to warm up by paddling the upper and lower Bow River, and then headed west to take up the challenge of a big water rodeo.

The glacier-fed river calls for all the whitewater gear we have, so while the rafting guides get their clients into wetsuits and lifejackets, Brad and I don drysuits, neoprene gloves, hats and booties, and crash helmets. As we perform the tricky no-eddy-bank-jump into the canoe saddles, I realize the current is really fast.

The water is a beautiful aqua-blue, but I have little time to contemplate the colour of this surging mountain river. The oar-powered rafts quickly pass us, so Brad and I have to paddle to keep up. This is no problem through the Class II and II+ warm-up. But then we encounter Cable Car Rapids, which gets its name from a cable that spans the river, and after scouting from the saddle we stampede the rapids. We ride standing waves that I would have avoided had I known there was a drier way.

Brad suggests I do a few practice rolls or eddy turns since I'm looking a little stiff. Secretly, I think I should be practising snorkelling or maybe taking up chess. Roy wants to show us a good time; but, as we are not paying customers, we don't expect him to hold up the show for us. We won't be able to scout, so it's going to be one helluva downriver run.

Hole the Size of a Truck

We're not stopping as we close in on Hopi's Hole, Class III+/IV. My mouth tastes like a desert. The kayakers are yelling, "Just keep left! The hole is on the right, but don't go too far left! There's a ledge . . . blah, blah, blah. . . ." I can't hear the rest over the roar of water rushing down a canyon. There's a mass of waves taller than me, numerous boulders, and one big drop as far as I can see. I'm backpaddling hard to avoid Hopi's Hole, which is the size of a truck, when I encounter a herd of boulders. "Where did they come from?" I ask myself. I try to cheat by going to the left side. Big mistake. I get turned sideways, and just barely make an eddy, where I regain my composure.

Everyone's gone and I have to make a tricky ferry to get out into the main flow. I catch Brad and Matt, who is in the rescue kayak, a long minute later. Brad suggests that I just head down the guts of the rapid the next time. I nod in agreement and look down at my knees to see if my bailer is going to be big enough.

We run some fun, technical stuff for several kilometres. I can feel saliva in my mouth again. Still, I'm concerned about keeping up to the rafts. They don't need to eddy out and bail or stop and get refocussed. I wish we had Roy all to ourselves.

The continuous Class III sets get tiring. My eyes feel strained as a result of constant vigilance. One small error in judgment and I'll be upside down. Since Brad is following Matt, an expert kayaker from New Zealand, I follow them. This helps my confidence.

Suddenly, just before a crucial manoeuvre has to be made, my bow kicks out. I'm heading for a big boulder with a large hole behind it. I back-ferry with all my might and make it safely into the eddy, where I bail like a paddlewheel. I think I'm the clown in this rodeo.

We catch up to the herd at the recreation site at Hunter's Creek. There's another rafting group having lunch, and they wave and yell. Their guide does a double-take at the sight of our Whitesells. I gather that our type of boats are not usually seen on this river.

As we round another blind corner, I bump one of our rafts trying to back-ferry. I get a rather dirty look from a raft rider. I feel like saying, "You're worried? I can't see anything with these rubber buses in front of me." I eddy out after hitting a few small holes and rocks that the raft has hidden from view.

Brad pops into the eddy behind and reminds me that Portage and Shotgun rapids are coming up. The river is now dropping at a rate of 15 metres per kilometre, and it's going to get wilder yet. Up ahead the rafts are pulling to shore. They're scouting. I'm amazed. I eddy in.

It's Portage–Shotgun and everyone is quiet. "You can see most of it from the railway tracks," says Roy. Portage Rapids is a IV+. It's 180 metres of major boulder gardens. A couple of the nastiest boulders, affectionately known as Black Bart and Shark's Tooth, guard the entrance to the upper sets. It's a tricky ferry at the top and then a mad zigzag in big waves. It could be a long, long swim, culminating in Shotgun — a chute where the river narrows to a mere 15 metres followed by a huge rolling boil and finishing with a wave called Table Saw. Even rafters get dry throats here. The Horse is definitely kicking now. I will portage.

The other kayaker and I portage beside the tracks, and at an ideal spot we stop to watch Brad follow Matt downstream. Brad has decided to take up the ultimate open-boater's challenge. He makes the back-ferry with ease, or so it seems, but then gets a load of water and starts to go sideways. He just barely makes it past a huge hole and we cheer. He's back in the stirrups. His red canoe looks ridiculously small in the jaws of this giant rapid. He manoeuvres through the rest of Portage and powers hard right to set up for Shotgun. He bucks through the boil, slips by Table Saw, and rides over the final standing waves. Everyone hoots and hollers, and I hear their cheers reverberating through the canyons.

I finish the portage, put my canoe in the water, and speed through more Class III/III+ rapids to catch up to the herd again. "How was it?" I ask Brad with a big smile. He is fluorescent with excitement. "My mouth was dry. Very

dry," he says. He loves being on the edge. His craving has been satisfied.

More wild, technical stuff follows, and as we bunch up again under Park Bridge, I'm amazed at how after four hours this bronco riding has become second nature. It's unconscious, pure poetry now.

At Rollercoaster, where the river narrows into a canyon of huge standing waves, it's a wild ride. Yippee! The rafts crash through. Brad's canoe disappears, reappears, and disappears again. "These are some biggies," I think as I enter the fray. But I stall out in a trough as I try to climb a third wall of water. My stern is about to be sucked into a hole when I use the well-known forward manoeuvre — the I-need-all-the-power-I-can-get stroke — to escape. I gain control and am immediately into the Last Waltz. It just doesn't get any better.

It's a short float to the take-out. We've made it. The ride is over. With great difficulty, I get out of the saddle and try to straighten my mangled legs. Some rafters come up and shake our hands. Roy jumps into his van and shouts, "Ya'll come back now, ya hear." We will. We will. But never at high water.

Spatsizi and Stikine Rivers
How I Spent My Summer Vacation

Patrick Mahaffey

I RECALL A VERY STRONG SENSE OF EXCITEMENT AND ANTICIPATED adventure as we hiked down into northern British Columbia's Spatsizi River valley on that first day. The weather was mild and the countryside was gorgeous, and it did not feel so onerous at first that we had a 3-kilometre portage to walk twice before we were even ready to begin canoeing! The trail descended into the valley, giving a wonderful view out across a fairly open valley with a definite northern or alpine feel to it.

From a high plateau to the Pacific Ocean, we were about to travel a river system from its source to its mouth — a first for all five of us. Where we began was only about 15 kilometres from the Spatsizi's source, and here the river is just a baby — only 20 metres wide. For the next three weeks we had 1,200 metres of elevation to descend and 530 kilometres to paddle. The Spatsizi, one of the main tributaries of the Stikine River, was chosen for its accessibility by car. Otherwise, it is necessary to fly into the Stikine.

Vehicle access is possible via a rough abandoned railway bed that runs along the Little Klappan River. It is a cautious four-hour drive each way. Hunters have found it easy to get into the previously inaccessible area, and the large ungulate populations are already suffering. The railway bed and a $3-million bridge across the Stikine are legacies of a grandiose scheme by the B.C. government in the 1970s to extend a railway line to the Yukon. The project was halted in 1977 amid scandals about cost overruns.

The Spatsizi rises on the eastern slopes of Skeena Mountain, close to the source of the Stikine River, then cuts through the Spatsizi Plateau on its way to join the Stikine. The valley is broad and flat-bottomed, with the river flowing steadily through many meanders. The entire 100-kilometre-long watershed is in Spatsizi Provincial Park.

Spatsizi means "red goat land" and its name derives from the reddish colour of the mountain goats who roll in the red soil of the Spatsizi. The first two of four nights on this river were spent by an oxbow lake at the foot of Red Goat Mountain. Dry, level camping spots proved scarce so this was a lucky find.

On the day off, we scrambled up the mountain to get a better sense of the lay of the land. As we gradually left the forest below, we were graced with a view of the river valley, the river bordered by natural levees and large shallow bodies of water beyond. Small wonder we were having trouble finding dry camping spots! This vista of mirror-surfaced river and ponds was rendered sublime by a fine misty rain and a double rainbow.

Moose are supposed to be common on the valley bottoms, but we saw only a pair of adolescents, as well as many tracks along the shores of the Spatsizi and Stikine. A few kilometres upstream from the confluence, a collection of log cabins, with a grass airstrip on the left bank, constitutes Hyland Post. It was established several decades ago and is still used by hunters, though it is a highly inappropriate type of facility to be inside the park. Hyland Post is a good starting point for climbing up onto the Spatsizi Plateau. We couldn't find the trail shown on the topo map, but there is a fairly easy bushwhack. You can walk unhindered across the treeless top, exploring the high, rolling tundra — home to herds of caribou and the big attraction for hunters. We didn't see any caribou or any wolves, which also roam the plateau.

Middle Stikine River

It was a momentous event when we arrived at the confluence of the Spatsizi and Stikine on the fifth day. The muddy waters of the Spatsizi take quite a distance to mix with the clearer waters of the Stikine, and the combined rivers produce a dramatic increase in width and volume. While the valley widens, the Spatsizi Plateau is still the predominate landmark.

The stretch from here to the Pitman River tributary, a 165-kilometre reach, is enlivened by a couple of long boulder gardens. We had been cautioned about them, but they proved to be only Class I and II rapids, so they were lots of fun.

Unfortunately, there is another hunting camp just below the confluence of the Pitman and Stikine, just outside the park's boundary. The ambience was eerie and grotesque, with discarded caribou antlers and scattered equipment and debris. A little further downstream on the Stikine, however, there is ideal camping on both sides of the river. Wolves had left tracks in the sandy right bank, so we chose to camp on the left and let the wolves have their solitude. That night we were treated to our first experience of nighthawks diving for insects. Like everyone, I'm sure, the mechanical buzzing sound made us think that there was a group of model airplane enthusiasts camped nearby.

Where Beggarly Creek joins the Stikine, the river flows through a powerful chute with a diagonal flow into a rock face. It doesn't leave much room for error and probably should be avoided by canoeists with less than intermediate ability. But not to worry, a swank portage trail, complete with a bridge across a creek, is well marked on the right shore. A section of whirlpools follows, and while not hazardous, it can spin your canoe around in a second. It was an unsettling taste of things to come on the lower Stikine.

A little further downstream, at the Klappan River confluence, we passed underneath B.C. Rail's abandoned truss bridge. With no deck or rails, it is an odd sight. If provincial plans for damming the Stikine Canyon go ahead, the reservoir here would rise high enough to flood this bridge.

The most famous feature of the Stikine River is its 100-kilometre Grand Canyon, which is completely impassible by open canoes. Two or three kayak groups, some with helicopter support, have managed to make it through this spectacular canyon, which in places is 300 metres deep. Needless to say, we approached the pull-out point at the highway bridge with caution, in fear of being swept into the abyss. The pull-out proved to be well-marked and quite convenient; the canyon itself beginning a few kilometres downstream.

With more time, we might have added the experience of backpacking along the top of the canyon. As it was, we only took time to examine the canyon from vantage points along the road from Dease Lake to Telegraph

Creek. The views were impressive, as were the sheer columnar basalt walls of the canyon. This is also where we saw our only black bear, grazing its way through fruit bushes along the canyon slopes. It appears that Grand Canyon was partly formed by outflows from numerous volcanoes in the Mt. Ediziza area to the south of the Stikine. The river may have been forced to cut down through successive new layers of lava, creating the steep walls.

Lower Stikine River

After avoiding Grand Canyon we camped at the village of Telegraph Creek, which used to be a transfer point during the Gold Rush of the late nineteenth century. Paddle steamers used to ply the Stikine, and it was the only practical transportation route into the northern interior of B.C. until the

Alaska and Stewart–Cassiar highways were built. The Tahltan natives, of course, have used the lower Stikine as a transportation corridor between the Pacific and the interior for millennia. The river has now returned to a wild, undeveloped condition, much like it was before European development.

In Telegraph Creek we gorged on Saskatoon berries. They hung so heavily from the bushes that we could pull them off fistfuls at a time. The only store and hostelry in the village was the River Song Cafe, which had a dormitory on the upper floor. It was full of German mountain climbers who had come here to climb the challenging Coast Range further west.

We launched onto the lower Stikine expecting a very different kind of river than the upper Stikine. We were not disappointed — the river was bigger and faster, probably 15 kilometres per hour. With the riverbanks festooned by dense alder brush, few good camping sites were available along the next eight-day, 250-kilometre reach of the river. We camped on sandbars that were probably under water during spring runoff. Nonetheless, these sites had splendid views of the river and the rugged Coast Mountains. Due to a good breeze, these river-view sites were cool and bug-free.

During our first day on the lower Stikine, headwinds were so strong that it was more practical to stop fighting them for a few hours by lying flat in the canoe and drifting sideways with the powerful current. But we were on the alert for Three Sisters Islands, which jut out in the middle of the river. They are probably 20 metres tall and give a nerve-wracking feeling of an approaching ocean liner. This vision is reinforced by the "bow wave" at the sharp upstream end of the islands that split the river in two. There are other obstacles, such as Buck Riffle, Bad Rapids and Dutch Charlie Riffle, but they proved to be trivial for an intermediate canoeist. They would cause paddle-wheeler boats some difficulty, however.

Next, the Stikine approaches the rugged Coast Range mountains and then veers south along their eastern edge. The river gradually widens and becomes a shallow braided channel, so careful navigation is important lest you get grounded midstream or end up stranded in side channels. Both of these things happened to us.

Other amazing features on this section of the river are three major glaciers — Flood, Mud and Great Glacier — which descend from the Coast Mountains. The first obvious campsite we saw during the entire trip was at the mouth of the Great Glacier's outlet stream, and it became our home for two nights. We lined a canoe up the stream and spent a couple of hours paddling in the cold rain in the lake at the toe of the glacier. This was a surreal experience, with the vertical cliff of ice rising 20 metres out of the water and many icebergs stranded in the lake. There were so many icebergs that we had a difficult time finding our way back to the starting point. Back out on the Stikine, we began encountering commercial fishing boats and fish-processing plants run by Tahltan natives. We also spotted a few seals — more than 50 kilometres from the ocean — who were also enjoying the salmon fishing.

At the Alaska border, the river takes a sharp bend to the west and passes through the Coast Range, while the shoreline forest, where the trees are enormous and dripping with moss, takes on a true rainforest appearance. The ongoing rain made the forest's ambience very authentic.

A worthwhile side trip was up the Ketili River, a narrow, slow-moving side channel, to Chief Shakes Hot Springs. We camped one night there and really enjoyed the soak, especially after all the days of cold rain. Developed and managed by the Alaska Forest Service, the site has a roof over one pool and a change room beside the other.

The last 20 kilometres of the Stikine are chockful of islands created by side channels. We canoed down the left side at Cottonwood Island, a narrow waterway overhung by immense trees, like a tropical jungle. We had to stop by a huge sweeper — a 1.5-metre-diameter tree had fallen, blocking our way.

Overall the river's transition to the ocean is very gradual, with the channel widening to nearly 2 kilometres at the mouth. That's a far cry from the 20-metre-wide river we had started on three weeks earlier. This reach of the river within Alaska is part of the Stikine–LeConte Wilderness Area. A few U.S. Forest Service cabins are located here and are free to use. We stayed at the Garnet Ledge cabin, an A-frame structure with all the amenities, including an ocean view. Garnet pebbles can be found upstream of the cabin.

Pacific Ocean

The delta of the Stikine has numerous low sandbars extending 20 kilometres into the Pacific. We set out for the 4-kilometre crossing to Wrangell Island at the start of ebb tide. It was not the best timing, considering we had to travel across its flow. Nevertheless, we steered partly into the flow and did quite well with a compass bearing, despite the fog. Taste-testing of the water showed that freshwater extends as far as the delta, which is more than half the distance to Wrangell.

As with most wilderness trips, it is a shock when there is an abrupt return to civilization. Such was the case when we rounded a point of land and entered Wrangell harbour. It is a typical West Coast port town, with a portion of the harbour devoted to Inside Passage ferry traffic. The ferry wharves are so large that we felt like ants paddling beneath them.

Going through the formalities of dealing with Customs proved to be a frustrating but amusing experience. Customs officials have the right to "enter our craft" and conduct a search, but the overweight official declined to board our canoes.

The float plane flight back up the lower Stikine valley to Dease Lake was a delight. The panorama was so stupendous, including a circle over the Great Glacier and up part of the Stikine Canyon, that it completely made up for the lack of views on much of our overcast trip on the river. What a finish to an amazing trip.

Tatshenshini River
A Treat from the Tat

Keith Morton

THE SOMBRE MOUTH OF THE CANYON LOOMED DARKLY IN FRONT OF US, and the scene was made even more intimidating by the grey clouds swirling over the hills. A few locals at the put-in at Dalton Post had made gloomy predictions about our life expectancy, and echoes of their predictions mixed unpleasantly in my head with the roar of the water ahead. We were about to enter a canyon with a fearsome reputation, and after only an hour on the river we'd hardly had time to get used to the handling of our heavily laden canoes. They felt like logs, and it was no consolation that they were better than the dugout canoe used on the first descent by Jack Dalton in 1890. Ahead we knew there was fast, cold water, steep canyon walls, boat-munching holes, and Class III–IV rapids for 10 kilometres.

The Tatshenshini River dropped away around an undercut corner, so "warp speed" was attained by the five tandem canoes (outfitted with spray covers) heading ashore to scout. As on all unfamiliar rivers, we needed to get a feel for the volume, steepness and type of geology. Being used to crystal-clear Alberta rivers, we now had to adjust to reading rapids where there was no "white" water because of the silt.

A challenging day of paddling followed. All of us were very much aware that one mistake could ruin our holiday and lead to a nasty bushwhack back to the road — assuming no one got hurt. We had organized the trip so that every canoe was a completely self-contained unit, therefore loss of a boat and gear would not hinder the rest of the party. No one wiped out, though we all had some close calls. Most of us got into situations we would prefer to have avoided, but all had the skill and/or luck to emerge from the difficulties unscathed. We made steady progress and by late afternoon had emerged from the canyon. Soon we were establishing camp on a gravel flat at the mouth of a tributary stream; our party unwound and settled in to enjoy dinner in the evening sunshine. A walk at dusk was rewarded with distant sounds of wolves.

The second day of paddling was so different we could have been on another river. Quiet Canyon held no whitewater; unlike the gloomy portals of its predecessor it welcomed us with a sunny golden glow. For the rest of the day the river meandered with a fast current through a wide valley surrounded by mountains. The valley floors and sides were forested but not appealing for hiking, so we drifted along with the fast current and enjoyed the scenery.

It was possible, however, to get up above the treeline from our second campsite. A steep climb through aspen woods took us to lush subalpine meadows, and then up onto a plateau 1,000 metres above the river. We were rewarded with views up and down the Tat and into the ravine-like side valleys. One of these was occupied by mountain goats, another held a valley glacier, curving sinuously down from a cirque on an inviting pyramid peak.

Protected Area

Back on the river the next day, a few hours of easy paddling took us to where the road to the controversial Windy Craggy Mine would have crossed the river. Mining this vast copper-ore body would have brought short-term monetary wealth but posed unacceptable risks of catastrophic long-term environmental and cultural damage. Acid rock drainage from copper mine tailings is always a problem, and the plans for its containment in reservoirs were highly questionable in this seismically active region. Destruction of the salmon runs by acid river water would wipe out the fisheries at the mouth of the river and have a very serious effect on the grizzly bear population. We were glad that, after an international outcry to prevent the development, sane minds had prevailed and made the area into a park. It now connects areas in Canada and Alaska to produce a protected area big enough to ensure survival of important species such as the grizzly. It felt good knowing future generations could enjoy this same unspoiled area.

Just upstream of the O'Connor River, we were roused from our reverie by a half-kilometre maelstrom of 2-metre-high standing and reflected waves. The river had been pushed against a rock wall by the outwash materials from a side stream, causing an abrupt change in width and gradient. After everyone had safely navigated this section, we were jabbering and laughing like excited teenagers, though a little sheepishly because it had actually caught us somewhat unawares. Camp that night was at Tats Creek, at the head of which would have been the notorious mine. It was there that we experienced the only rain of the trip, an evening thundershower.

A further half-day of paddling brought us to camp near the roaring, silty torrent of Melt Creek. It carried meltwater from the Melbern Glacier, grinding down from the Grand Pacific Pass 40 kilometres away. We knew the Grand Pacific Glacier tumbled into the Pacific Ocean, only 15 kilometres beyond the pass. We spent the afternoon on what became known as the Hike from Hell — trying to follow the creek up to the iceberg-laden melt lake at the toe of the glacier. Some long openings in the bush gave us periods of easier travel, but still we did not reach our objective. Wading through tributary streams led us to the sobering realization of just how cold the cold water was and how quickly it would incapacitate capsized canoeists.

Many tributaries had now joined the Tatshenshini, which was a kilometre or so wide. Braiding around gravel bars produced nasty boil-lines and eddies where currents rejoined. These necessitated constant vigilance; we often used upstream ferries to get across the turbulent areas more quickly. Big as the river was, we were about to join the Alsek River and triple the volume. We approached the confluence with considerable trepidation. As it turned out, with the prevailing water levels we were able to stay out of trouble and make our way down the churning brown Alsek to Walker Glacier.

Walker Glacier is the first of the glaciers that are easily accessible from the river. We spent a day clambering up the moraines and over the lower part of the glacier itself. The ice was incredibly broken up and did not present an inviting pathway to the peaks. This seemed to be typical of many of the glaciers we subsequently saw. Yet Walker Glacier provided some spectacular vistas even on a dull day.

That day was the last overcast one, but the following days were some of the most spectacular I have ever spent in a canoe. As we drew closer to the coast there were more and more glaciers in view. Some tumbled down steeply from the adjacent mountains, others oozed down as 6-kilometre tongues from the vast icefields of the St. Elias range 50 kilometres away. The most dramatic moment was rounding a corner to suddenly find Mt. Fairweather looming nearly 5,000 metres above us. This great ice-cream cone of a peak dominated the scene for the next three days. It was spectacular enough in its own right, but viewed across iceberg-laden Alsek Lake from our campsite, it was unbelievable. We spent two full days at the lake, canoeing among the icebergs and exploring. Even after these magical days, nature furthered rewarded us with the sight of a full moon rising over Mt. Fairweather.

Our final morning was foggy, but having explored the area we had no trouble finding our way around the icebergs to the outlet of the lake and the Alsek River. Paddling among the ghostly shapes was another unexpected treat from Mother Nature. By lunchtime the fog had cleared and we were almost in sight of the fish plant and airstrip at Dry Bay. Another half-hour and we were carrying our canoes up the bank onto the airstrip. Eventually we had the gear reorganized and all the seats and thwarts removed from the canoes so they would nest inside each other to fit in the plane. The aged DC3 charter arrived in a flurry of dust, and much to our surprise, a stewardess emerged. Apparently cabin crew are a requirement, even on bush charters! Our five nested canoes fitted in easily and we were soon winging our way over the river and the mountains, with spectacular views as far as Mt. Logan. In a little over an hour we were back in Whitehorse where our vehicles awaited. Friends had brought them back from Dalton Post, so we didn't even have to endure a vehicle shuttle. Pizza and beer finished off the final day of a dream trip — then all we had to do was drive 2,500 kilometres back to Calgary.

If You Go

Our trip was a resounding success and one of the best I have ever been on. However, I should caution readers on several points.

First of all, the vast majority of parties travel in rafts, which provide a much wider margin of safety. Our canoe group consisted of five very competent tandem pairs. Three members had paddled the Grand Canyon in canoes, while everyone else was used to Class III–IV water, and to living in the wilderness. Only with this level of both skill and experience could there be an acceptable safety margin. A capsize in the very fast and cold water would

be a very serious event, to be avoided at all costs. Most of the participants wore drysuits and the remainder wore wetsuits. Without this protection a swimmer would very quickly become helpless and seriously hypothermic. Even with this protection, they would still get very cold. Other factors that contributed to our success? First, we had good weather, so we were comfortable and well rested, and could therefore meet the paddling demands. Other parties have gone into the area and had day after day of rain and never seen the mountain views with which we were blessed. We were there for the last week of July and first week of August, but June should be drier. Water levels were moderate. Also, all the canoes, which were well outfitted, were our own. Rented boats might be a different story. All gear was properly sealed and tied down to act as buoyancy; several canoes had additional buoyancy bags. And we saw only one bear — a long way off on a gravel bar — but we did see lots of bear signs. We were careful to make lots of noise when hiking.

Logistics were easy. We drove to the put-in at Dalton Post, about three hours from Whitehorse. The DC3 charter back to Whitehorse from Dry Bay in 1993 cost $3,500 plus GST, split among ten people. We spent 11 days on the river, which gave enough time to hike and spend several days at the same spot. The river is very fast, and the 200 kilometres could be paddled in six days if one wanted to, but that would be a waste. You could, of course, spend a month in the region. You must contact Glacier Bay National Park (U.S.) and Kluane Park authorities in advance for a time slot and permit; quotas were introduced so that groups are well spaced on the river.

Soper River
Baffin Island Enchantment

Bruce W. Hodgins

IT WAS AN EARLY ARCTIC EVENING IN MID-AUGUST. AS THE LAST TWIN Otter flight lifted off from the natural tundra runway strip, winging east high over the hills of the rugged Meta Incognita, we were struck by the sound of silence and by the sheer beauty of these Panorama Flats where three small streams tumble down out of the hills from three directions to form the Soper, or Kuujjuaq, River. West over the shallow Soper from our large, spread-out campsite, sheltered by little shrubbed knolls and hummocks, rises the huge, half-egg-like curved monolith that is Mt. Joy, lush green along its lower steppes, brown and barren near the summits. Our site was two-thirds of the way north, along the sweep of the mountainside. The sky was clear, a deep blue. The sun was low to the southwest, but with the slow arctic sunset still many hours away. The night would be brief. Next to no bugs existed to disturb us. We were alone, our two small groups, deep in the interior of southern Baffin Island, in the enchanting Soper Valley.

No, not alone. Hardly ever alone. Within minutes of feeling that silence and sensing solitude, we saw that across the river, on the flat lower terraces of Mt. Joy were a dozen or more caribou, some walking, a few trotting, some eating from the shrubs, two or three motionless, watching us without alarm. For the rest of our trip, caribou would nearly always be with us, somewhere in sight; overall we probably saw about 500 but never a huge herd. The valley in late summer is one gigantic pasture, never crowded, never full. The caribou always seemed to be on the move, slowly eating and moving their way down the valley.

We set up our tents, cooked and consumed a long, slow dinner (on stoves, of course, since there was no dead wood), and lolled about, soaking up the atmosphere, clicking cameras in all directions, re-establishing old friendships. Then we hiked up to one of the nearly open waterfalls on a secondary stream, then went to bed, still in the warm evening light. It had been a very long day.

In 1993 this was a special Wanapitei canoe trip, our first on the Arctic Islands, in Inuit country. There were 13 adults, with six canoes and an inflatable rubber kayak. Although we were the official leaders, we knew the others now as close friends, and some as relatives. We had tripped with nearly all of them before, some on five or more other trips, in the Temagami area, on the Macmillan and Porcupine in the Yukon, the Clearwater in northern Saskatchewan and Alberta, on the Attawapiskat to James Bay, on expeditions usually of two weeks. This trip would be different, as it was only a week long and not very hard.

That morning most of us had been in Toronto, Ottawa or Montréal. By midday we were in Iqaluit, served a great lunch and toured about town by our co-outfitters, Matty McNair and her North Winds. Then we had flown, in three flights, low across the blue waters of Frobisher Bay, which was festooned with white ice-chunks left over from the winter, then up and over the great ridge of the Meta Incognita, named in 1576 by Martin Frobisher, even before Québec City was founded.

There was another group with us at the spacious Panorama Flats. We had known for a couple of weeks that they would be there. The good folk of Soft Science had arrived the day before to film a video on the Soper for the Canadian Heritage Rivers System and for the Territorial Park people. The Soper had just recently secured official National Heritage status; the valley (and the windswept Trail corridor over the ridge from the Bay) had also recently become a park, the first territorial one in the eastern Arctic. Between our two groups there developed an easy camaraderie. They could use us, occasionally, as summer subjects for their film; they too were experienced trippers and we found their informal banter great fun.

Soper Aesthetics

The trip was not to be hurried. In fact, Lake Harbour, our destination up a fiord from Hudson Strait, was only just over 100 kilometres downstream — well, almost downstream. Actually the Soper enters the sea over a low reversing falls, one fiord west of Lake Harbour; the Harbour is reached by a rough 3-kilometre road over the ridge from the southeast corner of Soper Lake. The trip was to combine river canoeing with a few light rapids and one portage around a falls together with many hikes up the lush sides of the valley and onto the barren, awe-inspiring ridges. It did not disappoint us. The

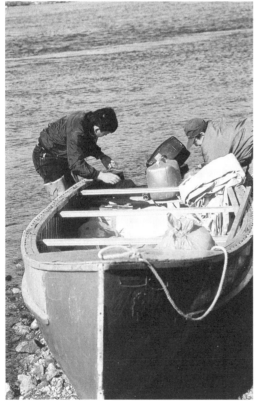

Soper is a canoe trip featuring aesthetics — landscape, vistas, green open foliage and flowers, flowing water and caribou at pasture.

The biggest problem — apart from the wet, cold weather later on — was getting our canoes to the put-in. Until very recently there were no canoes on Baffin Island. Even standard whitewater kayaks were few and nearly all in private Iqaluit hands. We did learn that an American organization had flown in a half dozen ABS canoes a few years earlier; they ran the Soper a few times and kept the canoes in Iqaluit for their own use. Fortunately, Wanapitei had a lengthy group trip this past July in Ungava ending at the Soper. Canadian Airlines flew that group to Baffin for hiking in Auyuittuq and brought along the canoes for a small additional charge. That is how we obtained our six canoes, but despite local assurances that it was possible, we could not squeeze three 17-foot ABS craft into the Twin Otter and have room for six passengers too. Hence, the third flight. The canoes are now stored at Lake Harbour for any future use on the Soper.

But for now, our first full day in the valley was spent mainly in hiking, indeed climbing, Mt. Joy, exploring its secrets and looking down into the Joy and other valleys beyond. We ascended one lush terrace after another, passed the caribou, scrambled up the higher rock ridges, up past a small pond, lunched by its delightful little outlet creek, and then climbed up to the barren summits themselves. Our descent was slow, the sights diverse. We saw falcons and arctic hare. We exulted in the now-fading flowers, all in an arctic heat wave, with temperatures reaching 26 degrees Celsius. Not a cloud in the sky. Though we didn't know it, this was the last day of Baffin's summer. That night it crashed to 3 degrees Celsius.

The next morning broke overcast and remained cool as we set off into the shallow waters of the Soper. For about the first 3 kilometres it was all in and out of the cold water, at times up above our knees pulling, pushing, lifting, sliding, gliding. Then there was a lift over a significant but too-shallow rapid that would be fun to run in higher water. After that we proceeded on through fast water and easy rapids to the confluence with the Joy River. So far we had been leapfrogging the film crew — some in their paddle raft and some walking on shore, then all in the raft through a gentle but foamy white rapid. Both groups gathered on the right bank amid the many passing caribou, just past the place where the waters merged, during a glorious, too-short hour when the clouds parted. We looked back for a last time at Mt. Joy and the upper valleys.

We moved on downstream, ahead now of the film crew; we did not see them again until just before we left Lake Harbour. The Soper now had plenty of water and was moving fast, often through low gorges, with light rapid following light rapid — at least one of them a Class II.

As we set up camp in a deep bunker opposite the mouth of the Cascade Creek, the storm clouds gathered. Tents and, though with difficulty without trees, the great kitchen tarps were carefully secured as the winds increased. Many of us hiked up the ridges behind, while a few crossed to the left and ascended the steep Cascade Valley, past falls after falls, including one 30 metres high that was "discovered" by Dewey Soper, the Dominion research biologist who, in 1931, was the first Euro-Canadian to ascend the river that was later named after him. It poured at the beginning of dinner, and the hikers arrived back from the falls drenched but happy to see the great tarp in place and holding.

The next day was very stormy, with cold rain blowing up the valley from the sea. With considerable difficulty, we reached the flats at the mouth of the Livingston (as large as the Soper, it seemed), set up camp on the "lawn bank" in the early afternoon, joining up with a couple of intrepid trekkers we knew from home and their dog. During a blessed 3-hour break in the bad weather we hiked up the Livingston amid sunshine, past the beautiful Shelf Falls and, far up this wide side valley, past shallow rapid after shallow rapid. Caribou were grazing on all the downs; we later watched many swim across the Livingston River.

The night was wet and very stormy, and cold, down close to zero degrees Celsius. So was most of the next day. But our spirits were lifted when we visited a sheltered grove on the right bank of a flower-bedecked stand of ancient "poplar trees." The trees were said to be over 200 years old and the tallest on Baffin Island, some reaching 3 or 4 metres in height. We also saw ancient Inuit tent-rings. We saw an Inuit, the first we'd seen on our journey, heading upstream by outboard in the deeper wider stretches of the Soper.

The next day the weather cleared but remained very cold. We had one great stretch of rapids and stopped around noon for a magnificent hike on open rock outcrops, frolicking everywhere over hill and dale, past quartzite knolls, searching for and finding open, bare deposits of mica just lying about and considerable blue lapis lazuli (a mineral used as a gem or as a pigment). That early evening we reached Soper Falls (a Class V rapids), camping on the left at an official site with open shelter, above the rocky chute. We stayed two nights. In our full day there we hiked a lot along the ridges of the lake below, and fished a bit, for small char. A few Inuit passed, upstream and down, picking berries and taking the occasional caribou; they generally left small outboards on the upstream side of the carry.

Finally, we portaged and paddled barren but awesome Soper Lake, through a heavy mist, to the landing, from where we walked into ever-so-picturesque Lake Harbour, famous for its great soapstone carvers and its wonderful hospitality. We ate a huge Inuit dinner, hosted at home by Sandy and Inneak Akavak. We stayed two nights at the Co-op, and arranged to be taken down the fiord by Inuit boaters to the sea and the great icebergs. There was more rain and fog, so we left later than expected by air for Iqaluit. But it was so worthwhile; we had memories, scenes and fellowship to last forever.

The Soper. Not a difficult trip, not a trying trip, a warm then a cool trip — perhaps we were a bit late in the season — an arctic canoe trip with the caribou, in a fantastic landscape, and all with friends, visitors and through Inuit lands.

Thelon River
Where Time and Light Stand Still

Max Finkelstein

"GET UP! THERE'S A GRIZZLY BEAR IN CAMP!" THOSE TERSE WORDS, uttered through clenched teeth, cut into my dreams. Jim and I crawled out of the tent into the brilliant stillness of an arctic dawn. All traces of sleep evaporated instantly once our bleary eyes focused on the silver-tipped barrenland grizzly nonchalantly investigating the gear we had stashed under our canoe. Lacking any clear plan of action, we aimed shouts at the bear: "Stupid bear!" "Get out of here!" and "That's our stuff!"

The big bruin looked up, snorted, and shambled up the beach towards a willow thicket. At the edge of the thicket, about 10 metres away, he turned to face us, stood up on his hind legs, slowly shaking his head from side to side.

Three thoughts filled my head. The first was that I was looking at the photo of a lifetime — if only I had my camera. The second was that we might be in trouble. The third was that I had had both these thoughts several times before on this trip. The bear hunkered down into the waist-high willows and disappeared. We urged the other four members of our expedition out of their tents and waited. All was quiet; it was the deep silence that can only be found in the barrenlands. Fifteen minutes passed. Then we saw the bear, 100 metres away, loping along the beach. A collective sigh of relief. But hearts were still pounding hard an hour later.

The bear had ignored Katherine's muffins, which were sitting on the upturned canoe, and instead gnawed on a bottle of liquid soap. Perhaps this was an indication of the quality of the muffins, we gently chided Katherine.

Our grizzly came on the last day of our canoe trip down the Thelon River in the Northwest Territories. It was an apt finale for a magical trip — and a reminder that we were merely visitors. We had interrupted the bear on his regular river patrol. The bear didn't invade our camp; rather, we had intruded on his domain.

The Thelon flows through a land barely out of the Ice Age, a land unchanged by humans, where you can travel for weeks and not see another person. This was the last mainland area of Canada to be explored. David Hanbury, an English gentleman-explorer, was the first European to canoe this river. In 1899 he paddled upstream from Hudson Bay, following the Thelon, and then paddling up its major tributary, which now bears his name, eventually reaching Great Slave Lake. Hanbury wrote in his diary that "The sense of freedom the Barren Ground gives . . . cannot be described." This is still true today.

According to Hanbury, the Inuit called this river the *Ark-i-linik*, meaning "wooded river." They travelled up it from Hudson Bay to gather driftwood to build kayaks and komatiks (sleds). The Dene people who frequented its upper reaches referred to it as *Thelewezzeth*, or Thelon.

The combination of abundant wildlife, great fishing, beautiful scenery, all set in one of the world's largest, least-disturbed ecosystems, makes the Thelon a top wilderness canoeing destination. The upper Thelon and the Hanbury, the two most commonly used approaches, require many portages. But the scenery is spectacular, particularly in the canyons where these rivers tumble off the Canadian Shield into the sedimentary rock of the Hudson Bay lowlands. Below Thelon Canyon, it's a portage-free paddle all the way to Baker Lake, almost 600 kilometres. Days flow into days as the Thelon sweeps by spruce forests, barren ridges of frost-shattered rocks, sand beaches that look transplanted from tropical desert isles, red sandstone cliffs where rough-legged hawks and gyrfalcons swoop and soar. The current carries you past staring muskox, imperturbable moose, patrolling grizzlies, white wolves, and caribou beyond counting — through a land where time and light stand still.

A Walk on the Tundra

For most of its length, the Thelon River flows through the Barren Lands. But the Barren Lands are anything but barren. The tundra is covered with a dense mat of lichens, mosses, herbs and shrubs. In July, sprinkled on the tundra like constellations in the night sky, are wildflowers — white mountain avens, purple louseworts, pink dwarf fireweed, yellow arnica. Look down at your feet. You are walking on the arctic forest. Though you might not recognize them as such, there are plenty of trees here — white spruce, dwarf birch and willow form dense mats in sheltered areas. The trees are just very small. I counted the rings with a geologist's loop on a twisted spruce just 2 inches across. It is 140 years old.

A walk on the tundra is a breathtaking experience. The land, vast and empty, stretches unbroken under the circle of the sky. Not a single branching silhouette breaks the skyline; no leaves rustle in the arctic breeze. At each step, your boot crushes a thousand brittle, curled greyish-white lichens. The

aromatic, spicy aroma of dwarf Labrador tea and arctic heather fills the air. Climbing now to the top of an esker where cushions of mountain avens, white and cheering, nestle in a small depression, eking out a tenuous existence on the scant soil. Over here is a patch of arnica, sunshine-yellow daisy-like flowers supported on spindly stems. A tuft of muskox wool clings to the willows; wolf tracks pattern damp earth; caribou bones litter a grassy slope . . . A ptarmigan suddenly flies up in front of you. Listen. Can you hear her chicks peeping? Over there is an *inukshuk*, two stones stacked on a large lichen-encrusted boulder to mark the way to somewhere. How long ago was it built? Owl pellets are scattered on the ground around it.

Ancient Campsites

When David Hanbury ascended the Thelon, he was greeted by Inuit camped upstream of Beverley Lake. Today these traditional campsites are easily spotted. Circles of boulders, once used to hold down skin tents, cover the highest bluffs. (Modern campers leave behind rectangles of boulders.) The Inuit left many artifacts behind: the cracked long bones of caribou; flakes of quartzite used as scrapers and chisels; a piece of wood, carefully shaped into a smooth curve, once part of the framework of a kayak; a tiny wooden double-bladed paddle, perhaps a child's toy; wooden stakes still embedded in the ground where they once pinned a caribou skin for scraping. The Inuit came here in summer to hunt caribou. How long was this campsite used? When was the cycle of the seasons broken? As the caribou and muskox are part of this land, so too are the Inuit.

In the short time since Europeans have travelled this land, they have also left their mark. In a grove of spruce trees are three weathered wooden crosses and the remains of a tiny log cabin. John Hornby, English gentleman and legendary northern traveller, and two friends wintered here in 1927. Hornby, who took pride in his ability to live off the land, normally took only tea and flour on his trips. But when the three travellers reached the Thelon in the fall of 1926, the annual caribou migration had already passed. All three starved to death before summer arrived. John Hornby, who had performed miracles of survival, made one fatal miscalculation in a land that gives no second chances.

The Thelon Game Sanctuary

On an earlier trip on the Thelon, one with a happier ending, John Hornby reported: "There is a large uninhabited area where muskox are plentiful, swans and geese nest, and caribou have their young undisturbed by man . . . if it is desired to protect the game in this part of the country it is essential to take measures to prevent traders from encouraging natives to hunt in this district. A few years, perhaps, and it will be too late."

David Hanbury also advocated the protection of game in this area: "On the Thelon there is a stretch of country into which no human being enters . . . thus there still remains one spot in the Great Barren Northland which is sacred to the muskox. Here the animals remain in their primeval state, exhibiting no fear, only curiosity . . ."

J. W. Tyrrell, the famous Canadian explorer, paddled down the Thelon in 1900, surveying for a possible railway line to Hudson Bay. He reported: "For the preservation of the muskoxen — which may be so easily slaughtered . . . I would suggest that the territory between the Thelon and Back rivers be set apart by the government as a game preserve."

In 1927, the Thelon Game Sanctuary was proclaimed by the federal government. Ironically, it included the very spot where Hornby, the sanctuary's proposer, was at that very moment starving to death. Today, the Sanctuary encompasses 56,000 square kilometres, an area larger than Nova Scotia. It is the only area in the Northwest Territories where hunting and trapping and mining are prohibited.

The future of the Thelon Game Sanctuary is in jeopardy. There are increasing pressures to open the Sanctuary to mining exploration (uranium and diamonds have been found just outside the Sanctuary), Aboriginal hunting, snowmobiling and other uses.

The Sanctuary was created by an order-in-council, and the stroke of a pen is all it takes to change its regulations and boundaries, or to make it disappear on a map, legislatively speaking. The future of the Sanctuary is a complex issue, as the boundary between Nunavut and the rest of the Northwest Territories runs through its centre. A draft management plan for the Sanctuary east of the boundary has been prepared, and is currently being revised by the Keewatin Inuit Association. Management planning west of the Nunavut boundary will likely take place in the near future when Dene land claim issues are resolved. Ensuring the sanctity of this northern protected area is a concern for all Canadians, and it will speak to future generations as a testament of what we, as Canadians, really value.

Close Encounters

It is virtually impossible to paddle the Thelon without encountering wildlife. On the first morning of our trip, we awoke to see ten muskox — black dots moving across the tundra. We scrambled to set up our spotting scope, not believing our good luck, certain that these would be the only muskox we would see during the entire trip. But by the end of the trip, the count was over a hundred. Once we saw a herd of 29, dozing beside the river like huge, dark boulders. As our canoes drew close, a big bull, weighing at least 600 pounds, snorted and stood up. Soon the herd was galloping across the tundra, the sound of their hooves beating a staccato rhythm. It was a scene from the Ice Age. We would not have been surprised to see woolly mammoths appear on the horizon.

Umingmak — the bearded ones, in the Inuit language — personify this land. Tough, yet vulnerable, they are perfectly adapted to the harsh environment, and remain on the tundra all winter. Their woolly coats, made of extremely dense underfur covered by long, coarse guard hairs, are such perfect insulation that muskox are impervious to the coldest arctic blizzard.

In addition to muskox, we saw white arctic wolves, chippy "sics-sics" (ground squirrels), golden eagles, bald eagles, peregrine falcons, gyrfalcons, rough-legged hawks, parasitic jaegars, all four species of loons, blazing white tundra swans, flocks of moulting Canada geese, and stately sandhill cranes. But the animals that will forever remain in our memories are the caribou.

Each summer the Beverley caribou herd, over 300,000 strong, migrates up the Thelon Valley. We paddled through a land alive with caribou. Caribou hair floated on the water, forming dense mats in the eddies, and in our soup. Caribou lined the beaches. Picket fences of antlers were silhouetted in the morning sun behind every ridgetop. We saw several large groups of caribou swimming across the Thelon. With their broad splayed hooves for paddles and hollow hair for flotation, caribou are excellent swimmers. When they reach the shore, they shake themselves like dogs, the spray forming a halo of sparkling diamonds suspended in the morning sunlight.

Days flowed into days as the Thelon carried us past red sandstone cliffs, Lookout Point, the larch forests of the Finney River, and the maze of the Ursus Islands. We stopped to hike to Musk Ox Hill, a pingo (a hill with a core of ice thrust up through the permafrost) located about 5 kilometres from the river. It shimmers on the flat barrens like a distant, snow-capped mountain. However, as we walk towards it, it begins to shrink in size to its true dimensions — a hill about 20 metres high.

Past the turbulent waters of the Thelon Bluffs, we are swept down to Beverley Lake, the first of three vast tundra lakes on the route to Baker Lake and civilization, still hundreds of portage-free kilometres and weeks away.

Perhaps the essence of the barrens was best expressed by Saltatha, an old Chipewyan chief, replying to a priest's description of heaven: "Is it more beautiful than the country of the muskox in summer, when sometimes the mist blows over the lakes, and sometimes the water is blue, and the loons cry very often?" The tundra overpowers and empowers you with its vitality. There is peace here, and a beauty that penetrates beyond the mind and heart, right down to the soles of your feet.

But it won't stay like this. Not unless everyone works together to keep the river and the Sanctuary it flows through as they are — unique and irreplaceable. At a meeting in Baker Lake to discuss the possibility of the Thelon as a Canadian Heritage River, James Ukpaga said: "If something is not done soon, the river and the land are going to be damaged by large development, be it mining or hydro or other kinds, and because we are the inland Inuit, the only kind of country food that we can get here is caribou and fish . . . any type of large development would distort the river and . . . then we have nothing."

Morse River
Journey Across the Barren Lands

Michael Peake

IT WAS LIKE WAKING UP ON A DIFFERENT PLANET. SOMETHING WAS wrong. Then they started. A seeming eternity away, a pack of arctic wolves began howling, their overlapping songs trailing off into infinity. Their wilderness chorus told us two things: one, we were still in the Northwest Territories, and two, the cursed wind had stopped blowing. Three days of roaring, ceaseless gales pinned us on the barren shores of the lower Back River. At 4:30 on the morning of the fourth day, that seemingly endless rush of wind had been replaced by a vacuum of silence.

It was Day 47 of a 55-day trip that would forever change the way we looked at canoeing, the land and ourselves. Simply called Journey Across the Barren Lands, for that's what it was, this trip had taken the six of us (Sean and Geoffrey Peake, Peter Scott, Peter Brewster, Dr. Bill King and me) from the scrubby shores of northern Saskatchewan to where we were now, 320 kilometres from the Arctic Ocean end of the mighty Back River in the most remote corner of mainland N.W.T.

This trip, which we undertook in 1985, had a special purpose beyond the call to adventure. We subtitled the trip The Morse River Expedition. We wanted to honour the Dean of Canadian wilderness canoeing, Eric W. Morse, whose writings and trips during a lifetime of wilderness canoeing had set a standard for all paddlers to follow. We felt the most fitting way to laud a northern paddler of his stature was to name a river after him. In retrospect, some of us feel as if we were just instruments in this undertaking, for, like the trip itself, the entire project had a charmed quality.

In Canada there is one major prerequisite for naming a geographical feature after someone — that person has to be dead. And while Eric was most honoured by our efforts, he did not feel ready to meet that particular stipulation. That's when the first of many fortuitous events occurred. The right to name a feature in the N.W.T. had just been transferred from federal jurisdiction to territorial. Yellowknife had no restrictions on geographical naming since there were no regulations in place. With the help of notable paddlers like Pierre Trudeau, a tripmate of Eric's on several occasions, who wrote letters of support for the project, and some ever-present good timing, we were able to run the usually formidable bureaucratic waters with relative ease. Geoffrey Peake, the originator of this naming idea, had located a river that he felt was appropriate. It rose on the height of land between the Thelon and Back rivers and flowed into upper Garry Lake. While only 100 kilometres long, this river was to be incorporated into a 1,600-kilometre journey that would include parts of three major rivers in the barrens of the Keewatin District.

Our chartered Twin Otter left Lynn Lake, Manitoba, the end of the rail line, on June 22, heading north. The land beneath us, which we were viewing for the first time, was an incredible panorama of lakes, hills and diminishing trees. We landed on Selwyn Lake, named by the Tyrrell brothers in 1893. This lake, which straddles the Saskatchewan–N.W.T. border, seemed a logical place to start. (The first half of the trip our group was composed of Sean and Geoffrey Peake, Peter Scott and me. Peter Brewster and Bill King would join us halfway through.)

The plane nestled into a sandy beach on a small, spruce-covered island. Its quick and noisy retreat left a buzzing in our ears that was slowly overtaken by a soft wind and the almost imperceptible squeal of delight from the resident mosquitoes. Just a few metres away from where we pitched our tents we discovered a small grave. The weathered posts there had fallen over;

as we put them back up, we felt as if this was both a sign and a reminder. I wrote in my journal that night, "It is our country but it is not our land."

We followed the Tyrrells' route over several portages into Wholdaia Lake, named by Samuel Hearne (Wholdaia is Chipewyan for pike and is on the Dubawnt River system). We can still vividly recall reaching the first rapid, just a trickle really, but nonetheless a rapid on the legendary Dubawnt. In those nervous, early days it took longer to prepare for the rapids than to run them. Dubawnt, which means "wide, shallow," was just that. We slithered down this easy-flowing, sandy-banked river, getting comfortable in these incredible new surroundings. We soon learned that this is a land of extremes. Two days later we hit ice on Barlow Lake, one lake before we were to make our turn west and head towards the Thelon. We climbed to the top of a large hill at the north end of Barlow. The view was both terrific and disappointing. The scenery was magnificent, but our proposed route was ice-clogged. We made a slight detour, and by portaging and paddling nearby ice-free lakes, we were back on track.

Off the Beaten Track

It was here that we left the Dubawnt and our familiar way of travel. We were off the so-called beaten track as we headed over a height of land. Trekking between river systems rather than staying on one river is something we have

done on every major trip since. While much harder and slower, it offers a different way to look at the land — and for it to look at you.

We took a rest day on Day 15 and camped on a barren island shaped like a flying saucer. A good thing we did rest, since the next day brought us into battle with another ice-clogged lake. It wasn't real ice. It was thick, heavy slush with occasional hard slabs, too thick to paddle through but too soft to walk on. What to do? Wait until it blew away or melted? Not a chance. We began three days of very laborious dragging along the shoreline.

This was to be the first of many morality tales: When the going gets tough, a lot of interesting things happen. This vignette included violent weather followed by vibrant, arching rainbows that bathed us in intense colour. We also saw caribou racks, ancient remains of a boat, and a hare's tracks suddenly joined by wolf tracks that ended in a patch of sand out of which only the wolf tracks emerged.

We finally made the Thelon and raced down its fast-flowing waters until we encountered the only large navigation obstacle on the entire river — Thelon Canyon. Following an exhilarating series of linings and runnings, we emerged and were just a short distance from the crossroads of the Barrens — the junction of the Hanbury and Thelon rivers. The late sun cast a dramatic caramel tinge over the landscape, peregrine falcons wheeled overhead, and we could smell herds of caribou. It was a glorious moment and a wonderful way to end the first half of the trip. Our other two canoeists flew in two days later, and then the six of us set off down the easy-flowing Thelon with our canoes packed with fresh food and treats for the final 28 days.

We revelled in the Thelon, enjoying the muskox, grizzlies and caribou that swam in front of our canoes. We sat on a beach just downstream of the ruins of John Hornby's cabin; a little while later, however, we reached the Ursus Islands, our turning-off point for another round of portaging and traversing another height of land. This time we were heading for the Morse River. As we made our way up through the ancient and rolling Akiliniq Hills, the age-old meeting place of the Back River and Thelon Inuit, we felt we were catapulted into the deepest recesses of wilderness. We were travelling through, as I wrote in my journal, "a chain of lakes that only existed in our minds." It was peaceful, beautiful, surreal.

As we reached the headwater lake out of which the Morse drains, we were greeted by stormy winds. Inside the billowing tents our faces glowed red with the price of weeks of hard work and a sense of accomplishment. A carefully wrapped bottle of cognac — a gift from Eric Morse — was opened and consumed in a gasping round of swigs. We toasted Eric, ourselves and the extraordinary land. The next day, which was appropriately perfect, we built a cairn to commemorate the naming of this river. As we were piling the rocks, a muskox strolled by with a look of puzzlement. The following morning, in the rain and cold, we headed down the Morse, a medium-sized river with substantial drops at the top and bottom. The next day, however, was a beauty and we filled the empty Courvoisier bottle with Morse River water and hatched plans to end this trip in a fitting way.

The Morse flows into Garry Lake where it joins the Back River. While it is a demanding river, it's the weather that proves the most difficult factor. After stopping at Escape Rapids for an off day, a windy and cold one, we discovered that it was just the first of three of hard, driving winds. We were going nowhere until the chorus of wolves signalled that the final push was upon us. With some hard paddling we made our rendezvous at the mouth of the Back in Chantrey Inlet on Day 55.

Upon our return to Ontario, we discovered that the N.W.T. government had officially named the Morse River on August 1 — amazingly, while we were on it. The cognac bottle was presented to Eric Morse at a special party we had to commemorate him and the naming of the river. Eric spoke of his travels through the lonely land and his love for it. Six months later he died. But his river and his legend are still flowing.

South Nahanni River

10 Reasons Why You Should Stay Away
from the Nahanni

Neil Hartling

B‌y reading this article you'll save yourself a lot of emotion, blood-pumping adrenaline, needless excitement, confounding mysteries, confusing myths, unwanted romance and maybe even a few dollars.

You won't like the South Nahanni for the following reasons:

1 ➥ Since the Nahanni River is only readily accessible by tiny aircraft, this acts as a bottleneck, thereby preventing the average person, of which there are many, from travelling the river — to say nothing of those who may be prone to air sickness. In 1995 the Nahanni had only 600 river travellers, a fraction of the number on the "wilderness" Tatshenshini, in Yukon and Alaska.

2 ➥ Nahanni National Park officials have introduced a departure regulation system that seriously limits the chances of bumping into other people while on your trip. This could be catastrophic. After all, what will you do when you run out of cigarettes or all of your toilet paper gets wet? Who will you hit up for more coffee or sugar? Any river worth visiting will have other

paddlers on it in July and August, so you are better off on one of the lesser-known rivers that doesn't have a limiting system. This way you have a more secure chance of meeting other groups.

3 ↩ Government publications say this about the Nahanni: "It flows past natural hot springs . . . Canada's deepest river canyons . . . Hills of soft calcium sculpted by the elements . . . Features so unusual and unique that the UNESCO Committee of the United Nations nominated Nahanni National Park as the first 'World Heritage Site.'" That's government for you. These are the same people who collect taxes — are you going to believe them?

4 ↩ The fact that the Nahanni has a greater diversity of landforms than nearly any other river in the world is bewildering. You travel to the wilderness to relax. Encountering new panoramas around each corner is stressful. Who needs diversity?

5 ↩ You often hear about the Nahanni's canyon walls rising up 3,000 feet, but no one mentions the stiff neck that results from viewing such vistas. Nor does anyone talk about developing a crick in your neck from sighting Dall sheep high in the mountain crags.

6 ↩ Virginia Falls may be nearly twice the height of puny Niagara Falls, but who needs that kind of noise. A wilderness trip is supposed to be quiet and peaceful, not full of thundering crescendos. A person can hardly sleep for the noise.

7 ～ Speaking of lack of sleep, at the summer solstice there are close to 24 hours of daylight. Such conditions don't allow for a proper night's rest. And there are problems later in the season, too. Your travelling companions will probably be waking you up at 2:00 A.M. to look at gaudy displays of the aurora borealis, or northern lights — a sort of eco-laser light show.

8 ～ Yes, the Nahanni has a history as old as the North and as interesting as a haunted gold mine. The legends that pervade the Nahanni are captivating, even spooky. Aboriginal legends abound, and there are tales of lost prospectors whose bodies were found headless. While names such as Headless Creek, Deadmen Valley, Funeral Range, Burial Range and Broken Skull River add a special aura to the dramatic backdrop, they are distracting. How can you concentrate on the enjoyment of a wilderness trip with such a macabre atmosphere?

9 ～ People who rave about hot springs and actually enjoy soaking in them after a day's paddling are soft. Who needs those kind of people on a canoe trip?

10 ～ The Nahanni has attracted the likes of Pierre Elliot Trudeau, Pierre Berton, Gordon Lightfoot and Prince Andrew. What do these guys know? They can go anywhere. Any more visits from such illuminati and the riverbanks will be crowded with paparazzi.

For your own good, I say, stay away from the Nahanni. You won't like it. If you don't, you might succumb, as I did, and be forced to return time and again. Don't make my mistake. I haven't been able to stay away for over a decade; I was even forced to write a book about the Nahanni. It is, obviously, too late for me, so I will continue to sacrifice my summers and travel the canyons of the river with the hauntingly beautiful name. It's a tough job — but somebody has to do it. . . .

Snare–Coppermine Rivers
Following John Franklin's 1820 Expedition

Shawn Hodgins

After 23 days of paddling, portaging and tracking, we had finally reached the last portage over the height of land. From here the downstream descent would begin. It was the end of a long hot day in the land of the midnight sun. Many of the group were, unfortunately, too tired to appreciate the beauty of our surroundings. From here it was down the Starvation and Coppermine rivers to the Arctic Ocean. The next 18 days would be much easier and more relaxing, as the hard work was basically over. The preceding 23 days had, however, not always been easy ones.

Our group of ten paddlers had gathered about a month before in Temagami, Ontario, at the Wanapitei Wilderness Centre. After an adventurous drive across Canada we had begun our canoe journey in Rae, at the northwest corner of Great Slave Lake in the Northwest Territories. Our trip from Rae involved climbing the Snare River and then following the historic route of John Franklin's 1820 expedition from the site of abandoned Enterprise on Winter Lake, up Winter River and over the height of land to the Starvation River, which flows into Point Lake on the Coppermine. The final two weeks would be a descent of the Coppermine River to the village of Coppermine on Coronation Gulf. All in all, a trip of about 1,000 kilometres and six weeks on the water.

The actual paddling began in Rae, the land of the Dene. From this area of mixed spruce forest the trip took us to the so-called Barren Lands and home of the Inuit in the Arctic. There is something very memorable about canoe trips that involve more than simply following a river downstream from A to B. Linear travel seems to be something quite common for current recreational travellers, particularly in the North. Our trip was no exception. We had the luxuries of modern transportation to whisk us back to where we began in just a few hours. Travelling upstream and crossing between various watersheds did, however, give us a greater appreciation for the unique environment we were travelling through. As well, it gave us some sense of the exploits of travellers before us, and also perhaps a vague sense of what life was like for the many generations of local inhabitants who have travelled this land for thousands of years.

For many in the group it was their first trip to the N.W.T., and certainly to the "barrens." Travel through this far from barren land is a truly memorable experience, and one's first sight of it can be very moving. Those who visit the barrens have a strong desire to return. Those who live there often wouldn't live anywhere else. Although in some respects a desert, the area is dotted with thousands of lakes, ponds and rivers. The ever-present permafrost means rapid runoff from winter snows and summer rains, as the ground can absorb very little water. The arctic summer is short and intense. The 24-hour sunlight and spring runoff combine to create an ideal home for a wide variety of wildflowers, shrubs and bushes, as well as mosses and lichens. The North also provides a summer home for thousands of nesting birds and a surprising number of mammals from arctic hare, foxes, bears, wolverines and wolves to the massive caribou herds that roam the barrenlands.

For those who love to travel by canoe, it is rare that any trip is not memorable. Naturally, it is often the most recent trip that you recall most vividly and fondly. Some trips, however, stay etched in your memory for much longer. A whole combination of factors leads to this: companionship and group dynamics, physical challenge, scenic beauty, natural resources and the weather. Ironically, hardships, while not necessarily enjoyed at the time, may be remembered fondly afterwards. A lengthy trip may also be much more vivid. Time gives you opportunity for reflection. Even if you are travelling with a group, this time is available.

Footwear a Critical Commodity

The Snare–Coppermine was one such memorable trip. Our six and a half weeks of food meant heavily loaded canoes and three trips across each portage. Travelling upstream can be an arduously slow task; the Snare, at times, was a powerful and deep river with a swift current and rapids. During the first several days we were able to follow winter roads and trails between some of the lakes on the Snare. After this, the current and rapids became too strong and frequent. It seemed advisable to depart from the river and follow small chains of lakes and creeks, eventually coming back to the Snare every couple of days. Although easier than fighting the current, it still meant hard work with an average of five or six portages a day, and only 10 or 12 kilometres of distance gained. Although the spruce forest was sparse, the lack of trails meant we still had to be careful not to get off track. We would often scout out portages without gear before setting off. Footwear also proved to be a critical commodity. Constantly in and out of the water, and portaging through alternately wet and rocky terrain turned several new pairs of shoes to mush in a few weeks.

After two weeks of northward travel we reached Snare Lake, an east-west widening of the river about 40 kilometres in length. We briefly visited the small isolated community of Snare Lake, a relatively new community largely made up of people wishing to escape the troubles of Rae by returning to a more traditional way of life by living off the land. The location had long been a summer gathering spot but now hosted a number of small log houses.

After a respite from portaging on Snare and Roundrock lakes we again headed upstream towards Winter Lake. We passed the site where Fort Enterprise was once located. It was Franklin's winter site in 1820–21 before his expedition headed down the Coppermine to the Arctic. It was also to here that they straggled back starving and expecting food; none was to be had, though help did eventually arrive for the survivors.

North of the Treeline

The portage into Winter Lake marks the treeline. This is a rough line north of which trees do not grow. It was here, as we climbed the rise towards Winter Lake, the trees appeared to fall back and the barrenlands opened up before us. Unfortunately, with the barrens came the blackflies, but there were other compensations. One of the real joys of travelling in the barrens is the vivid northern wildflowers, and though we were late in the season, we could still enjoy their colours.

The trek up the Winter River involved short paddles between wading, tracking and portaging around rapids. After the Winter, we pond-hopped and creek-walked our way towards the height of land. These portages, between the spectacular Big Lake and Starvation Lake, took us about a day. There were no trees to mar the way, but walking on the rough, rocky terrain was slow. Surprisingly, it is very easy for a person with a pack to just fade into the landscape. Wind can also pose problems. One prays for wind to keep the bugs down, but without tree cover the wind can be incredibly powerful, making travel difficult. Even in the best four-season tents you can find yourself crouching inside, holding the poles so the tent won't collapse around you.

The one-and-a-half-day downstream run on the Starvation River was enjoyable and beautiful, with spectacular small waterfalls and runnable rapids. It was in this section of our trip that we saw our first caribou. Caribou are a real symbol of the barrens; they roam the North in herds numbering in the thousands. For those who have never seen a caribou herd, it is not something easily forgotten. In our case, we were not lucky enough to see huge herds, but were content with numbers in the hundreds. Running with the caribou were occasional white tundra wolves, ignored most of the time by caribou unless they got too close.

The Starvation River flows into the southeast end of Point Lake. This is one of the many fly-in locations for trips on the Coppermine River. Autumn can come early in the North; for us it arrived as we entered Point Lake. With occasional exceptions our weather turned from hot and sunny to cold and damp for the next several weeks. Point Lake is about 120 kilometres long and, as with many large lakes in the North, can pose problems for the canoeist. In order to avoid the strong winds we often paddled at night or in the early hours of the morning, a task made much easier with the long hours of daylight. Point Lake is followed by Red Rock and Rocknest lakes before the river begins its descent to the Arctic Ocean. We spent just over five days traversing these large lakes, reaching the Coppermine on Day 30. During our crossings we occasionally threw in fishing lines and caught several very large lake trout.

Little Has Changed

The Coppermine was one of the earliest northern rivers to attract the attention of Europeans. In 1770–71 Samuel Hearne explored the river for the Hudson Bay Company, largely because of the persistent rumours about abundant natural copper. Fifty years later John Franklin travelled down the

Coppermine and mapped along the Arctic coast. Occasional other travellers journeyed on the river over the next 140 years, but it wasn't until the 1960s that "modern" recreational canoeists began to be attracted to it. During the 1970s and 1980s increasing numbers of paddlers travelled to the Coppermine to experience its wondrous beauty and enjoyable whitewater.

Little has changed on the Coppermine since the time of Hearne and Franklin. One can paddle down the river reading their journals and notice little difference. This lack of change is rare, and we thoroughly enjoyed reading the journals as we made our way downstream. After exiting Rocknest Lake, the Coppermine rushes over several difficult rapids; these are followed by a day of swift current and frothy whitewater. Then two or three days of gentle flat water, then crossing the Arctic Circle, all before the final descent to the Ocean.

The river bends sharply north at Big Bend. A route into the Coppermine from Great Bear Lake exists here. Soon after this obvious landmark the first of the named canyons occurs, and the major whitewater of the trip begins. At Rocky Defile the large river is forced between narrow cliffs of several hundred metres in height. Large, but normally runnable rapids occur within the canyon walls. Below Rocky Defile the river is marked by a series of major named rapids and kilometres of unnamed rapids, fast current and towering cliffs. Numerous birds of prey, such as falcons, hawks and eagles, nest in the cliffs. The river makes its way through the ancient Coppermine and September mountain ranges, which provide excellent opportunities for hiking. Names such as Muskox, Escape and Sandstone Rapids and Bloody Falls are reminders of bygone eras.

During the final 80 kilometres from Muskox Rapids to Bloody Falls the river drops 200 metres. Bloody Falls is the only definite portage for canoeists, though the many large rapids can end in cold swims even for those with splash covers. Both Rocky Defile and Escape Rapids gave some members of our group the unexpected chance to experience the cold water. Along this stretch of river are numerous chunks and veins of natural copper that gave the river its name, and which proved to be such a disappointment to Hearne.

At Bloody Falls, the site of the 1770 Inuit massacre by Hearne's more southern Aboriginal guides, we encountered many local Inuit from Coppermine camped and fishing for arctic char. The spot is still a favourite for catching char when they are running up the river. We only managed to catch four, but the aluminium motorboats heaped with fresh char and the numerous poles with drying fish were a sign that the locals were much more effective than we were.

For our time at Bloody Falls, Days 40 and 41, the weather made an abrupt change and the temperature rose dramatically into the high 20s. From Bloody Falls to the Inuit hamlet of Coppermine (Kuglutuk, population 1,000, of which 90 percent is Inuit) is about 15 kilometres. By the time we reached the settlement the mist was rolling in off Coronation Gulf and the temperature had dropped to only a few degrees above freezing. Coppermine is a wonderful community and it is well worth staying a few days instead of simply rushing off back home.

Although the expedition had been both physically and mentally challenging, the spectacular beauty of the environment and the pleasure in being lucky enough to experience it over an extended wilderness trip was unforgettable.

Bonnet Plume River
A River Gone Mad

Paula Zybach

W E HAVE BEEN GRADUALLY WORKING OUR WAY NORTHWARD, SAMPLING increasingly wilder rivers. The Bonnet Plume, starting high on the Yukon side of the Mackenzie Mountains at latitude 64 degrees N, flows 260 kilometres northwest to the Peel and then 290 kilometres north to Fort MacPherson at the edge of the Mackenzie Delta in the Northwest Territories. Its attraction lay in the promise of challenging whitewater, wonderful untrampled remoteness and great hiking. It sounded too good not to do. There was also the black cloud of mining development hanging over it. Once accessible by road and sullied by mining, most of its allure would be lost.

Getting there was half the fun for us. The Dempster Highway was a pleasant surprise of varied landscapes with lots of wildlife, little traffic and days of great hiking in the Ogilve and Richardson mountains. Here we discovered flowers that were new to us and saw our first white wolf. Even an unexpected two-day wait for our plane in Fort MacPherson was made interesting by friendly townsfolk who were happy to tell us of their memories and legends of our chosen river. Because they travelled the Bonnet Plume in winter to hunt and trap, they knew of a hot spring that we were not able to locate.

When off at last, we flew with the midnight sun, crossing a forest fire, up the Snake River, over a pass and then following the Bonnet Plume. It was a two-hour breathtaking flight through canyons and past glaciated peaks. At one point our pilot's eyes widened as he looked down. Tapping Anton's shoulder to get his attention, he asked, "Do you like that stuff?" Leaning the plane onto its left wing tip, we held on with death grips, peering down at the 7 kilometres of swirling water in Rock Slide Canyon. Here, the river has had to cut a new way through the rock debris left when half a mountain collapsed. "Yes, we like whitewater!" Our stomachs were in our throats, not from the prospect of paddling Rock Slide Canyon, but from flying sideways.

At 2:00 A.M. the pilot had just off-loaded us on Bonnet Plume Lake where we proceeded to set up camp. We were further north and earlier in the season than on any previous trip, and the unpacking led us to laughing at our selves. The first thing unpacked was a good flashlight, complete with new batteries. It would be weeks before night would return to this region. That weight in the barrel should have been chocolate!

A violent hailstorm the second night set the stage for our trip. We had entered a crystal-clear mountain stream at moderate flow, but now, as we approached Rock Slide Canyon, the water was running over the banks and in the willows. Daily rains made the river very pushy; we were one canoe loaded with three weeks of supplies, running very technical whitewater. It was exciting and exhilarating, but twice we found pieces of ABS canoes that had not made it. These grim reminders had a humourous side, though; each had been bitten clean through by a bear, just above the skid plates. Odd toys for curious tastes.

Two small falls necessitated portages of only 100 metres each, the first of which was festooned with a bumper crop of blueberries and fresh bear signs. It was thus a noisy site as we struggled to make ourselves louder than the pulsating roar of water. We had no unpleasant encounters.

Alpine Gardens and Undulating Ridge Walks

The canyons were a slalom run performed between colourful cliffs, and if the whitewater lived up to our expectations, the hiking surpassed them. It was easy to pick out routes up the mountains that required only a few kilometres

of bushwhacking to get above the treeline. Elevation gains of only 60 metres would lead us through alpine gardens and onto perfect, undulating ridge walks. There were lots of signs of Dall sheep, but they eluded us on this trip.

Along the river we passed foraging black bears and caribou. It is easy to forget what you learned in past caribou meetings, so we attempted to sneak up on our first one with camera readied, only to be flagged by a tail shot. After that we assumed a nonchalant manner and let their curiosity rule. It worked. One even followed up along the shore then headed cross-country where the river swept around a large corner. He awaited us at the next bend.

Although we saw only individual caribou, we realized that there were many because at one spot we saw what looked to be a graded roadway leading uphill from the river. Stopping to investigate, we found a very heavily used track, 2 metres wide, going up from a natural fording place. Thousands of hoof prints had beaten it into existence.

As we came slowly to the end of the mountains, leaving the whitewater behind, we exchanged drysuits for rain gear and woollens. There were more moose encounters now and each moose, disgruntled by the steadily deterio-rating weather, was in an uglier frame of mind than the one before. One cow with calf advanced menacingly as we swept past.

We wanted to do more hiking, so we spent a rest day just below Gillespie Creek, hoping for the weather to clear. This area, viewed through sheets of sleet and mist, looked like jagged, 1,000-metre-high Shield country that begged exploration. It became obvious that the bad weather was here to stay for a while so we decided to go with the flow and carry on.

Theoretically, the dangerous rapid sections were behind us. The rest should have been a Class I braided float. However, as the rains continued, every creek became a raging torrent and the water level rose dramatically. We paddled among hundreds of uprooted trees, passing partially submerged islands.

Above the Maelstrom

A good campsite and safe sleep saw us return to the river the next day and still the waters rose. This day was a spine-tingling exercise in survival: 96 kilometres of aggressive back paddling on a river gone mad. Only the headlands remained visible as the tree-clad islands were drowned beneath a surging sea of brown. At one point almost the entire river went crashing downhill through mature spruce forest. We found a path through and continued our search for secure, solid land. An upstream backwater above an inside corner brought us a safe place to stop. It was a difficult scramble up a sand cliff, pulling all our gear up behind us, but it was a blessed 5 metres above the maelstrom.

The next day we rode the back-slope of the flood crest down the Peel River. The trip reports we had read had not exaggerated this descent. The horizon line was never more than 30 metres ahead, giving the constant sensation of sliding into free fall.

Peel Canyon awaited us next. Sheer black rock walls painted with splotches of orange and gold lichen made for an amazingly beautiful but dangerous ride at this water level. A diagonal ridge of standing waves backed by a 46-centimetre sheer line was its threshold. Once in, we were funnelled through, enjoying the straight stretches but extremely wary at the corners, as they hosted larger, wandering whirlpools.

Out of the canyon we found a new adversary in the wind. A noon-time high of 5 degrees Celsius with 80-kilometre-per-hour gusts from the north lashing sleet upon us was not pleasant. The current was powerful and diagonal to the wind, causing dangerous cresting waves. We soon admitted defeat and headed into the forested benchland for shelter, only to find that four Swiss tourists had beaten us to it! They had come down the Snake River in inflatable canoes but seemed happy to share their spot if we would contribute another tarp. We had a nice evening of swapping stories.

The last days of paddling were cold but relaxing. While the scenery was no longer stunning, it was no less interesting. As we approached the Mackenzie Delta we began to pass Tetl'it Gwich'in fishing camps. Drifting along the last morning, an unidentifiable sound grew in our ears. Anton realized it was coming from two birds, flying downriver on the left shore. The 2.5-metre wingspan and distinctive black and white markings left no doubt that they were whooping cranes. They were more than 1,000 kilometres northwest of their normal range! Together they swirled in an aerial ballet, keeping about 10 metres above the treetops, rising and lowering to follow the contour of the land exactly. Even as they disappeared downriver they remained audible. After a few minutes they doubled back to give us a second show before turning west and away over the hills. For me, this encounter was the highlight of the trip.

Excitement fuelled ambition, and so when a lack of possible campsites added to the drive, we pushed on to Fort MacPherson. We had been flushed downriver by the forces of nature. Pulling out with seven days of food still packed, we had a head start to the preparations for our next river. But no other will ever be quite the same as our adventures on the Bonnet Plume.

Yukon River
Finding the Real Gold

Kirk Wipper

THE VERY MENTION OF THE YUKON RIVER INSPIRES WORDS LIKE MAJESTY, romance, hardship, frustration and even greed. My exploratory journey with Neil Hartling using a North canoe for the first time introduced me to the spell of the Yukon. The use of the replica fur-trade canoe for that 650-kilometre journey along such an historic route appealed to my adventurous spirit. It was indeed an experience that I could not possibly forget.

When our small group of six stood on the bank of that swift-flowing river below Whitehorse Rapids in the city of Whitehorse, I could not help but reflect on the number of people who had struggled along the Chilkoot Trail and perhaps stopped at the same spot that we now occupied. Earlier hardy groups were filled with hope that they would find adventure, freedom and, especially, gold. I wondered if they realized that the real gold was everywhere — the magnificent mountains; the clear, open skies; the cold, clear tributary streams; the amazing remnants of mining attempts; the encampments of Aboriginal people; and, of course, always the unpredictable, changing river itself.

On a rainy, cool morning we put our heavily loaded canoe in at Johnsons Crossing on the Teslin River, a tributary of the Yukon. This was planned in part as first-time exploration and further because Lake Laberge is often not good for canoe travel. Our crew of six came from different places but soon fused into a paddling team. It turned out that I was the lone Easterner!

Finding a camp spot on the Teslin was not at all easy because the combination of clay and heavy rain became a challenge. Further along, site selection was reduced to gravel bars or locations occupied by trappers, miners or members of the police force.

When we joined the main stream of the Yukon River, the colour of water changed as did the strength of the current. This allowed us to move at a brisk pace. Old records of the Yukon are an exciting resource since they reveal a continuous series of historic sites. It is still possible, for example, to identify the numerous places where the remarkable Yukon River boats loaded firewood to keep the voracious steam engines in action. As we trav-

elled the unpredictable currents, we marvelled at the fact that the captains of those boats could wend their way to Dawson City and back again. However, they did not always succeed against the hazards of fire, collision, running aground, mechanical breakdown and other perils.

History Comes Alive

Hootalinqua is one of many magical locations along the river. Here a detachment of the Northwest Mounted Police established their headquarters in an attempt to maintain law and order in this often-harsh territory. Here, too, there was spruce for winter storage of the riverboats. Using simple, creative techniques they were able to haul those very large boats up long timber skids with homemade winches. A riverboat still rests on the skids as evidence of an extraordinary scheme invented so long ago.

Further downriver we encountered small clusters of aboriginal shelters where many of the old traditions were much in evidence. Cemeteries with spirit houses remain reasonably intact on hills overlooking nearby waterways. Dried and smoked salmon along with moose hips on racks were signs of preparing for the approaching winter. This was especially evident near the abandoned village of Little Salmon. Impressive were the handmade signs to encourage visitors to respect the land even though few people used the river in this pristine territory.

Nonetheless, much to our surprise, we overtook three European adventurers who were attempting to replicate the early Klondike voyageurs in the days of the gold rush in 1896. To do this, they had chosen a crude raft that did not appear be a viable mode of travel. The inspiration to undertake such an adventure came from an article in *National Geographic*. Unfortunately, these travellers had not planned well and not only were they thoroughly stuck in a dangerous position, they were also seriously behind time. They simply had no chance to make it to Dawson City before winter. Because they were hopelessly jammed between a treacherous point of land with a large pile of trees and stumps and the banks of the Yukon River, we resolved to assist them. Our effort was dampened because of the extreme stubbornness of their "skipper," but by finally disregarding him, we succeeded to free the raft after a full morning of hard work!

There are locations where streams rush out from the base of the mountains along the river. It is almost certain that many an eager prospector stopped at such places to explore for the elusive precious yellow metal. For us these streams meant fresh, cold drinking water, which was always welcome on our long paddle. Occasionally a large chinook salmon would leap from the current where the smaller stream joined the larger river. Sadly, however, the chinook salmon population has dropped dramatically in recent times.

Carmacks, named after the enterprising George Carmack, is a main stop on the Yukon. A bridge at this narrowing of the river accommodates a 24-hour-a-day flow of valuable ore by special transport to the smelters much further south. The thunder of those vehicles passing nearby makes sleeping in a tent extremely difficult.

Just beyond Carmacks are the notorious Five Fingers and Rink rapids. It is difficult to classify these stretches of turbulent waters because of their unusual configuration. It is certain, however, that care is mandatory in navigating both locations. They are relatively short and manageable on river right. How the large riverboats made it through this section is hard to imagine; history reveals that many of them were damaged or even destroyed in the attempt.

Below the Pelly River, Fort Selkirk was established but was quickly inundated and destroyed by spring floods. The fort was moved to its present location by Robert Campbell in 1848 where it was inhabited for more than a century. Now a historic site, it speaks eloquently to life in the great Northern frontier. One note scribbled on a cabin wall reads: "I made it back, old friend, once more — I might try again but I really don't believe that will be possible. Anyhow I will always love you."

The swift, shifting waters of the Yukon are constantly gnawing at its banks as if to expand its northern empire. Nowhere is this more vividly demonstrated than at Stuart Island along the right riverbank. Once a thriving community, it is now occupied by an elderly mother and her son. Bravely and hopefully, this woman still maintains a productive garden even though nearby the river takes many feet of soil from the island each year. Changes in the main current are responsible. Each year some of the buildings are swept into the current of the relentless Yukon and the two occupants stand by helplessly wondering when . . .

Wildlife can be frequently sighted along this truly amazing river. Bears suddenly startled, bound up steep, scree-laden slopes and lynx occasionally stalk the river shores seeking food. The bald eagle circles high above the river valley detecting the slightest movement of potential prey below. Along the river, especially above Yukon Crossing and in the more distant Wrangell Mountains, a streak of white volcanic ash known as Sam McGee's ashes serves as an exclamation mark in this wild, historic region.

Mixed Emotions

It is a long journey from Whitehorse, and so the first signs of Dawson City and the Klondike River are entirely welcome. But the desecration along the Klondike is indescribable and disheartening. Essentially there is no longer a river at all. The entire valley has been dug, blasted and dredged mercilessly in the quest for gold. Machinery used throughout the period of exploitation lies rusting, although there is occasional evidence of recent attempts to recycle the tailings to pick up what was missed earlier.

Dawson City, on the other hand, is a charming frontier place, and little imagination is required to understand its boisterous and romantic past. Diamond Tooth Gertie's saloon and theatre present a graphic dramatization of what once was; the town now shows a fine variety of original weather-worn buildings. Not far away, it is possible to hear the poems of Robert Service at his cabin or the adventure stories of Jack London.

Recalling this Yukon River journey always brings to this paddler a renewal of the notion that there will always be gold along this river. It comes in many moods, patterns, textures and legends and boasts a singular wild northern beauty that simple cannot be surpassed!

Section Two

25 Distinguished Paddler Profiles

Bill, Joyce, Paul and Becky Mason
The First Family of Paddling

"THE CANOE IS THE SIMPLEST, MOST FUNCTIONAL, YET AESTHETICALLY pleasing object ever created. In my opinion, this is not a statement that is open to debate. It's a fact!" wrote Bill Mason in his classic book *Path of the Paddle*. "It follows that if the canoe is the most beautiful work of human beings, then the art of paddling one must rank right up there along with painting, poetry, music and ballet. In the ever-varying conditions of wind, waves and rapids, the possibilities for acquiring skill in the control of the canoe with poetry and grace are unlimited."

Bill Mason (1929–1988) was Canada's canoeist. "There is one thing I should warn you about before you decide to get serious about canoeing. You must consider the possibility of becoming totally and incurably hooked on it . . . My addiction to the canoe began at a shockingly early age. I cannot remember a time when I was not fascinated by the canoe. My parents tell me that at the age of five or six, my weakness for canoes began to show." This enthusiasm for paddling, which took him throughout Canada, would never wane.

In the early years, he would quit his job as a commercial artist in Winnipeg each spring and spend the summer canoeing throughout Manitoba and

Northern Ontario. In the fall he would return to his art job, and the cycle would begin again.

In 1959, Bill married Joyce Ferguson, and they moved east. Here, he soon began making a living documenting his life's passion. Wife Joyce, son Paul (b. 1961) and daughter Becky (b. 1963) were his frequent paddling partners, as well as contributors to his two cornerstone books on canoeing, *Path of the Paddle* and *Song of the Paddle*.

An accomplished writer and painter, Bill Mason also had a successful film career. His 25-year association with the National Film Board saw the creation of such memorable films as *Rise and Fall of the Great Lakes*, *Cry of the Wild*, the *Path of the Paddle* series, and his final film, *Waterwalker*. His 18 films garnered more than 60 national and international awards.

When Bill found out he had an inoperable form of cancer, he went on a canoe trip on the South Nahanni River with his family. On his return he continued work on *Canoescapes*, a book-length collection of his paintings (completed by his family and published after his death).

Joyce Mason, who continues to live at Meech Lake, in Québec, is director of Bill Mason Productions Ltd. She continues to support and advise in all of Mason Productions' endeavours.

Paul is a freelance cartoonist, accredited whitewater instructor, experienced wilderness canoe guide, and serious playboating addict (a bronze medallist at the 1993 Whitewater Rodeo World Championships). With Mark Scriver, Paul co-authored *Thrill of the Paddle: The Art of Whitewater Canoeing*, an advanced canoeing book that focuses on whitewater skills, a progressive follow-up to his father's *Path of the Paddle*. Paul and wife Judy, a teacher and canoe instructor, and their daughters, Jamie and Willa, live beside a canoeable creek in Québec's Gatineau Hills.

Becky acquired her paddling skills and her love for canoes and the wilderness from her dad. Every spring you are sure to see her out on Meech Lake, breaking up the ice to get her first Classic Solo canoe course started. After teaching all summer, then canoe-tripping until freeze-up, she stows her paddle for the winter and paints her canoeing memories and experiences. Becky is married to fellow artist and canoeist Reid McLachlan. They live close to Joyce and Paul and his family in Chelsea. Becky has designed the family's webpage, which showcases artwork and canoeing information concerning Bill, Paul, Reid and Becky. The website address is www.wilds.mb.ca/redcanoe.

In 1995, Paul and Becky, with the help of Joyce, Judy and Reid, completed the revised edition of *Path of the Paddle*.

Alex Hall
Guide in the Land Before Time

At more than 3.4 million square kilometres, the pre-Nunavut Northwest Territories comprised over one-third of all of Canada. The first professional canoeing guide to operate in the N.W.T. was Alex Hall, owner of Canoe Arctic Inc. Established in 1974, it is now the oldest wilderness travel company operating on the N.W.T. section of Canadian Shield, where the taiga's lichen woodland and the tundra's endless sweep roll on and on to the horizon. "I've had the privilege of canoeing more miles in the Northwest Territories than any other person," he explains. "Some summers I paddle more miles than I drive all year." Alex has canoed more than 40 different rivers — all the major ones and some known only to a select few — many a number of times. (He has travelled on the Thelon River more than 40 times.)

Some trips are long. In addition to two eight-week solo sojourns, he and a friend once spent 78 days canoeing 1,800 kilometres from the 60th Parallel to the Arctic Ocean without resupply.

Alex spends most of his summers in the N.W.T.'s Barren Lands — 1.3 million square kilometres which are neither flat nor barren. "The Barrens have been described as a 'cold desert,' but for Alex they are better described by the Cree word *Kistikani*, 'the garden,'" writes M.T. Kelly, a winner of the Governor General's Award for Literature. "Their harvest is wonder."

Born in 1942, Alex first learned to paddle at Camp Ahmek in Algonquin Park. He now operates his Fort Smith, N.W.T.-based guiding company with

his wife, Lia Ruttan, whom he met on a 1981 Canoe Arctic trip. They were married in 1984 and they have two sons, Graham and Evan. The most travelled person in the Barrens has three recommendations for other northern travellers, who generally are much too rushed: 1) put in early in the summer; 2) plan on modest distances (no more than 160 kilometres a week); 3) take out well before the mid-August change of weather.

Trained as a wildlife biologist, Alex has an affinity for all creatures, especially tundra wolves. He was instrumental in helping save the Thelon Game Sanctuary, which was threatened by the mining lobby in the late 1980s. This sanctuary, slightly larger in area than Nova Scotia, is the largest protected area in Canada. The final paragraph of James Raffan's Ph.D. thesis states: "My hope for the Thelon Game Sanctuary is that it will remain undeveloped in perpetuity and that there will always be an Alex Hall to keep it safe from harm."

Alex Hall describes his love of canoeing: "The canoe is the most practical, efficient and satisfying way to travel through wild country, particularly on the Canadian Shield, where you can go almost anywhere. I think of that country every day of my life. One of the things I like best about canoe travel is that you are completely self-reliant. There is no dependence on mechanical devices. It is utterly simple. For me, the canoe means complete freedom — the ultimate escape."

Claudia Kerckhoff-van Wijk
Determination, Focus and Will to Succeed

CLAUDIA KERCKHOFF-VAN WIJK, TEN-TIME NATIONAL WHITEWATER
kayaking champion, cross-country marathon skier, owner and director of a
thriving outdoor adventure business, wife and mother, is the personification
of balance.

Sport has been a major part of Claudia's life since childhood. By the age
of 13, she was Ontario's junior cross-country skiing champion, as well as a
national champion in whitewater kayaking. At 16, she became the first
woman to win the Canadian Ski Marathon, a popular 100-mile cross-country
trek between Montréal and Ottawa. Despite such early success, she soon rel-
egated skiing to hobby status. Kayaking became a career.

She was introduced to paddling at the age of three by her parents, Hermann and Christa Kerckhoff, provincial and national kayaking champions. (He competed in the 1972 Olympics.) They were also members of the first group to descend the Grand Canyon in kayaks. "I travelled all across the country with my family in pursuit of rivers," Claudia remembers, "but the sport didn't excite me because there were no other kids my age who were paddling." Her enthusiasm for kayaking didn't emerge until her parents developed the Madawaska Kanu Centre (MKC), a whitewater paddling school on the Madawaska River near Algonquin Park, in 1972. Claudia won her first national slalom championship when she was 13. It was a title she would successfully defend for the next ten years. She also won bronze in the 1982 World Championships.

After retiring from competitive kayaking in 1985, Claudia took over the running of MKC from her parents. With husband Dirk van Wijk, also a former Canadian canoe champion, and an experienced canoeing and rafting guide, Claudia now operates MKC as well as Owl Rafting on the Ottawa River, introducing the exciting sport of whitewater kayaking to thousands of enthusiasts each year. While both businesses have the potential to increase in size, that is not Claudia and Dirk's intention. "It's a conscious decision to stay the size we are," she explains. "Quality is more important than quantity." They have gained a worldwide reputation with this approach. MKC's slogan has proven itself: "It's a rapid education."

Determination, focus and the will to succeed have always been the Claudia Kerckhoff-van Wijk trademarks. On what paddling means to her, Claudia says: "Paddling has been my confidence builder. I believe everyone needs to be good at something to build her or his personal confidence in approaching every aspect of life. Paddling gave me this, and more. I had talent, courage and a desire to succeed. I feel lucky to have been able to use paddling as my venue, which took me all over the world, meeting different people, being in the outdoors, and feeling healthy. A great lifestyle."

Roger Pearson
Impelling Canoe Experiences

Rᴏɢᴇʀ Pᴇᴀʀsᴏɴ's ɪɴᴛᴇʀᴇsᴛ ɪɴ ᴄᴀɴᴏᴇɪɴɢ ʙᴇɢᴀɴ ɪɴ ᴛʜᴇ Uɴɪᴛᴇᴅ Kɪɴɢᴅᴏᴍ at age 16, when he built a wood-and-canvas kayak. His career in the sport almost came to an untimely end when, on a maiden voyage, with the River Tess in flood, an encounter with the centre span of an old stone bridge caused his kayak to capsize.

His rigorous introduction to canoeing took place through a program at the Outward Bound Sea School in Aberdovey, North Wales. This provided not only a chance for skill development but also an introduction to the philosophy of Kurt Hann, the school's founder, who believed, "It is wrong to coerce people into opinions, but it is your duty to impel them into experiences."

Following professional work as a naval architect in various parts of the world, Roger brought his interest in "things that float" to Newfoundland. In the early 1970s, he became the founding president of both the St. John's Canoe Club and the Newfoundland Canoe Association. He has served regularly on the executive of the NCA since that time.

With instructor certification at the 1976 Atlantic Instructor Canoe School, Roger initiated canoeing leadership and skill development programs throughout the province. Under his direction, the first nationally accredited Canadian Recreational Canoeing Association instructor program was conducted in Newfoundland in 1978. Roger has subsequently been a course conductor for all but one of the Newfoundland Lakewater Instructor Canoe Schools.

Soon after his arrival in Newfoundland, Roger worked with a group of fellow canoeists to construct a fibreglass canoe mould. Twenty years and many hundreds of canoes later, this mould continues to calve boats, giving pleasure to many new paddlers.

During the 1980s, Roger became involved with the flatwater racing dimension of the sport and established a competitive division of the St. John's Canoe Club, serving as coach–manager for many years. This desire to share the thrill of competition with others led Roger to support the Games for the Disabled in St. John's and to organize canoe racing events for the blind.

Having become less interested in the rugged portaging associated with lakewater paddling in Newfoundland, Roger can now be found among the whales and puffins on the east coast of the province, the eagles of the coastal areas of Terra Nova Park, or the seals of the western fiords. He has also formed an association with the Mi'kmaq of the Conne River Band, who are planning to build a traditional 26-foot seagoing canoe and paddle from Newfoundland to Nova Scotia in celebration of their heritage. When they set off on their voyage, Roger Pearson will be with them in spirit if not in person.

Eric Morse

A Pioneer of Northern Wilderness Paddling

Hᴇ WAS THE UNEQUIVOCAL CANOE-TRIP LEADER — THE BOURGEOIS. Fᴏʀ six decades, he canoed the lakes and rivers of the Canadian Shield. In his last 30 years, he retraced the early fur trade and explorers' routes from Montréal to the mouth of the Mackenzie, from Hudson Bay to Alaska, and from Winnipeg to the Arctic Ocean. Eric Wilton Morse (1904–1986) was a pioneer of recreational canoeing in northern Canada.

Born in India, his introduction to canoeing in Canada as a teen had an immense impact on the rest of his life. After graduating in Modern History from Queen's University, Eric served in the RCAF during World War II, retiring as squadron leader in 1945. He then became the first national secretary of the United Nations Association in Canada, and in 1949 began 22 years as national director of the Association of Canadian Clubs.

But it was at an Ottawa dinner party in 1951 that the legendary Voyageurs group was formed. Their trips on the Churchill, Camsell and other waterways in the 1950s and '60s made front-page headlines. Eric's interests eventually led him further north, and for 20 years, with a younger group of companions, he canoed the rivers of the Yukon and N.W.T. — the Thelon,

Coppermine, Kazan and others. "His enthusiasm was so infectious that he lured others along like a Pied Piper," says his wife, Pamela, who was a frequent member of those trips. "Eric also made it something of a mission to encourage young people to set themselves challenges in choosing canoe routes, and to be exploratory and innovative," she adds. "He made history come alive for them."

Eric wrote many papers, articles and books, including two classics: *Fur Trade Canoe Routes of Canada, Then and Now* and *Freshwater Saga: Memoirs of a Lifetime of Wilderness Canoeing.* But there was much more to Eric Morse.

"He also gave us all the inspiration to take care of this precious natural heritage that we have been left in the Barrens, to respect its fragility and to look upon it as a gift to be carefully used and carefully preserved," said Angus Scott in his eulogy at Eric's funeral. "As you know, his life's work has been recognized by membership in the Order of Canada, by the degree of doctorate of letters conferred on him by Queen's University, and by the river in the Northwest Territories which now bears his name."

Angus, who paddled with Eric on half a dozen long trips, continued: "I saw Eric as a rather unusual combination of stoic and romantic. The stoic part of him was perseverance, determination, courage, and the drive to forge ahead under adverse conditions of climate and geography and sometimes human constraint. On the romantic side was that sense of adventure . . . that enabled him to enjoy the thrill of whitewater, the challenge of discovery, the peace of a sun-filled morning on a still lake under a blue sky, miles, many hundreds of miles from the nearest road or railway."

"Eric was 72 when he made his last canoe trip in the Barrens — a really punishing route through divide country. As I recall, we reckoned we walked about 75 miles, what with two carries per portage," says Pamela from her home in Wakefield, Québec. "He went on canoeing and skiing for another eight years, and even in 1986, just before his death, he was contemplating another trip down his beloved French River."

When Eric Morse received his honorary degree from Queen's University, the citation stated: "He taught a whole generation of Canadians the importance of recovering our heritage and using it wisely."

Ken Madsen
Wilderness Advocate

Born in 1950, Ken Madsen began canoeing in the early 1970s on the Dease River in northern British Columbia. As he paddled more, a personal transformation took place. "Experiencing the wilderness and seeing grizzlies in the wild turned me into a devoted paddler and wilderness advocate," he explains. Ken's most satisfying advocacy achievement, to date, occurred in 1993. After four years of dogged determination — crisscrossing Canada and the United States giving hundreds of presentations, vigorously lobbying governments, and constantly speaking out for wilderness preservation — Ken Madsen helped save the Tatshenshini River in northwestern B.C. Instead of the ill-conceived Windy Craggy copper mine, the million-hectare Tatshenshini–Alsek Wilderness Park became a reality. It has since been nominated as a United Nations World Heritage Site.

A former teacher, Ken is now a Whitehorse, Yukon-based writer, photographer and outdoor educator. When not involved in environmental work and river conservation in the Yukon — which he has been doing since 1980 — he is paddling. Ken has plied waters in British Columbia, Alberta, the Northwest Territories, Alaska and the western United States, Mexico, Costa Rica, New Zealand and Australia. "But nothing in the rest of the world compares to the wilderness rivers of the North," he explains. "I always return to paddle in the Yukon."

Ken made the first Canadian descents of Turnback Canyon on the Alsek River and Grand Canyon on the Stikine River, as well as the first complete descent of the entire Stikine, from its headwaters to the Pacific Ocean. He's also been involved in many other first descents throughout the northwest — Bates, Kusawa, Nakina and Skagway rivers, Primrose Canyon, and Tats Creek, to name a few. It is the Alsek, however, that will be with him forever. Ken and his partner, Wendy Boothroyd, named their son Malcolm Alsek.

In addition to writing many magazine articles about rivers and the environment, Ken has authored two books about paddling, *Rivers of the Yukon: A Paddling Guide* and *Tatshenshini Wilderness Quest*.

Ken Madsen explains the significance of wilderness: "Paddling a wilderness river allows me to see more clearly where I stand in the grand scheme of things . . . an insignificant creature on an amazing planet. That feeling reinforces the importance of preserving wild lands — and the wild creatures and evolutionary processes that are dependent upon them."

Mark Scriver
Heralded "Hair" Boater

MARK SCRIVER CONSTANTLY PUSHES PADDLING'S LIMITS. ROUTES ONCE considered unrunnable are simply a new challenge for Mark. Seeking out "hairy" whitewater (gnarly, foamy rapids), steep creeks and treacherous waterfalls, he finds ways to make easy routes hard and hard routes harder.

He was Canada's premier representative at the 1993 World Whitewater Rodeo Championships, where he placed second, performing masterful paddling tricks. He went on to win the event in 1995 and again in 1997. As Whitewater Canada's vice-president of rodeo, Mark is helping to develop this fledgling sport and was responsible for Canada hosting the 1996 Pre-World and 1997 World Rodeo Championships near Beachburg, on the Ottawa River.

Born in 1960, Mark began canoeing at an early age, graduating to whitewater in 1980 and playboats eight years later. He taught whitewater

instructor training programs for the Ontario Recreational Canoe Association, as well as instructed flatwater and canoe-tripping courses.

In 1993, Mark led a group making the first open canoe descent of the Firth River, in the Northwest Territories. He has also run *big* drops (about 8 metres) in the eastern United States and Canada. "Mark is an amazing technical paddler," says Paul Mason, himself an accomplished rodeo and "hair" boater. "He is the best I know of in Canada."

Since the early 1980s, Mark has guided trips on rivers such as the Nahanni, Tatshenshini, Hood, Mountain, Hess, Seal, Moisie, Dumoine and Clearwater.

He and his wife, Marilyn, enjoy spending time in canoes and kayaks with their sons, Ian and Paul, both of whom are, to Mark and Marilyn's relief, showing a keen interest in boating and the outdoors.

Along with his friend and paddling partner Paul Mason, Mark wrote *Thrill of the Paddle: The Art of Whitewater Canoeing*, an instructional book that covers in detail all aspects of whitewater canoeing and tells of many interesting exploits Paul and Mark have had on such rivers.

About whitewater, Mark Scriver says: "There isn't one aspect of canoeing that I don't enjoy — flatwater, tripping, or even buying, selling and fixing canoes — but it's whitewater boating that I can't live without. Whitewater: if it's worth doing, it's worth overdoing."

Steve Cook
Teacher and Tutor

By Sheena Masson

IF YOU HAVE EVER PARTICIPATED IN A CANOE CLINIC IN NOVA SCOTIA, you may recall a big older man with white hair, out-of-control eyebrows and a twinkle in his eye. You might also recall his exceptional paddling skills, wild stories, and manic harmonica playing. Once you have met Steve Cook, you're unlikely to forget him.

Steve (b. 1923) is a familiar figure in the paddling world of Nova Scotia, but his considerable contributions to canoeing in general may be less well known. He has been an instructor at innumerable flatwater clinics and in every flatwater instructor school in the province, except two. He has also taught touring schools and clinics and whitewater clinics. All this has been accomplished since Steve began "paddling seriously" — when he was 52.

A few years ago he received his Level IV Whitewater. Now in his mid-70s, he is an inspiration to the rest of us.

"One of the difficulties of starting formal stuff when you're over fifty is that your body doesn't work the same as when you're forty or thirty. So I had to make some major adjustments," he says. "I had great difficulty in the beginning years doing the kneel-out position. I do all the fancy stuff now, but I sit right down on the bottom with my legs out front."

Steve got his start in canoe instruction in the 1970s through his work as director of Physical Education for Halifax City Schools. He initiated an extensive program in the high schools that introduced canoeing to hundreds of students, and he decided to become an instructor himself in 1973, through the Canadian Camping Association.

At that time there was no provincial canoe organization, and over the next few years Steve worked with other dedicated paddlers to establish Canoe Nova Scotia. He was the first CNS president and has been involved ever since. Between 1985 and 1990, he designed and taught a ten-day adventure training course for the Armed Forces that included canoe instruction.

Steve retired from the school system in 1983 and says he dragged along the best things from his job. He allows that whitewater is a lot of fun, but he prefers canoe touring: "It is what canoeing is all about, because you go places that you can't get to any other way. Exploring in a canoe is the ultimate." The Christopher Lake system and the Tusket River are two of his favourite trips. "For a small province, we still have a lot of unspoiled areas, and there are many special places you can only get to in a canoe."

A highlight of Steve's touring experience happened while fishing in the mist. He had paddled toward the sound of geese, and suddenly the huge flock descended all around him. He kept still while hundreds of birds swam about his canoe. Eventually he had to move, causing the flock to fly off in panic. "My hat was knocked from my head, as was my paddle from my hands, and by the time they were all in the air I was soaked to the skin, with three inches of water in the canoe."

Steve plans to keep teaching canoeing "until they won't let me anymore." His newest pupil is his young grandson. "One of the things I have enjoyed the most about canoeing are the people. My closest friends are all canoeists. They're a special brand of people. That's one reason why I keep at it and hope I can do it for quite a while yet."

James Raffan
Wordsmith Makes Connections

For James Raffan, wilderness canoeing affords the paddler an opportunity to hear the rhythm and music of the land and water. "Somewhere about the middle of a long wilderness journey, I awake and revel in a sleeping-bag that smells of outside and old socks. It's early. I gaze left and see my partner, a heap of blue nylon; no sign of life except the rhythmic rise and fall of her shadow on the opposite wall. Delaying the torment of putting dry feet in wet boots, I sit up, untangle the sweater that has been my pillow, draw it on, and unzip the door just enough to savour one of the best-kept secrets of wilderness-morning," he writes in *Summer North of Sixty — By Paddle and Portage Across the Barren Lands*. "Outside, warm, familiar air in the sweater is replaced by an infusion of the coolness and possibilities of a new day. I am alone with uncluttered thoughts. Yesterday, we hauled canoes over a frozen July river-bed; today, we will leave the boats and maybe hike among tundra wolves and caribou. Tomorrow, if the weather allows, we'll pack up and

parallel the shore of this grand lake, at a rate of thirty-two strokes per minute — transcendental monotony that bonds us to this place and lifts into imagination the essence of these experiences."

Born in 1955, James (Jim) Raffan has developed many talents along the way. A Ph.D. and former associate professor of Education at Queen's University, in Kingston, Ontario, he is an accomplished writer and editor, philosopher and storyteller, photographer and adventurer, naturalist and biological researcher, guide and inveterate rambler, and a biographer (*Fire in the Bones: Bill Mason and the Canadian Canoeing Tradition*, as well as the chapter "A Child of Nature: Trudeau and the Canoe" in the 1998 book *Trudeau's Shadow*). His most recent book is entitled *Bark, Skin and Cedar: Exploring the Canoe in the Canadian Experience*. He is also husband of Gail Simmons, a seasoned paddler, and father of their daughters, Molly and Laurel.

In *Wild Waters: Canoeing Canada's Wilderness Rivers*, Jim begins to explain how the canoe fits into Canadian culture and our imagination: "Standing on the barren shores of the Coppermine River, overwhelmed by black-flies and mosquitoes, I felt, for the first time, like a visitor in a river world. . . . I learned what wild really means." He concludes: "Rivers are at the very heart of this nation. Without them, who would we be? We must preserve them, and to do that we must take effective, united — and informed — action. At stake is an irreplaceable treasure that is very much a part of who we are."

Of canoes and canoeing, Jim Raffan writes: "Canoeing more or less defines who I am. Patched boats in the backyard affirm soul truths. My home, Canada, is not an abstraction; it is kindred canoe spirits and a constellation of sun-alive, star-washed campsites, linked by rivers, lakes, and ornery portages; scapes of the heart, rekindled by sensations that linger long after the pain is gone. When I meet someone, I wonder what they would be like on a trip. When it comes to problems, nothing can be as bad as the world's worst portage (on the L'eau Claire River in Québec)."

Brian Creer

B.C.'s Teacher Extraordinaire

"I WAS INVITED TO GIVE A CANOE WORKSHOP ON VANCOUVER ISLAND, British Columbia. When I arrived I found there was an accomplished white-water instructor among the group," said Bill Mason about Brian Creer in *The Path of the Paddle*. "We teamed up to demonstrate eddy turns. As we bore down on a wild-looking whirlpool-type eddy directly above a nasty-looking rock-studded drop-off, I suggested we change paddle sides so I could make the entry into the eddy with a nice safe bow cut and brace. He overruled the change and insisted on a bow pry entry. I thought to myself, 'Oh man, I sure hope that guy back there knows what he's doing.'

"It was my first big maneuver with a stern paddler with whom I had never paddled before. With considerable apprehension, I threw in the most violent bow pry I've ever attempted. It was all or nothing. Much to my surprise, the canoe leaned way over toward the eddy and spun right around on my paddle, ending up high in the eddy. My first feeling was one of relief and

a touch of pride at a pry eddy entry very well done. Then, as I glanced back at my partner, who sat there smiling, I realized that it was mostly his doing. He must have been leaning out there in the most solid brace imaginable."

"We paddled together on a number of occasions," says Brian, fondly remembering his times with Bill Mason, "and discussed the differences between western- and eastern-style river running." Since 1955, Brian (b. 1915) has taught thousands of people the special pleasures of paddling.

"I started canoeing on saltwater when I was fifteen years old," he explains, "and over the next fifteen years followed the learn-by-doing method, which of course is very slow and painful and risky, but does give one a solid background of experience."

Brian spent 16 years as a high-school physical education teacher and helped create the Instructor's Committee of the Recreational Canoeing Association of B.C. in 1972. He has taught canoeing as well as ocean and river kayaking at the Strathcona Education Centre on Vancouver Island, Capilano College in Vancouver, and for the Vancouver School Board, among others. Of the latter, he says, "My enthusiasm for this program — ten weeks of canoeing, followed by eighteen weeks of kayaking and scuba diving, followed by ten weeks of river kayak-ing — was greatly enhanced when it became apparent that my students also improved academically during the years I taught them."

Bill Mason had this to say about Brian's programs: "I came away very impressed with his aggressive style and teaching methods and would probably agree that he turns out a superior brand of whitewater canoeist — if they survive."

Brian Creer explains why teaching canoeing is so important to him: "Canoeing provides a financially viable medium for introducing young people to one of the small number of activities available which bring out desirable personality characteristics such as respect for the power of the natural environment and responsibility for the lives of one's fellow participants."

Omer Stringer
Master Canoeist

Omer Stringer (1912–1988) was a perfectionist. He loved to hone his considerable paddling skills and refine his trusty equipment. His paddle, made of black cherry, featured a long, sleek, narrow blade; the grip was perfectly smooth, and underneath was a flat spot for graceful one-handed running pries. An immaculate 15-foot red Chestnut canoe, with "Omer" stencilled in white on the bow, was his craft of choice for more than 50 years.

Born in Killaloe, Ontario, Omer was raised in nearby Algonquin Park. He was five when legendary Canadian artist Tom Thomson died mysteriously nearby; the well-known "Stringer" home was on Potter's Creek near Canoe Lake. His father, John, was a park ranger, and Omer followed in his canoe wake, becoming an experienced guide by the age of 15.

"Through years of paddling, Omer became a respected, world-recognized stylist," says niece Karen Stringer. "He claimed he was really a 'lazy' canoeist, but then he would touch his paddle to the water, shift his weight slightly, and

spin the little Chestnut 360 degrees. It was magical to watch." Compact and athletic, Omer was influential in making sitting or kneeling in the middle of the canoe, with the hull low in the water, an acceptable solo paddling style.

During World War II, Omer served with the RCAF and was stationed in India and Burma, where he was involved in the development of radar technology. When he returned to Canada, he was instrumental in building Camp Tamakwa on Tea Lake, in his beloved Algonquin Park. (He later received the prestigious Director's Award from the Friends of Algonquin Park.) While working as a high-school teacher, Omer also continued to teach canoeing. He gave countless demonstrations, especially for the Ontario Safety League.

These were always filled with fun and highlighted with pranks such as headstands on the bow seat.

Throughout his life, Omer ceaselessly built and remodelled canoes. He altered a 15-foot Chestnut Chum by removing the inwales, increasing the canoe's depth and raising the bow height to produce a more responsive, manoeuvrable "sports car." He later became involved with the Beaver Canoe Company, his name gracing its many products. (A confirmed traditionalist, he insisted that "nothing feels like a cedar-strip canvas canoe.")

"We will always remember the magic created by this man, his red canoe, and the waters of Algonquin Park," says Karen Stringer. "Those of us who knew him well will never forget the soft and husky voice, and sparkling blue eyes of this true outdoorsman and master canoeist."

John B. Hughes
Island Mentor

IT WAS DURING HIS FIRST CANOE LESSON — AT THE CHARLOTTETOWN YMCA in 1971 — that John Hughes became hooked on paddling. He was in his twenties and canoeing appealed to his desire for self-propelled recreation. He bought a fibreglass canoe and developed his paddling skills along the inland waters of Prince Edward Island. Two years later he became a certified instructor after attending the first Atlantic Canoeing School, held near Yarmouth, Nova Scotia.

Born in 1939, John today teaches physical education and environmental studies, and lives in Corran Ban with his wife, Vera, and daughter, Susan. He has helped conduct many paddling skills courses on the Island, as well as organizing numerous canoe trips in P.E.I., New Brunswick and Nova Scotia. In addition to being chairman of the P.E.I. branch of the

CRCA and representing his province at many national meetings, task forces and seminars, he has conducted certification courses for Red Cross leaders, scouts and schoolteachers.

To broaden his paddling horizons, John embarked on two endeavours. First, at the age of 40, he took up marathon paddling. In 1995 he and his paddling partner, Shawn Shea, competed against 160 other teams to win the Red Cross Multi-Sport Relay (paddling, cycling and running). Second, in order to learn more about the magic and grace of canoes, John built a cedar-strip using an authentic Mi'kmaq birchbark canoe as a model.

Of paddling and canoes, John Hughes writes: "I have always had a desire to explore out-of-the-way places. Together, the canoe and this country's many waterways provide the ideal combination. When travelling by canoe you seem to blend in rather than being an intrusion on your surroundings. I've always had great respect for the ability of our Native Canadians to build such an ideal watercraft from their natural surroundings. My canoe-building project was an attempt to preserve one of the original models they used in this area."

George Luste
Tripper, Bibliopole and Wilderness Symposia Organizer

High energy is George Luste's specialty. While his vocation is teaching high-energy physics at the University of Toronto, his avocation — a profound love and appreciation of the North — also involves a lot of energy. His extensive northern canoe trips are legendary; his Wilderness and Canoeing symposia are highly acclaimed; and his mail-order Northern Books is a bibliophile's dream.

George was born in 1940. His first canoe trip was a solo venture down Ontario's Abitibi River to James Bay in 1963. It is believed that in 1969 George and five friends were the first group of modern canoeists to travel the full length of the Dubawnt River in the former Northwest Territories, 1,200 kilometres from its headwaters to Baker Lake. George Luste is one of the most cited paddlers in the definitive *Canoeing North into the Unknown — A Record of River Travel: 1874 to 1974*, by Bruce W. Hodgins and Gwyneth Hoyle. In addition, George is an avid winter tripper, using skis and snowshoes to reach special northern destinations.

Though an experienced solo paddler, George also enjoys travelling with others, showing them the wonders of a wilderness canoe trip. For many years his craft of choice was an aluminum canoe. "His love for the Grumman dates from early in his canoeing career . . . when he was working at the Chalk River nuclear station on the Ottawa River," says friend and veteran tripper Toni Harting. "When George married, the first item he and Linda bought was not a sensible piece of furniture to put in their new home, but a canoe — an aluminum one, of course." However, he now increasingly uses canoes made of modern materials such as Kevlar and ABS.

The annual Wilderness and Canoeing Symposium, which began in 1986, now attracts close to 800 canoeing afi- cionados from around the world. "The aim of the annual midwinter get-together in Toronto is to share an appreciation of our northern wilderness," George explains. "This takes the form of presentations from individ- uals who represent a mosaic of varied north- ern experiences. Some have travelled there by canoe or kayak, by dog-team, or on foot. For others it is their home or where they once lived." George's Northern Books, which deals in used, rare, and select new books on the North, Arctica, Canadiana, Wilderness, and Canoeing, is also world-renowned.

Another of George Luste's callings is that of protector to Canada's invaluable waterways. One of his favourite rivers, Ontario's Missinaibi, is under threat from unwarranted development, so he is currently fighting hard for its integrity.

In *Canoeing North into the Unknown*, George Luste states: "Canoeing in the northern wilderness of Canada can be a profoundly satisfying experience, resulting in an emotional bond with this primordial landscape. It offers phys- ical exposure to the elements, hard work, a visual symphony of vistas, and the inner solace that only solitude can give."

Mark Lund
From Pool Bum to Internet Provider

Born in 1951, Mark Lund learned to paddle in Red Deer, Alberta's new indoor pool in the early 1960s. His first canoe trip, as a 15-year-old, was an overnight 60-mile adventure on the Red Deer River. "Just one canoe — me and my buddy Greg Bissell," Mark remembers fondly. "I often wonder why our parents let us go!"

A few years later, Mark joined the Red Deer Canoe and Kayak Club and became involved with a keen group of Alberta whitewater paddlers. He participated in the first Whitewater Nationals held in western Canada, on the upper Red Deer River in July 1972. Mark and his partner, Glen Moore, finished fourth in the men's wildwater C-2 event. Around the same time, Mark and a group of Red Deer College canoe team members researched and prepared for publication the first Alberta canoe guide, *Canoe Alberta*. "We paddled some 2,500 kilometres that summer, and we were able to complete the first draft," says Mark. "The first print run was a hundred copies. They were gone in less than a month."

Mark was the canoe coach at Red Deer College in 1972 and a year later became the first full-time paddling instructor at the new Blue Lake Centre, north of Hinton. That same year, he and other paddling enthusiasts from the Red Deer, Edmonton and Calgary canoe clubs saw a need to organize and formalize open canoe paddling instruction in the province. The Alberta Recreational Canoeing Association was created, with Mark as education chairman. Since then, he has also served as president and environmental chair for ARCA, as well as western regional vice-president for the Canadian Recreational Canoeing Association. (He is currently a member of the selection committee for the CRCA's Bill Mason Scholarship Fund.) Mark was co-chairman with Ted Bentley when the Whitewater Nationals returned to Alberta in 1976 and has been president and race chairman for the Alberta Whitewater Association.

In 1975 Mark began teaching in the Outdoor Education Program at the University of Alberta. In 1978 he helped found Edmonton's Ceyana Canoe Club. He continued to teach at the U of A until 1984, at which time he moved across town to Grant MacEwan Community College. He continues to instruct in the physical education program, including activity courses in paddling, swimming and nordic skiing, and core courses in pedagogy and leadership, critical thinking, outdoor and environmental education, and physical fitness. His wife, Lois, is a family paddling expert. In 1995, Mark Lund helped launch paddling into cyberspace as an information provider for canoeing and kayaking on the Edmonton Freenet (look under the Sports and Fitness menu). His most recent publication adventure was in the world of self-publishing — *Mark's Guide for Central Alberta Paddlers*.

Mark Lund's paddling highlights: "I have two real highlights. One, all the wonderful paddling students I have had the chance to help, and the many of those who have become good friends and supporters of our sport and the out-of-doors. Two, all the wonderful places I have been able to go to by canoe in Canada — from the Broken Islands, the Yukon, the Nahanni, the Churchill, Lake Superior, to the many, many rivers of Alberta. Even after nearly thirty years of paddling in Alberta, there are still new streams and new reaches to explore. And new friends to meet."

Kirk A.W. Wipper
Kanawa Trust

Kanawa is a bridge — a bridge between languages and cultures. Originally a West Indian Arawak word for dugout, it is the root of the Spanish *canoa*, from which we get *canot* and canoe. Kanawa is also the world's largest collection of canoes, kayaks and rowing craft. The Kanawa Collection was conceived, developed and lovingly cared for by Kirk A.W. Wipper. "Watercraft was humankind's most important conveyance outside of walking," he explains. More than 600 craft and associated artifacts — traditional wood-canvas canoes, skin boats, cedar-strips and lapstrakes, as well as an extensive assembly of aboriginal craft from North America and abroad — are in the collection. Three truly outstanding craft from the Kanawa Collection are an Aboriginal birchbark canoe with moose-hunting scenes scraped on its bark; the last canvas-covered "Indian Maid" canoe made by the Chestnut Canoe Company of Fredericton, New Brunswick; and a double-cedar canoe (circa 1860) with its outside cedar planks running longitudinally, while the inside layer runs crosswise.

Kirk was born in 1923 to humble beginnings at Grahamdale, near The Pas, Manitoba, but he became a prodigious athlete who learned to paddle early. He went on to become a teacher, and after serving in the North Atlantic with the Navy during World War II, he continued his studies and became a professor at the University of Toronto. For 38 years, from 1950 to 1988, he was instrumental in instilling a profound love of outdoor pursuits in thousands of students. Kirk was inducted into the U of T's Sport Hall of Fame as a builder and athlete in 1991. (One Kirk Wipper Trophy is for distinguished leadership and performance in wrestling, another is for environmental concern by a student.) Three years later he was honoured by the Canadian Heritage Rivers System for his outstanding contributions to canoeing.

Kirk has been co-director of the first National Canadian Canoe Instructor School, founded by the Canadian Camping Association; past Ontario and national president of the Royal Life Saving Society; a founding member of Canoe Ontario; and president of the Canadian Recreational Canoeing Association, from 1989 to 1997. He was instrumental in the development of the CRCA's Outdoor Education Centre in Merrickville, Ontario. The CRCA's national magazine, dedicated to the promotion of paddling in Canada, is also called *Kanawa*.

Kirk Wipper started the Kanawa Collection in 1955 at Camp Kandalore, where he was owner-director from 1957 to 1980. Of Kanawa, he writes: "In its contemporary use, the canoe and kayak become a medium to experience peace, beauty, freedom and adventure. These values are of utmost significance in a world which has lost much of its contact with the profound lessons found in nature. To travel the paths in natural places makes all the difference and in this the canoe and kayak are essential partners."

The Kanawa Collection is now housed in the Canadian Canoe Museum in Peterborough, Ontario.

> Tho' they rest inside, in our dreams they'll glide
> On the crests of streams of yore.
> In the mid-day sun, they'll make their run
> and night on a distant shore.
> The travellers are gone their unmatched brawn
> Who plied the maples ways
> But their craft we keep tho the paddlers sleep.
> Their stars we seek today.
>
> — from *Kanawa*

"Miramichi" Bill Palmer

A River Ran Through Him

From 1915 to 1996 Bill Palmer and the Miramichi River were inseparable. His first trip on the fabled New Brunswick river was in the early 1920s, in a rowing canoe. For more than seven decades, Mr. Miramichi — an educator, instructor, and inspiration — was instrumental in introducing thousands to the joys and pleasures of canoeing. For 18 years, he supervised a University of New Brunswick-sponsored canoeing school. He also helped form Canoe New Brunswick in 1970 and found the Atlantic Canada canoe instructor's school. Through the years he conducted hundreds of clinics for novices and experts, Girl Guides and Boy Scouts, church groups and the general public. For his considerable efforts, "Miramichi" Bill Palmer was made a lifetime member of Canoe New Brunswick; two years later he was named Honorary Chief Instructor.

A lifelong military man, he served with the RCAF in World War II and retired from the Armed Forces in 1964 as a squadron leader. A former member of the Canoe Museum, Bill procured many rare canoes for the Kanawa Collection, including the last "Indian Maiden" manufactured by the Chestnut Canoe Company and a 30-foot long eastern dugout canoe. After receiving the Canadian Recreational Canoeing Association's Award of Merit in 1990 for his contributions to canoeing in Canada, Bill, then in his late seventies, took up canoe racing.

While the broad and beautiful Miramichi River still runs through northeast New Brunswick, on September 18, 1996, "Miramichi" Bill Palmer passed away. He was 81.

"Canoeing can be extremely educational as well as hard physical work," Bill Palmer once said, "but when everyone pitches in, there's a new esprit de corps. This emerged in every class, and is one of the finest results of good hard enjoyable paddling."

Wally Schaber
Founder of Black Feather and Trailhead

By James Raffan

QUIETLY AND IN HIS OWN IRREPRESSIBLY METHODICAL WAY, WALLY Schaber (b. 1950) has had as much influence on the growth of canoeing in Canada as anyone of his generation. Founder of Black Feather Wilderness Adventures (1971) and subsequently, with partners, the Trailhead group of stores in Ottawa (1977, 1982), Toronto (1984), Mississauga (1992) and Kingston (1995), Wally's canoeing roots go back to the Ottawa YMCA Camp On-da-da-waks on Golden Lake, in Bonnechere Country south of Pembroke, Ontario, where he was a camper and staff from 1960 to 1969. In 1969 the decision was made to close Camp On-da-da-waks on Golden Lake and begin it anew as a wilderness base camp near the headwaters of the Dumoine River on Ten Mile Lake. Wally and half a dozen other staff members took part in attempting this initiative, but it did not succeed; however, it did create the beginnings of Black Feather's mailing list in 1971.

Branching out from On-da-da-waks and high school in Ottawa, Wally entered the Honours Bachelor of Environmental Studies program at the University of Waterloo, where he met Jack Pearse, professor of Recreation

and founding director of Camp Tawingo. During his summers at university, Wally worked as a canoeing guide at Camp Tawingo, leading trips into the Kipawa region of western Québec — an area that would provide his bread-and-butter canoe routes when he mounted his first Black Feather Wilderness trips from his mother's basement in 1971.

While exploring new routes for Black Feather, often paddling with his neighbour and friend Bill Mason, Wally also became the first licensed canoeing guide in Nahanni National Park in 1976. Since then, as his business interests grew and more and more people were introduced to canoeing and to wilderness canoeing trips through his influence, Wally has built an enviable paddling résumé: Nahanni (ten times), Coppermine, Mountain, Hood, Snake, Flat, Natla-Keele, Chicoutimi rivers, and he reckons he has paddled the mighty Dumoine River something in the order of one hundred times — in spring flood, in summer trickle, and at fall freshet, always enjoying the company of his friends and customers, always learning something new.

In addition to encouraging many people to share in his passion for canoeing and wilderness, Wally has written about canoes and rivers; he has contributed in large measure to various movies and instructional books, notably those of Bill Mason. He has been an active conservationist, attempting to influence attitudes in the outdoor industry and, along with Trailhead partners, he has been an innovative developer of canoe-tripping products under the Black Feather label.

Wally Schaber writes: "I'm not too philosophical when it comes to what I use or where I go when I access the wilderness. The canoe, the kayak, skis, snowshoes or even the mountain bike are all means to an end. I like to end in a place that's beautiful, clean, unimpacted and inspirational. I want to arrive there with good friends, to share memories or experiences as fresh as the moment. I want to feel I got there because of my own skills, at my own risk. The wilderness and the environment — weather, wildlife — are not there to confront me, nor I to conquer them; they are a puzzle to be sorted out by planning, experience and good tools. The seventeen-foot Prospector is the best vehicle to take you anywhere the waterways allow. But in my lifetime I predict wilderness as we know it will disappear. So, fellow travellers, enjoy it now; you are living through the last decade of wilderness travel."

Ric Driediger
A Self-Portrait

I LIVE WITH MY WIFE, THERESA AND OUR TWO CHILDREN, DANIEL AND Sarah, in Missinipe, Saskatchewan, a small community on the Churchill River. I'm the owner and operator of Horizons Unlimited Wilderness Services and Churchill River Canoe Outfitters. During the summer months my staff and I operate canoe trips and courses from around our base on the Churchill. We also run canoe trips throughout northern Saskatchewan, northern Manitoba and parts of the Northwest Territories. We have rental cabins and a lodge at our base in Missinipe, along with some fishing boats. Each summer we help hundreds of canoeists have a safe and enjoyable wilderness holiday.

My winter months are spent manufacturing the Bill Mason campfire tent (about 15 classic Bakers each winter), looking after my children while Theresa works, and dreaming about next summer's canoe trips.

Even though I am now primarily involved in administrating the two companies, it wasn't always that way. From the time I started my business in

1973, when I was 19, until I purchased Churchill River Canoe Outfitters in 1988, I would spend every summer from May until September in my canoe. When I first started guiding I would take groups out without being paid. I would do it so I could be paddling in the wilderness. After one trip, a participant asked what I wanted to be paid for providing guiding services. I was astonished! You mean I can get paid to be out here? At that point it was decided: this was what I was going to do for my livelihood.

During those first years most of the groups I guided were church groups with very little money (but it was while guiding a trip for one of those groups on the Churchill in 1978 that I met Theresa). I would figure out routes that were easily accessible by road. To make  it interesting, I tried to do as many new routes as I could. I found routes that were and still are virtually untravelled. I have paddled nearly 100 different routes, most of which are easily accessible. This knowledge has assisted me in helping others plan their own canoe trips.

Throughout all of this I fell in love with the Precambrian Shield of northern Saskatchewan. I have paddled in many regions of Canada and U.S., but I know of no wilderness area as big, as accessible, as empty, and as beautiful as here. Saskatchewan Tourism coined a slogan some years ago: "The Northern Saskatchewan wilderness is Canada's best-kept secret." In some ways I would like to keep it a secret, but my personality is such that when I find something special I want to tell everyone about it. I love helping others enjoy their wilderness canoeing experience; yet I long to be out there myself.

Once wilderness canoeing becomes a part of you, it is like an unquenchable thirst. The more you drink of it the more you desire it. You may try to quench the thirst by drinking something else, but wilderness canoeing will always call you back for more.

The Hodgins Family
A Paddling Tradition

IT ALL STARTED WITH STAN AND CECIL HODGINS IN 1915. THE TWO brothers bought a canoe called the *Ile of View* and paddled it on the Avon River, in Stratford, Ontario. Their first canoe trip was in 1916 on the Severn, from what is now Highway 11 almost to Port Severn, and up into Six Mile and Crooked Lakes. In 1926, Stan and his bride, Laura Belle, honeymooned on a two-week trip in Algonquin, arriving by train — there was no Highway 60. Then, for four summers they tripped in the Temagami–Lady Evelyn–Obabika–Mountain Lake area, latterly with Cecil and his wife, Margarite. Cecil's and Margarite's eldest son, Daryl, became a significant canoeist. He and Barbara have four children — Glenn, Eric, Murray and Andrea — all of whom are experienced trip leaders. Stan and Laura Belle had two sons, Bruce and Larry, both avid canoeists. Larry became, and remains, a keen northern trip leader, and Jacquelyn, one of his three children, is as well.

In 1956, after directing Camp Wabanaki on Beausoleil Island for 12 years, Stan and Laura Belle bought Camp Wanapitei on Lake Temagami. Bruce took charge of the program and its canoe trips, having led his first trip in 1948. In 1958 Bruce married Carol Creelman, and ever since, they have been instrumental in making Wanapitei a major centre for wilderness canoe trips. Bruce and Carol have led dozens of trips, for both youth and adults, throughout Canada, including many in the N.W.T., Nunavut, the Yukon, northern Saskatchewan, the Temagami area, and to James Bay.

Bruce has taught history at Trent University since 1965 and has been active in many canoeing and camping organizations (a past president of ORCA, active on the Canadian Canoe Museum Board and with Canadian Heritage Rivers). He has written widely and often about canoeing. He co-edited *Nastawgan* (1986) and *Using Wilderness* (1992), and co-authored *The Temagami Experience* (1989) and *Canoeing North into the Unknown* (1994). Carol, a physical therapist, published the *Wanapitei Canoe Tripper's Cookbook* (1982), which has gone through 11 printings and sold over 12,500 copies. (She has been declared "Canada's undisputed queen of the campfire kitchen.") Volume II was published in 1999.

Bruce and Carol have two sons, Shawn and Geoff. Shawn has become a distinguished northern canoe-trip leader and whitewater instructor. He was on Quebec's Eastmain in 1977 (the last trip ever able to canoe it) and has tripped extensively in Labrador, Ungava, Nunavut and the N.W.T. Shawn has been director of Wanapitei since 1997. In 1995 he married Liz McCarney, herself an experienced paddler.

Geoff and Pat Bowles were brought together by the canoe. They met at Wanapitei, canoe-tripped together at age 12, and have led many trips throughout the North. They are married and have three small children. The fourth generation has begun.

On the canoe in Canadian culture, Bruce Hodgins writes: "For me, the canoe and the canoe trip are central to my personality, my *amour-propre*, my very being. For me, the canoe does not stand alone, apart from its very diverse, strong but fragile and aboriginally peopled northern environment, one which affects me both emotionally and spiritually. The canoe on the waterways is vital to my northern landscape. Together, canoe and landscape form the deepest part of my Canadian heritage."

Bill Brigden
Designer and Builder, Olympian and Inspiration

Born in 1916, Bill Brigden began his prestigious racing career in 1948, twice winning, in record time, the 65-mile Les Voyageurs Annual Canoe Race from the Winnipeg Canoe Club to lower Fort Garry and back. Then, in 1952, Bill Brigden (stern) and Jim Nickel (bow) finished 11th in the 10,000-metre K2 kayak event at the Helsinki Olympic Summer Games. A few years later, Bill and Don Starkell twice won the Gold Rush Canoe Race held in Flin Flon, Manitoba. (The 1955 race covered 104 miles and in 1956 it was 140 miles.) "Regardless of the impressive showings, Bill was known to his fellow competitors as a hard-working, tireless athlete who had a rare gift — the stamina and endurance to master long events and yet the power and strength to win the shorter races," reads the citation in the Manitoba Sports Hall of Fame, where Bill Brigden was inducted in 1991.

In addition to his paddling feats, Bill is known throughout Manitoba for building hundreds of "Brigdens." Sixteen feet long and available in various

colours, these distinctive and marvellous canoes are durable and inexpensive. Made of gelcoat, polyester resin, fibreglass, cloth and mat, with oak gunwales, they are handcrafted one at a time. He created the 21-foot canoe that Don and Dana Starkell used to paddle 20,000 kilometres from Winnipeg to the mouth of the Amazon River over two years, 1980 to 1982 (read *Paddle to the Amazon*).

Bill also makes a variety of paddles, including straight-shaft and bent-shaft paddles with kayak-paddle-like blades. His first bent-shaft paddle design in the 1950s helped give him an extra advantage during canoe races. With a unique oval-shaped shaft, the paddle doesn't turn awkwardly in your hand. "I applied a kayak stroke to paddling the canoe," Bill Brigden says. "It is achieved by reaching forward with the grip hand, which forces you to twist at the waist and to pull instead of push." Bill built the double-bladed kayak paddle that Victoria Jason used for her 7,500-kilometre trip in the Canadian Arctic from 1991 to 1994 (read *Kabloona in the Yellow Kayak — One Woman's Journey Through the Northwest Passage*).

Bill and his wife, Marion, who have two sons, a daughter, and several grandchildren, have made countless paddling friends and memories over more than three decades.

Peake Brothers and Friends

Chroniclers of Wilderness Canoeing

IT'S THE CLUB OF CLUBS. WITH THE LATE ERIC WILTON MORSE AS Honorary Patron, members of the Hide-Away Canoe Club (HACC) are Michael Peake (b. 1952), Governor; Geoffrey Peake (b. 1960), Chief Guide; Peter Scott (b. 1960), Chaplain; Sean Peake (b. 1956), Director of Research; David Peake (b. 1953), Quartermaster; Peter Brewster (b. 1942), Piscine Director; and Andrew Macdonald (b. 1972), Director of Reconaissance. Since 1980 they have paddled and walked more than 10,000 kilometres along the routes of our forefathers. "We are Canadians," says Michael Peake, "who have taken the time and hard work to feel history in the stroke of our paddles and blisters in our boots."

Club trips have included the Missinaibi, Rupert, Dumoine, George, Povungnituk, Churchill, across Ungava (up the Koglauk and down the Payne rivers), Nahanni, Heart of the North (Great Bear Lake to the Coppermine River via the Hepburn River), Petawawa, Quetico, across the Arctic Mountains (from Ft. McPherson, N.W.T., up the Rat River and down the

Bell and Porcupine rivers to Old Crow, Yukon, and north to Ungava on the George River). In 1985 most of the intrepid HACC trippers spent 55 days and travelled 1,600 kilometres in the N.W.T. to name the Morse River (Eric Morse was alive at the time and very honoured; the river now adorns topographical map 66F – Pelly Lake). "We are trying to be worthy successors to the great legacies left by Eric Morse and the Voyageurs," Michael explains. "We believe that our rich and largely unknown history comes alive when retraced in the form of wilderness canoe trips. We pay homage to these men and their rich traditions, sense of fun, and respect for the land."

Descriptions of these trips as well as issues and concerns related to Canadian wilderness canoeing can be found in *Che-Mun* (Ojibwa for canoe), a quarterly journal founded in 1973 by Nick Nickels and published since 1984 by the HACC. The website is www.canoe.ca/AllAboutCanoes/che-mum. Club members also appear regularly in the media, including CBC and PBS.

The annual Hide-Away Canoe Club dinner is held December 28 — the date of Eric Morse's birthday. "We review the year's trip, and enjoy the firewood and water we've brought back from the previous summer's sojourn," says Michael. "Much of that water ends up as ice in a glass of good scotch."

Michael Peake explains the philosophy of the HACC: "The Hide-Away Canoe Club's motto, 'The time comes nigh,' is from Eric Morse. And its credo, which is credited to James Monroe Thorington, an early member of the Alpine Club of Canada, states: 'We were not pioneers ourselves, but we travelled over old trails that were new to us and with hearts open. Who shall distinguish?'"

Hap Wilson
License to Paddle

W**HENEVER** J**AMES** B**OND** NEEDS TO KNOW HOW TO OPERATE THE LATEST high-tech device, he relies on the trusty and reliable "Q" (the late actor Desmond Llewelyn). When Agent 007, aka Pierce Brosnan, was playing Archibald Belaney in the 1999 film *Grey Owl*, directed by Oscar-winner Richard Attenborough, he relied on outfitter and canoe guide extraordinaire "HW" — Hap Wilson — to learn to paddle properly.

A wilderness advocate and environmental activist, author and illustrator, Hap has guided more than 150 wilderness expeditions, which added together is more kilometres than the world is round. But unlike many wilderness adventurers, he doesn't collect canoe trips. Instead, Hap (b. 1951) marches to his own drumbeat. The philosopher Joseph Campbell said: "Follow your bliss — the heroic life is living the individual adventure." That's Hap. The former park ranger finds consolation in the wilderness, and the canoe is the conduit to that sacred place.

"Since my departure from high school in 1970, I've never taken a job that wasn't somehow related to canoeing, never punched a time clock, and

never been fettered by the nine-to-five tedium," Hap explains. "I often lose track of the days of the week, choose to live in what I call ordered chaos, and religiously forget to pay bills on time.

"My responsible existence is planned around wilderness trips. I can blame — or thank — the canoe for my revisionist ideology. Thoreau explained the shortcomings of society and the dangers of conforming to systemic monotony, and Grey Owl romanticized wilderness in a mischievous and provocative way. But it was the wanton destruction of my beloved wilderness by exploitive humankind that charged my passion to paddle, to explore, and to share with others that sense of spiritual freedom and purpose . . . and this could only be accomplished with the aid and assistance of the Canadian canoe."

Examples of Hap's meticulously hand-drawn maps, landscapes and figures, as well as his striking photographs, can be found in *Temagami Canoe Routes*, *Tripper's Log Book*, *Riviere Dumoine*, *Rivers of the Upper Ottawa Valley*, *Missinaibi: Journey to the Northern Sky*, and *Voyages*, which won the Natural Resources Council of America's award for best environmental book in 1995. In addition, Hap and his wife, Stephanie Aykroyd, an accomplished artist, photographer and canoeist, have co-authored *Wilderness Rivers of Manitoba* and *Wilderness Manitoba*.

To find consolation in the wilderness, Hap Wilson visits his cabin deep in the heart of Temagami. Hap writes: "For me and my family [Stephanie and son Christopher], canoeing is our preferred lifestyle — everything else is incidental. We share in the celebration of the wilderness as our real home, our life inspiration, and our future salvation as a species. It is our common goal to continue to promote canoeing as a corroborated means to salvage what's left of our wild heritage through our books, lectures and artwork. We do this for the children who, as of yet, do not have a voice to speak out with."

Neil Hartling
People Will Protect What They Love

He has paddled the fabled South Nahanni River close to 40 times, but one of the most memorable trips was a two-weeker — twelve days upstream and two days downstream! But Neil Hartling, founder and owner of Nahanni River Adventures, put that masochistic trip to good use. He successfully tested a prototype of his take-apart and put-together seven-person canoe. In fact, that test run led to what is now standard equipment with Nahanni River Adventures — sectional Voyageur canoes that can nest inside Twin Otter aircraft.

Neil was captivated by the canoe at an early age. Born in Edmonton in 1961 and living in various places in Canada, including the Maritimes and Ottawa, he attended his first summer camp on the Ottawa River at the age of eight. "I was drawn to the cedar-and-canvas beauties on the beach and captivated by the romantic notion of the canoe as a ticket to adventure," Neil remembers. "During my school years I would spend days imagining adventures that featured a canoe as the central theme — rendering me virtually unemployable in any other vocation."

Neil first built a fibreglass canoe in his Grade 9 shop class. After a few years of aimless paddling, he had the good fortune to study Outdoor Education under Garry Gibson and Dave Larson at Augustana College in Camrose, Alberta. And it was while Neil was finishing his Physical Education degree at the University of Alberta that he encountered another profound influence. "Mark Lund [an instructor at U of A] further mentored me into the fraternity of canoe builders, and I destroyed my parents' lawn and garage with the many building projects that ensued. Property values have not recovered," he says with a chuckle. "Along the way, I became fascinated with the business of adventure."

Soon after graduating, Neil started Nahanni River Adventures, which is now the largest river expedition company in Canada. In addition to the Nahanni tours, Nahanni River Adventures offers canoe trips on the Burnside, Coppermine, Horton, Stikine, Wind, Snake, Taku and Yukon Rivers, and raft trips on the Firth, Alsek and Tatshenshini Rivers. Once Nahanni River Adventures was established, Neil and business partner Randy Clement established Rocky Mountain Voyageurs, a company offering canoe trips on the Athabasca River in Jasper National Park. "With fifty guides at the peak of the season, we run expeditions from Alaska to Nunavut," he explains. "We offer environmental and historic interpretive programs to more than five thousand paddlers a season."

Based in Whitehorse and president of both the Wilderness Tourism Association of the Yukon and the Nahanni River Outfitters Association, Neil was instrumental in developing the regulation system in Nahanni National Park, thereby creating a practical approach to the challenge of sustainable wilderness tourism. "Outfitting areas are highly valued in the United States and we are not far behind in Canada," Neil says. "With this comes the responsibility to manage our sector of the tourism industry responsibly and keep the eco in eco-tourism."

Neil explains his unique business approach: "I enjoy sharing wild places with others. People will protect what they love. I like to think my work creates emissaries for the land. I know it also enriches the lives of those who travel to these enchanted rivers."

Kevin Callan
On Dealing with Bugs, Bears and Bad Weather

It was in Ontario's Algoma Highlands in the mid-1970s that Kevin Callan was first introduced to canoes. "I think I was twelve and my father took me along on his annual fly-in fishing trip. We didn't catch any fish on the main lake so we decided to borrow one of the lodge's old beat-up Grummans and portage into a smaller lake. It was loaded with speckled trout," Kevin remembers. "That day proved to me that the canoe was the best craft ever invented for heading into remote and wild places."

While Patrick Callan helped his son hone his camping skills, Kevin's canoeing skills are essentially self-taught. "My technique, especially in white-water, has come from a combination of trial and error, and from reading Bill Mason's books and watching his films over and over," he explains. "Apart from my annual trip with my high-school chums, workmates, and a few guided trips, I either paddle solo — which ends up to be most of the time — or head off with my wife and Bailey [a young springer spaniel]. My wife, Alana, has always been my best paddling partner — honest."

Although Kevin, who was born in 1963 and lives in Peterborough (the birthplace of the modern-day canoe), says he's not a collector, he does own six canoes: an 18-foot We-no-nah Kevlar Sundowner for big lakes and long portages; a 17-foot We-no-nah plastic boat for Class I boulder gardens; a Dagger Reflection for solo whitewater trips with Class II whitewater or easier; a 14-foot Swift Osprey for solo lake travel; and a Prospector from the Voyageur Canoe Company in Milbrook for everything else. Oh, and a half-restored Peterborough canoe for placing over the mantel once it's fully restored. "After all the work I've put into it, I wouldn't dare paddle it!" he says with a laugh. What does Kevin Callan use when he heads out to paddle rapids more difficult than Class II? He rents.

Overall, his favourite canoe is one that is affordable and safe. "I think too many people get caught up in the Tilley Hat Syndrome, where they buy expensive gear to help them survive," he says. "I think a proper state of mind helps you deal with bugs, bears, and bad weather — not high-priced gear."

His work as a forest technician, nature interpreter, outdoor educator and syndicated nature columnist hasn't kept him away from canoeing. In his method of making time for paddling, Kevin is reminiscent of a young Bill Mason, who used to quit his job every spring and then hope to get hired back again in the fall. For the past ten years Kevin has been a part-time instructor of environmental issues and wilderness ethics at Sir Sandford Fleming's School of Natural Resources. He really loves to teach. "In the spring I get laid off, so then I go paddling for five months and make a few dollars guiding, working at camps, writing magazine articles, and living off the dollars I make from my guidebooks," he explains. "Then I hope and pray that I get hired back at the college in the fall."

A frequent guest on radio and television, Kevin is an also an established author, having published six books (five of them with Boston Mills Press): *Killarney* (1990); *Cottage Country Canoe Routes* (1993); *Ways of the Wild: A Practical Guide to the Outdoors* (Broadview Press, 1993); *Up the Creek: A Paddler's Guide to Ontario* (1996); *Brook Trout and Blackflies: A Paddler's Guide to Algonquin Park* (1997); and *Further Up the Creek: A Paddler's Guide to the Rivers of Ontario and Quebec* (1999).

People read Kevin's guidebooks to find out what happened to him last season as much as to follow his carefully researched canoe routes. "He's a first-rate tripping partner, a solid and cautious canoeist, and a funny guy to whom funny things happen," says Noel Hudson, a good friend and fellow paddler. "Bears try to tip over his Mazda; nocturnal creatures slip into his sleeping bag; know-it-all guides wolf down tins of bad smoked oysters and have to be airlifted to hospital; he loses fishing contests to five-year-olds; and he makes truly bad morning coffee and risks mid-trip mutiny."

Because Kevin averages over a dozen wilderness trips a year, you'd be hard pressed to name a river in Ontario that he hasn't paddled. His favourite place to paddle? Anywhere he has never paddled before. His second-favourite place? Killarney Provincial Park.

Kevin Callan explains the pull of river trips: "I should rattle off some poetic philosophy of river travel that I've cherished since boyhood, but when I reminisce about the first time the current's pull proved irresistible, it was actually when a school chum and I floated down the local drainage ditch on slabs of Styrofoam. The incident had nothing to do with any soulful sentiment, a mystery waiting around every bend, or the ache of wilderness solitude that only the journey on a remote river could satisfy. I just wanted to play in the rapids."

Gary and Joanie McGuffin
Paddling's Leading Couple

From the time she was four years old, Joanie Wood spent summers at the family cottage on Muskoka's Lake Joseph. She became a well-rounded waterbaby — kayaking, sailing, swimming and scuba diving. At the age of four, Gary McGuffin was learning to paddle solo at the family cottage in Temagami. He spent hundreds of hours in his mother's 15-footer with Rusty, his cocker spaniel companion.

Joanie grew up in Thornhill and Gary in London. They met while studying Outdoor Recreation Technology at Seneca College in King City in 1980. They got to know one another while making handmade toys in Seneca College's woodworking shop. They graduated to constructing kayaks, carving paddles, and sewing sprayskirts and outdoor clothing. It was on their first canoe trip together, on the Matabitchuan, that they fell in love.

Their honeymoon, a canoe trip from the Atlantic Ocean to the Arctic Ocean in 1983–84, was documented in their book *Where Rivers Run: A 6,000-Mile Exploration of Canada by Canoe*. By this time the McGuffins had found a way to further their love of year-round adventuring and their concern for

diminishing wilderness, by combining Gary's photography with Joanie's writing and public speaking.

After a five-month cycling trip — from Tuktoyaktuk on the Arctic Ocean, to the Queen Charlotte Islands on the Pacific, to L'Anse aux Meadows at the tip of Newfoundland on the Atlantic Ocean — the adventurous couple returned to a place that called out to them: Lake Superior, the largest expanse of freshwater in the world. Having paddled and cycled along the North Shore on previous journeys, they eventually spent the summer of 1989 paddling the entire circumference of the lake's 3,200-kilometre shoreline. Their many subsequent explorations resulted in the impressive photographic book *Superior: Journeys on an Inland Sea*, which won the Great Lakes Booksellers Award. The region drew the McGuffins like a magnet, and in 1992 they moved to Batchawana Bay and now call Lake Superior home.

In 1998, the McGuffins and their Alaskan malamute, Kalija, embarked upon a significant journey to help protect Ontario's remaining ancient forest landscape. Their 1,900-kilometre canoe route, the Ancient Forest Water Trail, linked important roadless, old-growth forests from Ontario's oldest park, Algonquin, to North America's largest interconnected canoe routes region of Temagami to Lake Superior.

Through digital photography, satellite communications and internet technology, Gary and Joanie were able to share their story with the world. Thousands logged on to their website (www.adventurers.org), read their weekly accounts in Southam newspapers and heard their reports on CBC Radio. The story prompted many to become involved by writing letters encouraging the Ontario government to set aside more land for parks and protect the province's wilderness.

The year 1999 was a memorable one for the McGuffins. They produced a canoeing techniques book, *Paddle Your Own Canoe* (Boston Mills Press), and a daughter, Sila Kestrel, born on July 21.

Joanie and Gary McGuffin describe the lure of living on the shores of Lake Superior and their hopes for Sila: "We call this place home, feeling happy for clean water, fresh air, roadless forests, rivers to fish in, quiet campsites, and places where the only sounds you hear are those of the loons, wolves and wind in the pines. . . . And now having a daughter has brought our life full circle. Sila is a happy, healthy child who will find her own gifts and in the process take us on journeys we might not otherwise have ever imagined."

Section Three

A River Landscape for Canada

A National Waterway Management Plan

The Blueprint for Preserving Canada's Wild Rivers

Wally Schaber

Rivers are the life forces linking all wilderness in Canada with our freshwater and saltwater coastlines. Rivers offer pathways for journeys of discovery through all the natural regions of Canada, and even offer journeys that are metaphors for life itself.

So why don't Canadians preserve more rivers? Is it because we lack the willpower or foresight? Let me suggest three reasons.

One: We all find rivers far too useful as transportation routes, sewage dumps, industrial waste disposal systems, hydroelectricity generators, irrigation canals and recreational playgrounds to set them aside as "river parks" or "wilderness preserves." Rivers transport our problems elsewhere. Our problems disappear downstream.

Two: Planners and politicians have difficulty with wild river parks because rivers do not respect political boundaries, and because they sometimes offer risk-taking recreational opportunities, something the majority of people do not participate in.

Three: The prime reason against the advancement of nationwide wild river parks is that corporations, both private and Crown, in business to produce hydroelectric power have convinced the public we need these rivers as a source for our future energy.

Canadians consume more electrical energy per person than any other nationality in the world. Much of our over-consumption is due to the fact that our energy is relatively cheap and subsidized by tax dollars, and the belief that we have endless undeveloped sources of energy.

When the public is asked to choose between hydro-generated power and the other two alternatives — nuclear and fossil — not a river in Canada seems safe from a plan to generate power for the future. Conservation or alternative energy sources are not presented as practical options. Hydro-Québec is even less subtle about its priorities: It is in the business not just of supplying

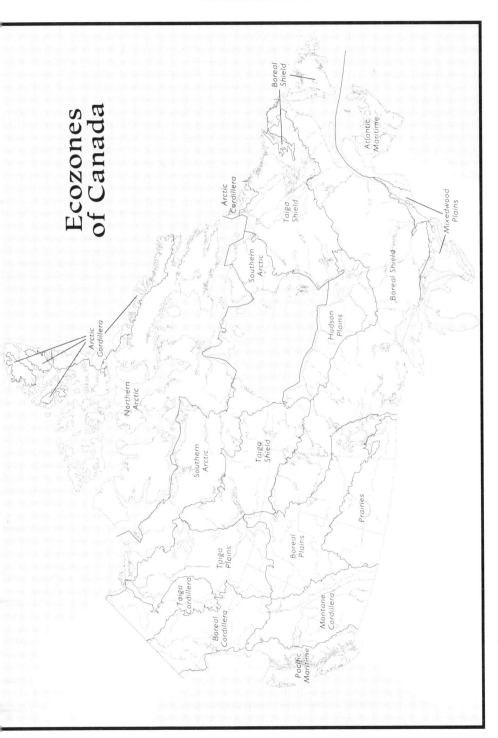

Ecozones
of Canada

Boreal Shield

Atlantic Maritime

Arctic Cordillera

Taiga Shield

Southern Arctic

Mixedwood Plains

Boreal Shield

Hudson Plains

Arctic Cordillera

Northern Arctic

Southern Arctic

Taiga Shield

Prairies

Boreal Plains

Taiga Plains

Taiga Cordillera

Boreal Cordillera

Montane Cordillera

Pacific Maritime

Québec's needs for the future, but of selling power to the United States.

James Bay I and II are Hydro-Québec's grandest creations, but smaller projects are scheduled for the Lac St-Jean area (Ashuapmushuan River) and the North Shore of the St. Lawrence (Moisie, Romaine and Ste-Margarite Rivers). Selling hydroelectricity to the United States is big business. All Canadian provinces with "excess" power export it (and fresh water may soon follow). Provincial hydro Crown corporations strongly encourage private hydroelectric generating companies to develop small stations that service local needs. In most provinces every river has been evaluated for its hydroelectric generating potential. If it is not economic to "capture" this power now, these powerful interest groups carefully guard their options for the future.

I don't think Canadians really care what form protection takes (they're all the same tax dollars), but they do care that leadership is shown to minimize duplication and maximize efforts to achieve a national goal. We now pursue wild river preservation through the Canadian Heritage Rivers System and Parks Canada. Provincially, each government has a strategy to add to the system, and some private landowners would gladly participate in a local watershed management plan for a public thank-you and a tax credit. But no one government or non-governmental organization has taken a leadership role to issue a national blueprint to focus everyone's energy on the same course of action. Based on extensive research, many conversations with paddlers as well as my own wilderness travels across the country, I put forward these ideas to further the process towards a nationally coordinated plan.

This complete waterway preservation system should include a river in each of the fifteen ecozones and many of the ecoregions of Canada as well as a river in each of the fifteen major watersheds. In addition to a vital natural history, each of these rivers must have a significant cultural, historic and/or recreational component. And each candidate should be chosen because of its existing or potential use to support the wildlife and aquatic populations indigenous to the area.

The ultimate goal is to have the rivers link our fifteen terrestrial ecozones with our five marine ecozones. That would mean our landscapes and seascapes would be united by a common bond — flowing water.

Based on this approach, here is a province-by-province and territory-by-territory inventory of preservation work to date, and my candidates for consideration in the National Waterway Management Plan.

British Columbia: A Province of World-Renowned Rivers

The Pacific Maritime ecozone encompasses a large rainforest natural region containing several subdistricts inter-related with the marine regions along the coast. There are four marine regions that could possibly be linked with the west-flowing rivers of the Coastal Mountains:

1. Hecate Straight, located between the Queen Charlotte Islands and the coast, includes South Moresby National Park, which has small remnants of island watersheds. The great rivers of the interior empty into deep estuaries along the coast. The most worthy candidate here is the Khutzeymateen River valley, the most important grizzly bear valley on the rainforest coastline.

2. Again, South Moresby, including the West Queen Charlotte Islands, preserves all east- and west-flowing island watersheds.

3. The interior of the Queen Charlotte Sound is well represented within Tweedsmuir Provincial Park; however, the Alexander Mackenzie Trail, both a water and overland route from the Fraser River to the coast, deserves more recognition and protection within a natural heritage system. In addition, Robson Bight, a critical killer whale habitat on the northeast tip of Vancouver Island, is a key marine coast site at the mouth of the Tsitika River. It is certainly worthy of special status representing this zone, but unfortunately most of the Tsitika River valley has been clearcut.

4. The Pacific coast of Vancouver Island, including the West Vancouver Island Marine Shelf, has two parks of significant size — Cape Scott in the north and Pacific Rim National Park in the centre. Strathcona Provincial Park protects the headwaters of both east- and west-flowing rivers, but does not extend to either coast. The Carmanah Valley has attracted considerable attention and deserves all the assistance inclusion in a national heritage system can offer. The lower Carmanah Valley has been protected in part by the creation of a small provincial park, yet the entire valley should be protected and included in the Canadian Heritage Rivers System. Many, many river valleys have been clearcut in the Pacific Coast Mountains. More living remnants of our natural heritage must be included in a true representation of this region.

The major rivers in the Montane Cordillera ecozone are the Fraser and Thompson, both historical routes to the Pacific Ocean. The largest parks in this region are Wells Gray, Bowron Lakes, Mount Robson and Hamber, all mountain parks except for the beautiful Bowron Lakes system. The Chilko-Chilcotin river system has been identified as this ecozone's number-one wild river park candidate since 1974. We still await some protective status for this beautiful area.

Numerous provincial parks along with Kootenay, Glacier, Yoho and Revelstoke National Parks contribute to the protection of representative rivers. The Canadian Parks Service manages its portions of the Yoho River (18.5 km) and the Kicking Horse River (49 km) as Canadian Heritage Rivers. We can only hope the B.C. government extends this wild river corridor further downstream.

British Columbia's finest examples of world-renowned wild rivers are found in the Boreal Cordillera ecozone. By far the most impressive wild river preserve in Canada is the Stikine. The headwaters of the Stikine and a major portion of the headwaters of the Spatsizi River are protected within Spatsizi Provincial Park. The Stikine flows across the Spatsizi, Tanzilla and Klastdine plateaus into Alaska. The threat of hydro development along the Grand Canyon of the Stikine as well as water pollution from coal and gold mines on watershed tributaries continue to cloud the future of this great river. Other beautiful rivers, such as the Finlay flowing east out of Tatlatui Provincial Park, the Nass and Skeena flowing south, and the Jennings and Teslin flowing north, find their headwaters in the Cassiar Mountains near the Stikine.

The great news about the Tatshenshini River, tucked away in British Columbia's northwest corner, is that it is now protected. The Tatshenshini begins in a rain shadow arctic desert, descends through the St. Elias Mountains into the coastal rainforest and ends in the Alsek Glacier caving area at Glacier National Park in Alaska. The Tatshenshini is also an exceptional wildlife habitat that includes one of the highest density grizzly and silver blue grizzly bear populations in the world. Congratulations to the B.C. government for protecting the entire Tatshenshini-Alsek region as a provincial park and nominating it as a World Heritage Site.

Alberta: Mountain, Foothill and Prairie Grassland Rivers

The major rivers that cross Alberta's share of the Boreal Plains ecozone are the Athabasca and the North Saskatchewan. The headwaters of both rivers are included in the Canadian Heritage Rivers System because they are protected within Jasper and Banff National Parks, respectively. The boreal plains sections of these rivers, especially of the Athabasca, are under great pressure due to large amounts of toxins entering the watershed from numerous pulp-and-paper plants. The Brazeau, Smoky, Clearwater, Bow and upper Red Deer rivers are all protected to some degree within the foothills and mountain preserves. Alberta could assist the system by extending provincial protection to one or more of these candidates.

There are also the rivers of the Prairies ecozone — the lower Old Man, lower Red Deer, South Saskatchewan and Milk. The Old Man begins in the southwestern Rockies and flows out onto the grasslands after gathering in water from eight major tributaries above Pincher Creek. The Old Man then combines with the Bow River to form the South Saskatchewan. At Pincher Creek is the controversial Old Man Dam, which has had devastating effects on the character and beauty of the upper river.

The section of the Red Deer River from Red Deer through the badlands of Dinosaur Provincial Park is relatively wild, offering excellent opportunities for wildlife observation and geological interpretation. An extension of Dinosaur Provincial Park to include an overnight Heritage River canoe trip would be an excellent addition to Canada's future system.

While the South Saskatchewan is the major river in this region, it has several control and diversion dams for irrigation and water control. Nonetheless, some parts of the river valley may still offer an environmental sample of what a river experience was like 125 years ago. (The Meewasin Valley Authority, for example, recognizes the recreational value of preserving portions of the South Saskatchewan in as natural a state as possible.)

The Milk River is unique in that it is the only river that has its headwaters in Canada but is part of the Mississippi watershed. The river valley supports an unusual abundance of bird, mammal, fish and reptile species. The flora is also lush and unusual for Canada. The Aboriginal peoples viewed the area around Writing-on-Stone Provincial Park as a spiritual place. All in all, the Milk River is a unique and premier candidate indeed.

Saskatchewan Promotes Canoeing as a Tourism Feature

Within Saskatchewan and Manitoba there are five ecoregions and the Hudson Bay marine region. Both provinces actively promote canoeing as a tourism feature and both have two rivers each in the Canadian Heritage Rivers System — the Clearwater and middle Churchill in Saskatchewan, and the Bloodvein and Seal in Manitoba. While both provinces are faced with the problem of an abundance of lakes and rivers in the north, there's a shortage in the south where irrigation is essential.

Saskatchewan, as an inaugural member of the Canadian Heritage Rivers System, contributed one of the first rivers — the Clearwater — outside an existing national or provincial park. Now the Churchill River, from Île-à-la-Crosse to Frog Portage, is also part of the system (the Churchill in Manitoba has been altered by the Nelson-Churchill hydro project). The Clearwater became Saskatchewan's first Wilderness River Provincial Park, coincidental with its nomination as a Canadian Heritage River.

The huge Boreal Plains ecozone is the heartland of Alberta, Saskatchewan and a small southwest corner of Manitoba. Prince Albert National Park in the spiritual centre of this region protects much of the lake and river district made famous by Grey Owl. All the larger provincial parks in northern Saskatchewan relate to rivers — Meadow Lakes Provincial Park (Waterhen River), Lac La Ronge Provincial Park (Churchill River), Nipawin Provincial Park (Torch River tributaries), Greenwater Provincial Park (Copeau River) — but none of these parks has a specific mandate for wild river protection. Meanwhile, precedent-setting legal cases have been fought over Saskatchewan's rights to proceed with the Rafferty Dam project without a federal environmental assessment. A clear voice for water preservation is needed among such conflicting demands.

One of the last national parks to be created below the 60th Parallel was Grasslands National Park, near Val Marie, Saskatchewan, in the Plains ecozone. This outstanding achievement should be interpreted as an optimistic sign for the potential of a grasslands Heritage wild river in the future. Water is a precious commodity in this region, which contains so few candidates for heritage status. Many of the rivers that do exist have already been altered so we must act quickly to protect one or two prime examples of a grasslands wild river.

Manitoba: Heart of Canoeing Heritage

One of the first mega hydro projects on Hudson Bay rivers was built in the 1970s on Manitoba's Nelson and Churchill rivers, resulting in mercury poisoning in dam-made lakes. Ontario is planning to build transmission lines to import Manitoba hydroelectric power, creating additional pressure to expand the Manitoba hydro system. Manitoba has done a good job preserving wild river representation in certain ecoregions to try to compensate for the devastating effects of the Nelson-Churchill project.

The Atikaki-Bloodvein Wilderness Reserve shared by Ontario and Manitoba is an encouraging example of co-operative planning. The Bloodvein River system flowing west into Lake Winnipeg is well protected within this new park. Other great rivers such as the Berens still run free in this watershed.

Dominated by Lake Winnipeg and Lake Winnipegosis, the Mid-Boreal Lowland and Interlake Plain ecoregions of the Boreal Plains ecozone should feature a heritage route designation similar to the Boundary Waters area, as all the major canoe trading routes passed northwest through Lake Winnipeg. From Lake of the Woods, the voyageurs paddled the Winnipeg River, mentioned by many explorers in their journals as the most beautiful river on their entire route to Lake Athabasca. Today, pockets of splendid remnants of the river exist between dams. While Lake Winnipeg is extremely unpredictable and treacherous for canoes, the voyageurs' original route out of the lake to the Churchill River system was via Cedar Lake and up the Saskatchewan and Sturgeon-Weir rivers. The Waterhen Lake and river route through the eastern portion of the Boreal Plains ecozone is considered the premier way to experience this area by canoe.

The Churchill, Nelson and Hayes rivers flow through the Hudson Plains on the final portion of their journey to saltwater. Only the Hayes River remains unaltered at present, linking two ecozones with the Hudson Bay marine region.

The Seal River, part of the Canadian Heritage Rivers System, is a most worthy candidate of the Taiga Shield ecozone. The beautiful Fond du Lac River from Wollaston Lake in Saskatchewan to Lake Athabasca is another premier candidate. However, radioactive waste spills from a uranium mine on Wollaston Lake show the need for better watershed protection.

Ontario Must Lead the Way in Wilderness River Conservation

The year 1993 was the 100th anniversary of the establishment of the provincial parks system in Ontario. With over a century of strategic planning under its belt, you would expect the Ontario parks system to be very sophisticated. And it is. Ontario's park planning strategy, originally proposed in 1978, calls for six classes of parks: wilderness, nature reserve, natural environment, historical, recreational and waterway. Ontario has divided the province into thirteen site regions and those regions into sixty-five site districts. Each of the thirteen site regions is to be represented by one wilderness park. The ideal waterways park system is to have one river (or a part of one river) representing each site district. The waterways park system has candidates dedicated to intensive use and others to low-intensity use. In a site district where major waterways are located in a wilderness or natural environment park, those rivers could serve a dual purpose, representing the waterways system as well. To date, twenty-seven rivers (or sections of river with a minimum length of a half-day downstream canoe trip in intensive-use areas) have been included in the Ontario Provincial Waterways Parks category. Not included are rivers protected within the Algonquin, Lake Superior, Pukaskwa

(National Park), Killarney, Polar Bear, Quetico, Woodland Caribou, Wabakimi, Opasquea or Lady Evelyn-Smoothwater provincial wilderness parks. Ontario is also a major contributing member of the Canadian Heritage Rivers System with the French, Mattawa, Bloodvein, Boundary Waters, Missinaibi, Humber and Grand rivers already included. Ontario, the province with the greatest demands for hydroelectric energy, could possibly add the ninety parks required to complete the provincial parks system — and soon, it is hoped. Many of these parks could be waterway parks and include portions of the Madawaska, Ottawa, Dog, Magnetawan, Temagami, Mississagi, Saugeen, Steel, Credit, Spanish and Don rivers.

This Provincial Waterway Park System is evolving into Canada's finest example of a completely representative system of recreational and natural region corridors. Yet, Ontario Hydro and other private power corporations have alternative plans for some James Bay and Lake Superior watershed rivers. Acid rain, clearcut logging, hydro power consumption and illegal water pollution from industry and residential sources continue at an alarming rate in Canada's most populated province. As a result, Ontario must lead the way in wilderness conservation simply because the rate of change is proceeding at an extremely fast pace.

Québec: Best Variety of Wild River Canoe Routes in the World

This province is endowed with eight ecozones, giving it the best variety of wild river canoe routes in the world. But Québec's political priorities certainly have not included conservation of wilderness preserves, especially wild rivers. Québec currently has three percent of provincial lands protected under any form of park or ecological preserve. The national goal is 12 percent, but it should be higher. With Hydro-Québec playing such a major role in the province's economy, it is very difficult to get other priorities considered for rivers in Québec. Antiquated environmental controls concerning the dumping of raw sewage, salt-laden snow and other waste materials into Québec rivers, combined with Hydro-Québec's long-range plans for more dams, cloud the future and quality of many prime wild river candidates in Québec.

The Boreal Shield ecozone includes all the rivers flowing into the Ottawa River and the lower St. Lawrence from the Laurentian Plateau. There are scores of worthy candidates, but not one is truly protected. I vote for the Dumoine River as my representative for this region. (Neighbouring rivers, the Coulonge and Noire, are in different stages of development by a private hydroelectric generating company.)

The Lac St-Jean–Saguenay River system is blessed with beautiful wild rivers, yet many have been logged and some dammed. The Saguenay itself has been declared a joint federal-provincial marine conservation area with the Saguenay–St. Lawrence estuary already receiving marine conservation area status. Small tributaries such as the Chicoutimi and Aux Écorses rivers, which flow into Lac Kénogami Provincial Park, are prime candidates to represent this watershed.

The Central Laurentians ecozone is the heart of Québec canoe country. Many good recreational parks promote canoeing as part of a multiple use plan with hunting, fishing, trapping and logging. The Jacques–Cartier River is a member of the Canadian Heritage Rivers System, and it is hoped that many more will follow. La Mauricie National Park protects a small portion of the Rivière Saint-Maurice while Parc Mt-Tremblant includes the headwaters of several wild rivers, as does Parc Grand Jardins. Unfortunately, the two prime rivers in this ecozone — the Ashuapmushuam and the Mistassibi — are not protected at all. The Ashuapmushuam is scheduled to be dammed in another major Hydro-Québec project that involves diverting the Aux Pékans River, a major tributary of the Moisie, into the Romaine River and damming the Romaine. All three rivers will be thereby seriously damaged. A third plan in this region calls for hydroelectric development on the Ste-Marguerite River.

The major river in the Québec part of the Hudson Plains is the Harricanaw. It has escaped the devastating effects of Phase One of the James Bay project, and should be protected as the last remaining example of a large, free-flowing James Bay wild river.

Québec shares the Arctic Cordillera, Taiga Shield and Boreal Shield ecozones with Labrador. Together they could co-protect a prime candidate, the Natashquan River, from its headwaters to the Gulf of St. Lawrence.

All major west-flowing rivers in the Taiga Shield have been or will be altered as a result of James Bay I and the proposed James Bay II hydro projects in this region. The headwaters of north-flowing rivers such as the Kaniapiscau begin in this region. One small watershed remains untouched, the Clearwater River from Lac à l'Eau Claire to Hudson Bay. We must preserve this small natural remnant in this region. The Southern Arctic ecozone is wild country and still unspoiled. Meanwhile, three great rivers — the George, Grande Baleine and Kaniapiscau — flow through, but they could all be destroyed in the proposed Great Whale project.

The Gaspésie, famous for its coastal scenery, Chic-Choc Mountains and salmon fishing, has many rivers managed for decades by rich fish and game clubs to keep them pure and wild. The Cascapédia and Bonaventure Rivers should someday find their way into the Canadian Heritage Rivers System.

But must future generations choose from only the scraps left over from a legacy of planning that gives little priority to conservation of rivers? Token contributions to a wild river system are not enough from Québec, the province with the most to offer.

New Brunswick: A Long History of Canoeing

New Brunswick has a long history of canoeing and canoe-building (Chestnut canoes), and has long promoted canoeing as the natural way to explore the province's wilderness. Several conservation programs are now re-establishing the next generation's wild river heritage. The Saint John River valley is receiving considerable restoration attention with positive results, and the St. Croix is now part of the Canadian Heritage Rivers System.

Nonetheless, major portions of rivers to be included in a heritage program of federal-provincial co-operation have to include the following three systems: (1) The Kouchibouguac River, which is protected in Kouchibouguac National Park, but the headwaters are not; (2) a portion of the Miramichi River watershed; and (3) the Restigouche River (fortunately, the Upper Restigouche, from Jardine Brook to the junction of the Patapedia, was nominated to the Canadian Heritage Rivers System in January 1995).

Nova Scotia: Good River Preservation So Far

The Southwest Nova Scotia Uplands ecoregion, which includes Kejimkujik National Park, the Mersey and Shelburne rivers, and a historic Mi'kmaq canoe route from the Atlantic to the Bay of Fundy, interacts with the Atlantic Coast ecoregion. The Nova Scotia Highlands ecoregion, which includes Cape Breton Highlands National Park and its many fast-flowing small rivers, intersects with the Magdalene Shallows marine region. While the Margaree has been nominated to the Canadian Heritage Rivers System, ideally a west-flowing river such as the Bear or Sissiboo could complete our initial representation of Nova Scotia.

Prince Edward Island: Size Is Deceiving

Canada's smallest province displays the ecological features of the Prince Edward Island ecoregion, which includes beaches, dunes, salt marshes, warm lagoons and remnants of Acadian forests. Fortunately, Prince Edward Island National Park helps protect that region, and the Hillsborough River is now part of the Canadian Heritage Rivers System.

Newfoundland and Labrador: Setting the Definition of Wild River

Newfoundland has eleven ecoregions. The Main River, which has its head-waters just outside Gros Morne National Park and flows east across the northern peninsula to White Bay, became a member of the Canadian Heritage Rivers System in 1991.

This is an excellent start to a river system that should include the following five components as a minimum: (1) A west-flowing river, such as the Humber River, linking the northern peninsula interior and the Laurentian Trough marine region; (2) a south-flowing river, such as the Grey River, linking the central interior with the Grand Banks; (3) a Heritage River or expansion of the national park boundaries uniting the Terra Nova River valley to Terra Nova National Park; (4) a wild river on the Avalon Peninsula linking the wilderness preserve with the coast; and (5) A northeast-flowing wild river, such as the Lloyds or Exploits river system. I'm sure Newfoundland wilderness recreationalists will want to expand this list.

Labrador has thirteen ecoregions. Parks Canada has made many overtures requesting national park lands from Newfoundland, but no formal response has been received. This rugged and scarcely populated coastline has *no* designated provincial parks. Excluding the Churchill River power development and the Goose Bay military operations, the entire area is an isolated, pristine wilderness. Parks Canada has conducted aerial wild river surveys on the Goose, Kanairiktok, Natashquan and Naskaupi rivers, and a few recreational canoeing expeditions explored the river valleys such as the Baie du Nord (nominated to the CHRS in 1992), but access is difficult. Meanwhile, kayaking and canoeing along the coastline using the coastal ferry service to access the Nachvak Fiord (Torngat Mountains) is gaining popularity among a few intrepid paddlers.

Ultimately, it will be the exquisite quality of the rivers of Labrador that sets the definition of a "wild" river. It is hoped that we may always have these benchmarks to measure how far we have strayed from the ideal. Perhaps a national park in each ecoregion could incorporate an east-flowing wild river within its boundaries for safekeeping.

Yukon: Spectacular Rivers that Need to Stay Wild

How lucky we are to have the Yukon, Northwest Territories and Nunavut. Just ask any of the German, Scandinavian, Italian, French, Swiss or American paddlers you meet on the most remote rivers of the Canadian North.

The rivers of the Yukon are all spectacular and it is hard to pick "the best." The Canadian Heritage Rivers System has already included a 48-kilometre section of the Yukon, which includes the historic stretch between Lake Laberge and the mouth of the Teslin River. Ironically, Whitehorse's raw sewage pours into the Yukon River, which ultimately flows into Lake Laberge.

A 90-kilometre portion of the Alsek River in Kluane National Park is also part of the Canadian Heritage Rivers System. Recently the 160-km section of the river, which includes the infamous Turnback Canyon, one of the wildest stretches of whitewater on the continent, was included in the Tatshenshini-Alsek Park.

Ivvavik National Park, formerly known as Northern Yukon National Park, protects the Firth River as its central feature. The rest of the Yukon's most popular rivers — the Hess, Bonnet Plume (nominated, thankfully, to the Canadian Heritage Rivers System), Big Salmon, South MacMillan, Wind and Coal, to name a few — have friends in the Yukon watching over their wild character.

Northwest Territories and Nunavut: Where Rivers Run Free

The Northwest Territories and Nunavut are areas where wild rivers run free, living examples of how these natural highways traversed vast regions centuries ago. Long before the Europeans arrived in Canada, Aboriginal people invented the canoe and kayak to explore and hunt throughout their territory. Europeans, driven by commerce and curiosity, adopted the canoe to explore and exploit Canada from coast to coast to coast via its lakes and rivers. Ironically, it may be the Native people's fight to acquire aboriginal rights to wild lands that slows down the primary resource industries enough to give the rest of us a chance to think logically about preserving our natural heritage. The N.W.T. and Nunavut encompass six ecozones. New national parks are planned for several of these ecozones, and the governments of the N.W.T. and Nunavut and Aboriginal groups are actively pursuing a full complement of designated Canadian Heritage Rivers.

Within the Taiga Cordillera ecozone, the South Nahanni River is already a member of the Canadian Heritage Rivers System and is a UNESCO (United Nations Educational, Scientific and Cultural Organization) World Heritage Site. But the boundaries of the national park should be expanded to include the headwaters of the South Nahanni River. The Arctic Red River is also now part of the Canadian Heritage Rivers System, representing the Mackenzie River watershed.

My choices for protected rivers in the Taiga Plains are the Anderson, Mountain and Horton rivers. In the Southern Arctic, the Coppermine, Ellice, Hood, Burnside and Brock rivers are all worthy candidates. In the Taiga Shield, the Fond du Lac and Snowdrift Rivers (the latter is in the proposed national park on the east arm of Great Slave Lake) are quality candidates. A good section of the Kazan River is now a member of the Canadian Heritage Rivers System as is part of the Thelon River.

The Thomsen River Valley, in the Northern Arctic ecozone, is the central feature of the proposed Banks Island Muskox National Park. The Silvia-Grinnel River flowing into Frobisher Bay is a another good example.

The Arctic Cordillera contains the Auyuittuq National Park Reserve and the Owl River Valley. The Soper River on southern Baffin Island is a member of the Canadian Heritage Rivers System. We also need representatives for the western high arctic, a polar desert, and the eastern high arctic, which encompasses the Ellesmere Island National Park Reserve-Lake Hazen watershed.

How Should We Proceed?

Four steps are recommended:

1. Refine our "ideal" wild river conservation system by consulting professionals, recreationalists, other conservation groups and government officials.

2. Produce a preliminary plan for discussion.

3. After receiving feedback on the first draft, we should work with existing conservation groups who are willing to help establish a complete national system of wild river "preserves," region by region.

4. Work to complete a national framework to identify protection needs for a complete system of nationally significant waterway candidates in the next few years. This protection plan calls for the establishment of national parks, provincial parks, municipal parks and even joint understandings between private landowners managing these significant natural resources for the public good.

The World Wildlife Fund, which has created an excellent blueprint for completing our national goals for wild spaces in the book *Endangered Spaces*, has focused non-governmental efforts to lobby governments for a common goal. Such a plan or supplementary plan needs to be created for individuals and groups.

These are lofty goals and their pursuit requires sensitivity, enthusiasm and patience. Let's pass on a legacy of protected wilderness rivers as they flow to the future.

How the Tatshenshini Was Saved

A Step-by-Step Plan to Launch Your Own Conservation Campaign

Ken Madsen

THE STERN OF THE RED KAYAK LOOKS LIKE THE TAIL OF A HUGE SPAWNING salmon, diving into the depths, swallowed by the turbulent river. Jody's body is buried under the wave. That indistinct yellow blob must be his helmet. His paddle is thrust straight up. Waves lick at the blade, like the dancing flames of a campfire. The image on the screen fades, replaced by a soaring bald eagle.

"As we paddled the last rapid in Turnback Canyon," I say, "we looked up and saw a bald eagle circling above the rock walls. Just downstream, a sow grizzly with a pair of cubs watched as we floated past. It brought home the real reason we had paddled the Alsek — not for the whitewater, but to show our love for this incredible wilderness . . ."

It's Thursday night and this must be Washington, D.C. And the congressman who introduced me is asleep in his chair. The "Tatshenshini Wilderness Quest" barnstorming slide show is almost finished. Only Monday in Seattle is left.

I started two months ago, in my hometown of Whitehorse, Yukon. With a changing cast of environmental companions, I flew through Alaska and across Canada. Sixteen cities later I found myself pounding down marble corridors, lobbying bored-looking congressional aides about a joint resolution to the House and the Senate. The resolution, sponsored by Vice President Al Gore, addressed preservation of the Tatshenshini and Alsek watersheds.

The slide show is finished, and I duck under a table groaning with crackers, cheese and grapes to unplug the extension cord. A black-tied waiter peers at me as he pours a glass of white wine. A buzz of conversation testifies that the presentation has impressed the Capitol Hill crowd. Among the representatives and staffers are a few river rats I'd like to talk to, but a young man lurches over and grabs my arm, spilling wine onto my running shoes.

"I'm from Congressman Owen's office," he tells me, his eyes glazed with enthusiasm and too much alcohol. "He's really into this issue. Call me. Together we'll stop those goddamn miners. But you have to call me!"

I'd rather be on the river.

We'd all rather be on the river. But what will the rivers of Canada be like in the future? Would we still want to be on the river if it was being "managed" by our industrial society. Dammed and logged and undrinkable?

Sometimes I feel like shouting "Screw it!" I have a list of secret streams buried in the wilderness where I can retreat from bulldozers, canyons where even the most zealous developer can't find me. But wild places are being hunted down today like passenger pigeons were during the 1800s, and my conscience won't let me hide forever.

Strange things happen to those who get involved in river conservation issues. I've set off across the continent clutching projectors, dissolve units and six trays of slides. I've been bored to distraction listening to the drone of bureaucrats. I've paddled through Turnback Canyon with a *National Geographic* helicopter blowing me upstream in a Class V rapid.

Strange things happen. But at least you can face your reflection when you look in the water over the side of your canoe, kayak or raft.

How and why does a river conservation campaign begin? How do you plan strategy? What are the principles of action?

The why part of the equation is easy. Just think back to the last wild river you paddled . . .

"Hey, Arno. Let's eddy out behind that creek."

"Right," he yells over his shoulder. He paddles forward, then jams a pry against the bow of the canoe. I hang over a low brace. We swing into the eddy and the bow crunches on gravel.

No matter how long you paddle, a well-executed eddy turn is a moment of pure pleasure. Even if you are on the northern Yukon's Snake River and there isn't another canoeist within 300 kilometres to admire your grace.

The first thing we see on shore are tracks. Grizzly tracks. Big grizzly tracks. (Has anyone ever seen small grizzly tracks?) The prints haven't had time to be blurred by wind or rain. They're fresh, perfectly formed. Fifteen minutes ago a bear waded across the creek and ambled down the beach.

This looks like a great campsite: flat tent sites, dry driftwood and a vista upriver. It's a terrific place to spend a night — but when I suggest camping here,

Arno Springer stares at me as if I just stepped off a spaceship from Mars. He looks down at the grizzly tracks and back at me. Then his shoulders heave in a what-the-hell shrug. He grabs his pack and walks up the beach to set up his tent.

I stay up late that night, baking cinnamon buns. The reflector oven is perched on a rickety grate beside the river. I toss a handful of twigs onto the bed of coals on top. A wisp of smoke curls upwards, then the dry wood ignites with a whoosh.

I lean against the canoe and wiggle my bum to make a comfortable hollow in the sand. There are no clouds, but the sky is smudged with the orange glow of forest fire smoke. There's a small fire in the narrow swath of forest that follows the river valley just downstream, with most of the haze from a myriad of fires burning somewhere over the horizon. I savour the pleasure of being in a land where the seasonal cycle of fire plays by its own rules. No water bomber will drop out of the sky to splash orange chemicals in this watershed.

The goals of river conservation work will vary in every region, but whenever possible, think big. Even if you love paddling for its own sake, remember that rivers are more than flowing water and boulders. Rivers are the lifeblood of the land. Don't be afraid to dream about an entire watershed with its full complement of native plants and predator-prey relationships.

I sat in an advisory board meeting about Canadian Heritage River status for the Bonnet Plume River in northern Yukon. "Mining can actually improve the environment," said a vice-president of Westmin Resources. Here, for sure, was someone who would agree with a former governor of Alaska who said, "You just can't let nature run wild."

The mining executive went on to describe his vision of the Bonnet Plume watershed (currently unroaded wilderness). He envisioned town sites, all-season roads and transmission lines. He spoke of pipelines, tailings ponds, and the possibility of power production from dams or coal-fired plants. He talked of the need for growth and the economic bottom line.

But he didn't mention the ecological bottom line. How much can the Earth take and continue to give back? Is there anyplace where three and a half billion years of evolution can be allowed to continue in peace?

In most parts of the world, wildlife habitat has been whittled down so much that all we can hope to do is save examples of species in zoo-like parks. In North America, grizzlies, cougars, jaguars, crocodiles, green sea turtles, wolves and wolverines have been exterminated from much of their range. Biologists tells us that we are in the middle of the Earth's sixth great extinction. The last one was the disappearance of the dinosaurs.

The howl of a wolf, a wolverine loping into the boreal forest, grizzly tracks — these are the signs of Canada's remaining wild lands. And, in fact, these creatures can be used as "umbrella" or "indicator species" — the canary in the coal mine. Their ranges are large enough that if we protect enough wild land to allow for their needs, the needs of many other plants and animals will also be met.

It is frustrating to fight conservation battles and watch a dozen new projects spring up each time we manage to knock one down. Why should the onus be on us to justify why Corporation X shouldn't further reduce our vanishing heritage of wild lands? It is time to lay out a vision so that *they* have to justify their actions.

If you would like to link your conservation project to a broader based vision of wilderness preservation, search out the Wildlands Project in your area. The Wildlands Project is a part of a North America-wide strategy to stop the disappearance of wildlife and the wild places they depend upon. In every region of the continent, grassroots organizations are working to preserve their vanishing biological diversity.

Protected areas across North America have failed to adequately protect wildlife habitat. Conservation biologists tells us that most of our parks have become protected "islands" in a sea of development. Wild places and their natural life forms have a right to exist, simply because they are. We need substantial wild areas, with buffer zones and natural corridors that allow for the movement of evolutionary and ecological processes.

How do you plan a river conservation campaign? The struggle to preserve the Tatshenshini and Alsek rivers was unique, but then, so is every watershed. Some of the lessons we learned will be applicable in all regions of the continent.

The Tatshenshini campaign started in the hearts of the people who are in the best position to appreciate a watershed — paddlers. At about the same time that I cobbled together a slide show and started publicizing the issue in the North, Johnny Mikes, a commercial raft operator, started telling his environmental friends in British Columbia about the river.

The first lesson is, become involved.

In the beginning, my audiences were polite . . . which is just about the worst response you can get at a public event. "The Tatshenshini is a special place," they'd say, "but do you know how much money has been spent by Geddes Resources?" They'd thank me for the show and say, "You don't really think you can stop the mine? Do you?"

The second lesson is to stay involved, but don't focus exclusively on results. Don't expect to change the world immediately. Don't even expect that people will listen to you. Persevere because it is the right thing to do. And so, even when it seemed hopeless, I went on writing letters, talking to the media and showing slides.

Get others involved. Early in the Tatshenshini campaign I drove down the highway to do a slide show in Haines — the Alaskan town through which Geddes Resources wanted to truck its ore concentrate. It wasn't much of a show, but I met a man named Peter Enticknap. Peter wasn't a whacko environmentalist; rather, he was a former businessman who had retreated from the high-pressure corporate world of southern California. In Haines he had found his paradise, and he was willing to fight for it. Peter became a tireless advocate. He badgered people from Anchorage, Alaska, to Washington, D.C., and helped put together an American coalition that became invaluable.

In Vancouver, Ric Careless became interested, and a group called Tatshenshini Wild was formed. Other environmental groups were convinced to join. What began as a few lonely voices snowballed into an international coalition whose total membership numbered in the millions.

Plan your strategy. What do you want to achieve? What steps will you need to take to achieve it? What information do you need to gather? How can you convince people? Be realistic . . . but not too bloody realistic! Significant environmental victories have been won through idealism and sheer bull-headed stubbornness.

Please assess your campaign strategy carefully. We're all getting tired of environmental groups who try to stop logging in sensitive areas by sending out reams of paper — unasked for and unwanted reams of paper. We need to communicate with one another, but keep your means in line with your goals.

Publicize the issue. North America is bombarded with entertainment options. Somehow you will need to get people's attention over the drone of television, video, radio, sporting events (the list is endless). One of the hooks we used was the adventure angle — paddling Turnback Canyon. Kayaking a remote Class V river had nothing to do with why the Tatshenshini-Alsek deserved preservation, but it was a way to get people to listen to what really mattered: the land.

You'll need to harass your local media — radio, newspaper and television. Sponsor public events. Invite personalities and give presentations. Take musicians on a river trip and ask them to create a concert based on their trip. Get visual artists to put together a show. Public events will not only get your message across, they'll spur other people to become involved.

Publicity, however, can be a double-edged sword. During the Tatshenshini campaign, some in the environmental community acted as though the goal of preservation justified any means. The Tatshenshini was called "North America's Wildest River." It had the biggest mountains, the most bears, the best wilderness. Everything was "world class." Hyperbole ruled. But if that particular corner of the world contains the ultimate that wilderness has to offer, how do we justify preserving other areas?

Wild lands don't need to be "monumental" in order to be treated with respect. Wetlands, tall grass prairies, foothills, tundra . . . they are all an integral part of a vision of North America that includes wildlife and wild places.

Take people who will help your cause onto the land. Most people will be touched by the spirit of wild lands if you can awaken their senses. They need to feel icy water, hear owls calling, taste silt in their coffee, smell the forest after a rainfall, see a beaver slap its tail. Artists, musicians, scientists, politicians, bureaucrats, potential donors, they all can help.

Part of your mandate is public education. It is easy to get caught up in the immediacy of an issue and forget about a long-term vision. Public events will help to inform people. Sponsor a series of articles or interviews in your local media: ask a mix of people, from scientists to artists to outdoor adventurers, to describe their own perspective. Schools are usually happy to let you invade their gymnasiums with slide shows or videos.

For us to live in some semblance of harmony with the natural world we need to assess the impacts of our way of life. We paddle plastic or fibreglass boats, wear petroleum-based clothing, and fly to the put-in of rivers. It is an individual choice to decide how much is excess, but our credibility will be at stake if we don't at least grapple with the question.

In order to succeed, you'll need to cope with the "M" word. You'll have to raise money. Once again, be creative. Use the talents of your friends and co-conspirators. Some will be good at thinking up imaginative schemes. Others will excel at calling people or businesses to canvass (badger) for support. Effective money-raising schemes will also publicize your issue.

Find a way to use your skills creatively. I don't enjoy meetings or the endless chase of letter writing. So, during the Tatshenshini campaign, I looked for other ways — paddling, photography, writing. We worked with the World Wildlife Fund and initiated a paddle-a-thon on the three rivers that would have been most affected by the proposed Windy Craggy Mine. We raised about $10,000 through pledges, but more important, created a slide presentation that allowed us to publicize the issue across the continent.

During our paddle-a-thon we agreed to invite *National Geographic* magazine to photograph our descent of Turnback Canyon. What should have been a private meeting between river and paddlers received a bizarre twist from our publicity efforts. I remember my feelings after the helicopter left us.

The racket of the helicopter dissipated, its last vibrations absorbed by the land. It took longer for my ears to stop quivering. We wanted the photographs and we wanted the media attention, but I was glad the damn thing was done. Why is nothing ever simple? Why do we need to import 1990s hype in a bid to convince people thousands of kilometres away that the mountains shouldn't be levelled? That the rivers shouldn't be poisoned?

I could hear the river again. I could feel the wind in my face and see a dark speck soaring above the canyon downstream. The wilderness washed over me, like the return of night vision after staring at a bright light.

We rode over a series of standing waves and squirted through the last constriction in the canyon. I leaned back on my stern deck and looked up. The dark speck was now a bald eagle, wings outstretched, circling. I gestured to everyone with my paddle. We were silent, as if afraid that we had already presumed too much by inviting the helicopter out here, as if our voices would be too much of an intrusion now.

We floated with the current for a few minutes. Jody pointed towards the bank. I saw a glistening thread of meltwater from an icefield and then three motionless shapes, a sow grizzly and a pair of cubs. They looked sleek and healthy, almost ready to crawl into a den for the winter. Their senses were no doubt assaulted by our colour, shape and scent, just as we had been by the rattle and stench of the chopper. They watched as the river swept us around the corner and out of sight.

If you jump into a river conservation campaign, you'll hike along paths and paddle down streams that you wouldn't encounter in your strangest dreams. Smile at the bizarre situations you find yourself in.

At times, even considering becoming involved in conservation matters is overwhelming. How can you compete with multinational corporations, with the Toronto Stock Exchange? How can one person's contribution possibly make a difference?

When you are feeling that way, asking those questions, remember Edward Abbey's advice: "Be as I am . . . a part-time crusader, a half-hearted zealot . . . It is not enough to fight for the wilderness; it is even more important to enjoy it."

I'm a firm believer in the "ripple effect." If you throw a rock into the ocean, the ripples will be felt, however slightly, across the world. Your actions will not be lost in the chaos of modern life. Somewhere, someone is listening.

The Canadian Heritage Rivers System
Ensuring That Rivers Flow Into the Future

Max Finkelstein

CANADA HAS MANY FACES. IT IS A MOSAIC OF LANDSCAPES AND cultures that, taken together, define our nation and our heritage. This image of Canada is different for each and every one of us, but there are common elements that we all share. Winter, wilderness, the North, forests . . . and rivers.

Rivers are part of our lives and our history. They are the threads that bind the fabric of nature and humanity together and make Canada Canadian.

But Canada's river heritage is threatened. We are changing our rivers. Damming them, paving their banks, polluting their waters, degrading the vital, yet fragile, ribbon of their shorelines, disregarding the human heritage along their banks.

Even wilderness rivers are no longer protected by their isolation. New roads bring motorboats, all-terrain vehicles and snowmobiles to rivers that until recently knew only the sound of paddles. The most remote and wildest of our rivers have been studied and surveyed for hydroelectric and water control projects. No river in Canada is unthreatened or untouched by our modern way of life.

Though our national parks system is over 100 years old, protection of rivers is a relatively new idea in Canada. In 1999, we celebrated the fifteenth anniversary of the founding of the Canadian Heritage Rivers System.

The CHRS is a national program to recognize and protect the vital heritage role of rivers in Canada. The CHRS was born in 1984 as the culmination of a vision of a national system of protected rivers. The objectives of the CHRS are to give national recognition to the important rivers of Canada, to conserve and protect the best examples of Canada's river heritage, and to encourage the public to learn about, enjoy, appreciate and become involved with Canada's rivers.

The first river to be designated to the Canadian Heritage Rivers System was the French River, in Ontario (1986). As of April 1, 2000, there are

37 Heritage Rivers across Canada (covering more than 9,000 kilometres), at least one in every province and territory. They range from wilderness rivers in the Arctic barrens to working rivers in Ontario's heartland, from rocky rivers rife with rapids on the "Rock" (the island of Newfoundland), to rivers flowing through walls of ice spawned by the glaciers of Canada's highest mountains in the Yukon.

The goal of the CHRS is to establish a system of Canadian Heritage Rivers that reflects the diversity of Canada's rich river environments and celebrates the importance of rivers in Canada's history and society. The dream is to ensure that rivers in Canada flow into the future, pure and unfettered as they have since the melting of the vast Pleistocene ice-sheets.

How the CHRS Operates

The CHRS operates on the principle of co-operation. There is no federal Act establishing the CHRS or protecting rivers in the System. In the late 1970s, Parks Canada invited all provincial and territorial governments, non-governmental conservation agencies and private citizens to work on a task force to develop a river conservation program that everyone could embrace. The result, the CHRS, is not a federal government program but rather a national program.

The program is overseen by the Canadian Heritage Rivers Board. On this Board the federal government is represented by the Director General of National Parks and by a delegate from the Department of Indian and Northern Affairs. The other voting members are either senior managers of the parks agencies of provincial and territorial governments or private citizens appointed by the provincial or territorial government. (There are now two private citizens on the Board representing New Brunswick and British Columbia.) The main function of the Board is to review nominations and decide if the nominated rivers meet selection guidelines, and to define policy and guidelines for the System. A small secretariat in Parks Canada provides administrative and technical assistance to the Board in implementing the program, and helps publicize the System.

How a River Is Selected and Nominated

Selection of rivers to be considered for inclusion in the CHRS is usually made through province- or territory-wide "system studies." These studies, which have been carried out by most provinces and all three territories, rank rivers based on their heritage values and the integrity of their river

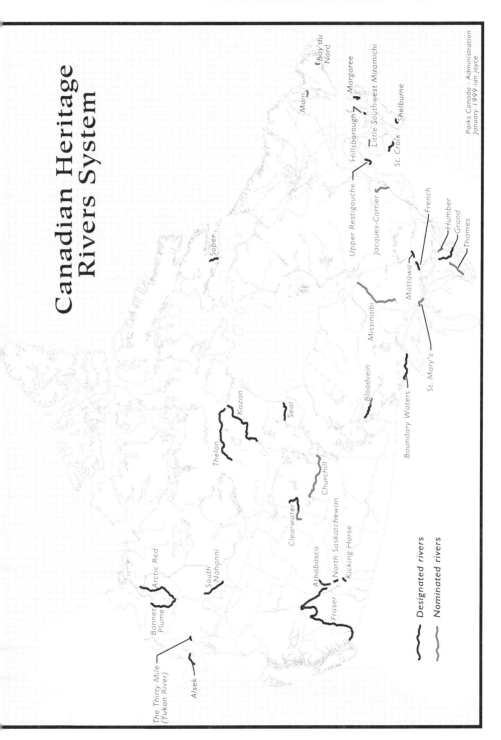

Canadian Heritage Rivers System

Parks Canada – Administration
January 1999 ian joyce

Bay du Nord
Main
Margaree
Hillsborough
Little Southwest Miramichi
St. Croix
Shelburne
Upper Restigouche
Jacques-Cartier
French
Humber
Grand
Thames
Soper
Mattawa
Missinaibi
St. Mary's
Kazan
Bloodvein
Thelon
Seal
Boundary Waters
Churchill
Clearwater
North Saskatchewan
Athabasca
Kicking Horse
Arctic Red
South Nahanni
Bonnet Plume
Fraser
The Thirty Mile (Yukon River)
Alsek

—— Designated rivers
—— Nominated rivers

ecosystems. Private citizen groups can also present to the provincial or territorial government a river they feel is worthy of nomination.

Background studies are then undertaken on potential Canadian Heritage Rivers by the managing governments to ascertain if their heritage values measure up to CHRS selection and integrity guidelines. The next step is to prepare a nomination document.

A river can only be nominated by the government that has jurisdiction over it. A potential Canadian Heritage River, or a portion of it, is nominated based on the significance of one or more of its natural heritage features, human history and recreational potential according to ten guidelines. These guidelines address the significance of a nominated river's geological formations, fluvial processes, unique or outstanding features, places of outstanding beauty, prime habitats and critical areas for rare or endangered species. Human heritage guidelines look at the significance of historical and archaeological sites along the river and the role of the river in Canadian history. Finally, recreational guidelines address the recreational potential of the river given its natural and cultural resources, and the ability of the river environment to accommodate recreational use. Although rivers do not need to meet all guidelines, only rivers that are truly outstanding examples of Canada's river heritage are admitted to the System. The flexibility in interpreting the guidelines means that rivers such as the pastoral Grand, in southwestern Ontario, and the estuarial Hillsborough, in Prince Edward Island, can earn a place alongside the mighty Yukon, in the Yukon Territory, and the world-renowned South Nahanni, in the Northwest Territories.

Nominations are brought forward by a member of the Board to be judged by other Board members. Nominations may and have been turned back by the Board, in cases where the guidelines for selection are not adequately met. But even when a nomination is accepted, it does not mean that the river is protected. Before a river can be formally designated to the System, the nominating government must submit for approval by the appropriate federal, provincial or territorial ministers a management plan, or "heritage strategy," that specifies just how the river will be protected and managed.

Management Plans: The Heart of the CHRS

Management plans are the heart of the System. The actions spelled out in these documents determine whether or not designating a river to the System means more than a fancy bronze plaque on a riverbank. Management plans are the responsibility of the government with jurisdiction over the river, and must show their commitment to protect the river. It must define a management area, which can range from a corridor along the main stem of a river to corridors along the river and all its tributaries, to entire watersheds. It must spell out policies and practices that will ensure that the particular values of the river for which it was nominated will be protected. It must outline a strategy to ensure that the river and its environment are sustained in a healthy state for the benefit of generations present and future. And it must generate a willingness and commitment from all stakeholders to share actively in ensuring the river's well-being.

Rivers in the CHRS range from rivers in national parks to rivers on public lands to rivers flowing through private lands. For the last group, which is becoming a larger percentage of rivers in the System, planners must deal with concepts such as conservation easements, stewardship, consensus-building, landowner's rights, public participation, citizen empowerment, land trusts and partnerships. Exploring these channels for preservation of rivers is where the future, and the challenge, lies for the continued growth and evolution of the CHRS.

Monitoring Heritage Rivers

The official designation of a Canadian Heritage River brings with it the responsibility on the part of the governing agency to monitor and report on the condition of the river. For each designated river, a checklist that describes the river's natural and recreational values, human heritage and water quality is prepared, and baseline information on the condition of resources is recorded.

Each year managing governments must report on the condition of the river, particularly changes in water quality and ecosystem health, changes in the condition of significant features (for instance, are the pictographs being damaged by visitors?), and on significant developments that could affect the natural, cultural or recreational attributes of the river. These findings are written up and included in each CHRS annual report. Every ten years a separate "state of the river" report is prepared by the Canadian Heritage Rivers Board.

What happens if a river is deteriorating or being unsustainably developed? If a river is deteriorating, the Board can remove its designation and conduct special assessments. To date, this situation has not occurred. The public, especially non-government environmental organizations, are the most powerful watchdogs to ensure that Heritage Rivers remain healthy.

The Next Ten Years

Expect to see more rivers flowing through private lands included in the System. Expect to see greater public input in selecting rivers, writing the management plans, and monitoring their condition. This is already happening. Citizens are getting involved in projects throughout the CHRS. They are monitoring water quality on the St. Croix, in New Brunswick, and developing public education programs along the Jacques Cartier, in Québec. Aboriginal communities who see the CHRS as a means of developing economic opportunities in ecotourism and protecting Aboriginal heritage are getting more involved. The Inuit community of Baker Lake lobbied successfully for the nomination of the Kazan in the N.W.T. Ecotourism and Aboriginal heritage were important elements in the nomination of the Soper River on Baffin Island, also in the N.W.T.

The spirit of co-operation that forms the basis of the CHRS will continue to expand, bringing all stakeholders — residents, recreational users, mining and industrial interests, and bureaucrats like me — together in the process of selecting, management planning and monitoring Heritage Rivers.

How to Get Involved

Even though there has not been, to date, a lot of direct public involvement in the early phases of CHRS planning, individuals and non-government organizations can recommend, in principle, rivers for consideration. Your best best is to get to know the Board member and river planners in your province or territory. Most provinces and territories now have completed system studies, so study them and find out where the gaps are.

Nominating a River

The rules state that nominations must be tabled by the province's or territory's Board member. But increasingly, nominations are being prepared with input from local and regional government and non-government organizations. This is in keeping with the direction and spirit of the CHRS charter. This document, signed on Earth Day (April 22) 1997, by ministers of all provinces and territories and the federal ministers for Canadian Heritage and Indian and Northern Affairs, reaffirms the commitment of all governments participating in the CHRS to continuing to support the program. It also reaffirms the rights of landowners and other stakeholders in the nomination and designation of Canadian Heritage Rivers.

The nomination process can be spearheaded by local groups, as was the case for the Thames, Detroit, St. Marys, Clearwater and the Grand. If you're interested in getting involved, get to know the local authorities, offer to volunteer or serve on a committee. Talk with planners and make sure you know exactly what's going on.

Management Planning

This is where you can really kick up your heels. Public meetings and hearings are where you can express your opinions on the management issues that the plan must address. Write letters and briefs to raise public awareness and support. In the settled areas of Canada, innovative means are being used to protect lands and rivers in place of direct land acquisition. Easements, land trusts, stewardship agreements — all these require public support. To get this support, you must first generate public awareness and concern. Innovative means such as signage, brochures, video and television coverage are also being used to market Heritage Rivers. Again, you can be part of the decision-making process.

So go to a public meeting. Read the nomination document. Fill out a survey. Write a brief or a letter. Serve on a committee. Get involved in making your community aware of the issues.

And Afterwards . . .

Monitoring Heritage Rivers ensures that their heritage values have not been adversely affected, and that the strategies in the management plan are being carried out and are working. The CHRS Secretariat co-ordinates monitoring and has produced a video and several manuals to help local groups become involved in taking care of their rivers. Carry the message of river conservation into your community. Organize a river clean-up. Talk to your river manager and find out how you can contribute to monitoring your river.

So What?

Heritage River status does not guarantee that a river will not be affected or changed. But it is the best opportunity available to ensure that our rivers flow to the future unpolluted and rich in life and human heritage, a future where rivers will evolve as they have done since the dawn of time. It is the best opportunity we have to ensure that the future of Canada's rivers will be one where our children will be able to swim in them without worrying about mercury and other contaminants, and dip their cups over the gunwales and drink the water. That is the dream.

Acknowledgments

The ideas expressed in this essay came from speeches, articles and conversations with the following people who have been instrumental in the founding and growth of the Canadian Heritage Rivers System: Michael Greco and Don Gibson of the CHRS Secretariat, who have nurtured the System since its inception and continue to mould its growth; Nick Coomber, a now retired planner with the National Parks Directorate of Parks Canada, who was one of the architects of the CHRS; and Lynn Noel, who has sung out all over this land about the CHRS and Canada's river heritage, and continues to do so.

To these people and others who dedicate their lives to protecting Canada's river heritage, the rivers thank you.

Canada Experientially
To Every Waterway a Story

Bob Henderson

"I have rolled out a new map, giving names to unknown indentations. I am Canadian." — Florence McNeil.

WE UNFOLD OUR MAP FOR THE TRIP. IT'S NOT NEW. IT IS TATTERED WITH cracks in the folds and obscured worn areas at its corners. Yet it all looks new to us, alive. The blue is the key. Fingers trace out a route of blue — of water — and do a subconscious hop at overland green intrusions. Details are examined with wide eyes. Then the eye looks still further outward. There are not many linear patterns — roads, settlements. It all looks sort of the same, green and blue, with occasional pencil lines and adjacent notes such as "watch for trail to the left at the marsh, do not go straight into marsh, must be winter route." There are some lakes with no names. We like that. It's both unsettling and exciting. We're in the bush and can travel in many directions. The bush is still largely a new map with unknown indentations.

The real adventure here is, can we belong? The unknown indentations are both geographical and cultural. Technically it has all been discovered, but discovery remains. The question is, what is that we seek? Is it to be over or against or with or of? What is it to be "of" a place?

The bush was home to the Aboriginal people. To many of our forefathers it was the New World. We are still looking for the New World, still hoping to have a discovery of Canada. We travel on water, true to the heritage of so much of this landscape.

We Canadians love our political and economic history, making it the cornerstone of university Canadian studies. But if Canada is anything in particular, it is geography and bush travel. Our history is as much David Thompson and J. B. Tyrrell as it is Sir John A. Macdonald and Tommy Douglas. All Canada refers back to water travel. But we have a hard time admitting this. We prefer to think of Canada as if it were a Chile on its side, with the bump of the St. Lawrence Valley and southern Ontario narrowing down to a sliver at the western tip at Victoria. Edmonton and Whitehorse are anomalies. As for everything else, all that water, much of it remains the "country back of beyond," as Robert Service once noted, or the "country way back in," as recorded of Labrador trappers by Elliott Merrick, a 1930s traveller, in *True North*. This is the Canada we have to discover, Elliott Merrick's "True North."

Discovery of Imagination

Sure there are resource extractions and airborne toxins leaving their insidious marks. So-called pollution hot spots abound. But despite this, there remains an integrity to Canada; a bush that remains, not a wilderness (a confused term from the beginning), but a "way of the North." This is the North that George Douglas, P. G. Downes and many other of this century's travellers were bent on discovering. This discovery calls for an imagination that brings spirits to the landscape and allows for the "movement in time" that "takes us out of time," such that we can be part of the history, part of the discovery of Canada.

Time can lose much of its control over us. Time, as linear concept, can become lost amid the wide imagination.for stories of the place relived and retold again and again. The trick is to know the stories and come to know the place experientially. What one discovers is what novelist John Steffler writes about the ghost of Labrador explorer George Cartwright in his compelling novel *The Afterlife of George Cartwright*. Cartwright discovered that time is like sound, "that the past doesn't vanish, but encircles us in layers like a continuous series of voices, with the closest, most recent voice drowning out those that have gone before. And just as it's possible to sit on bench in a city reading a book, oblivious to the complex racket all around, then to withdraw from the past and pick out from the cascade of noises the voice of one street vendor two blocks away, so for Cartwright it's possible at times to tune in a detail from either the past of the ongoing course of time and, by concentrating on it, become witness to some event in the affairs of the dead or the living." The more the stories of the land are known and told, the more time encircles us with its voices enlarging our present.

Literary theorist Northrop Frye asked us, in *The Bush Garden: Essays on the Canadian Imagination*, "Where is here?" This, he suggested, was Canada's central problem. "Who am I?" is secondary. But one can safely assume he never went out to discover it — the bush, that is. Certainly not to greet it. And if he had ventured outside his cities' "garrisons," would he have not discovered, as might be expected given his background, the same North that in 1838 fellow Methodist James Evans called, "a region of moral darkness and spiritual degradation."

Discovery is not just a matter of journey. It is more a question of how the journey is to be imaginatively taken. To discover "where is here," you must first go there, and then travel with a reflexive, engaging spirit. This open spirit of travel adds a challenge, to avoid the temptation of certainty that predetermines perceptions of the land and peoples, and to avoid as mind-scape a simplistic binary distinction between civilized and savage.

Our historical precursors, who rolled out new maps, faced this challenge in the New World. J. Wreford Watson, a geographer, wrote, "The geography of any place results from how we see it, as much as from what may be." For some, the journey brought only a landscape as reproduced in their own minds. Canada was to be seen as an extension of the Old World. The "scenery" was encoded by European traditions. For others, the journey brought a genuine meeting, an authentic complex communication of self and setting. The latter involves an adventure "to fit it" and not "fill out" from an Old World frame of reference. Explorer David Thompson, missionary Gabrielle Sagard and trader George Nelson all come to mind as examples of a more complex "fit it" mindscape. Alexander Mackenzie and John Franklin seemed lost in the Old World, while actually in the "New" World.

Anthropologist Robin Ridington wrote of his own meeting of Aboriginal peoples and canoe country this way: "I know . . . that I cannot dream up another culture that does not exist, but I also know that in order to understand . . . I must be willing to dream into it."

Roll Out a New Map

For the discovery of Canada we need to "dream into it," unfolding the map, giving meaning to indentations; the indentations that speak of heritage and those indentations in our perceptual and conceptual framework that will come to be challenged. Where is here? The following verse of Al Purdy is useful:

A.Y. Jackson for instance
83 years old
half way up a mountain
standing in a patch of snow
to paint a picture that says
"Look here
You've never seen this country
it's not the way you thought it was
Look again."

Here's a subtle reworking:

Take the water traveller, for instance
young or old
well into the trip at the end of a portage
standing with map in hand
staring out on the lake
as if to say to a partner
"Look here
You've never seen this country
it's not the way you thought it was
Look again."
and together they look.

And so we can come to roll out a new map.

What becomes of the pedagogy for this discovery of Canada? Indeed, where is here? Experiential learning is at the heart of this teaching and learning of place. The canoe and snowshoes are the means. The classroom and book learning will further the learners' knowledge, but not necessarily their comprehension. The travellers may come to know more and more with library and lecture, but that knowledge will not run deeper, not as a concrete apprehension. It is this deeper knowing, the concrete apprehension for the discovery of Canada, that is the focus of travel. Though this discovery of place is easily lost in a vague, sensual, preconceptual knowing with the balance of some academic rigour, it is rare that classroom learning provides any clarity for the genius of a place. It is necessary to balance the experiential exploration and classroom and library exploration for holistic inquiry. The student must be a traveller; the traveller must be a student.

Canoe travel that attempts to offer this balance is grounded in the notion that the student will never understand the writings of Canada's discoverers, explorers and settlers without time to share in that experience of life on the land, even in a most fleeting way. As was suggested to Edmonton journalist Stephen Hume, "Don't rely on books, you've got to go there." The comprehension of the diary of Catherine Parr Trail, the recollections of trapper Erik Munsterhjelm, the verse of Archibald Lampman's Temagami, the exploration literature of David Thompson, the letters of fur trader George Nelson — all demand that we live for a time unfettered by our modern urban sensibilities and craft.

Jack Warwick noted in *The Long Journey: Literary Themes of French Canada* that "There are distinct resemblances between early travellers' reactions to the journey 'enhaut' and those of modern writers," particularly, one might add, for those modern writers who attempt to travel "à la mode du pays." Today's journal writers, with time to absorb the bush and distance themselves from whatever scholastic, social or institutional routine has become commonplace, come to see that, like the earlier traveller, they might be looking or "not looking" for the New World of backcountry Canada. A resultant cultural identification brings a richer grasp of the "time out of time" experience, and one's writing finds a home as part of a continuing Canadian tradition.

In describing the writings of early North America, Wayne Franklin writes, in *Discoverers, Explorers, Settlers: The Diligent Writers of Early America:* "And they often turned to writing with an urgency which suggests that it was a means of self understanding, an essential way of shaping their lives after the facts. They seem, too, to have been painfully aware of the many problems which language posed for people separated as they were from their own world." How relevant these words fit for the canoe tripper and recorder of today.

The pedagogy of water travel as the discovery of Canada involves roots, spirit and imagination. Roots refer to the telling and living of the stories of the Canadian bush. It is an integrated task. Spirit is concern for the fundamental nature of one's inquiry, one's state of mind, which must be open to other assumptions and practices and to another time. Romantic poet John Keats thought of this quality of spirit as "negative capability" and wrote to his brothers in 1817: "Several things dovetailed in my mind and at once it struck me, what quality went to form a Man of achievement . . . I mean Negative Capability, that is when man is capable of being in uncertainties, Mysteries, doubts, without any irritable reaching after fact and reason."

Finally, a healthy imagination is a characteristic you must not only tap, but you must consciously think to advance. As poet Wallace Stevens wrote, "We have it [imagination] because we do not have enough without it." We must come to perceive beyond our own limited frame of reference so that both our awareness as historical and ecological beings comes to flourish.

With attention to roots, spirit and imagination, the traveller of Canadian waterways rolls out a new map with welcoming routes each with many unknown indentations. We can come to find the so-called New World that both baffled and was ignored by so many Euro-Canadian ancestors. "Where is here?" awaits our discovery.

A different version of this paper was originally published in *Celebrating Our Tradition, Charting Our Future*, edited by Glenda M. Hanna. Proceedings of the 20th International Conference of the Association for Experiential Education, October 8–11, 1992 in Banff, Alberta.

Contributors

Laurel Archer and **Brad Koop** met as canoe guides on the Churchill River in northern Saskatchewan. They now live in a log house on Lac La Ronge. They spend the majority of their free time canoeing and kayaking, whether on rivers in the Arctic, the Rockies, Mongolia, Costa Rica, or somewhere in between.

Sheila Archer was born in Regina, Saskatchewan, where she has spent most of her life. Since 1987 she has pursued a dual existence as both a practising visual artist and canoe guide/instructor for Churchill River Canoe Outfitters/Horizons Unlimited. Paddling Saskatchewan's wild rivers continues to be her passion, and she hopes to always to be able to jump into a canoe and surf the "Big Smoothy," one of the many great waves upstream from her summer home on the Churchill River at Missinipe.

Gino Bergeron is working towards a master's degree in French Literature at the Université du Québec in Chicoutimi. He looks forward to taking his son and daughter on lots of paddling and winter camping expeditions.

Dave Bober and wife **Mary** live in central Saskatchewan, where they make their living raising beef cattle. Dave enjoys wilderness tripping with family, friends and youth groups. He is a member of the Wilderness Canoe Association and Saskatchewan Wilderness Paddlers. A number of his stories have appeared in *Nastawgan, Kanawa,* and local newspapers.

Lawrence Buser published an adventure travel magazine, *Great Expeditions,* for ten years. He also organized adventure tours to exotic destinations for the public and educational organizations. He first met Chris Harris when he started his business. Several years later, when Chris was running his own tours to the Bowron Lakes, Lawrence took paddle in hand and toured the lakes with Chris and a number of other adventurers. He loves nature and writing, and makes his home in Vancouver.

James Cottrell teaches at Killarney Junior High in Edmonton, Alberta. He passes over the North Saskatchewan River on his way to and from school. He claims that it is the energy of the river that fuels his imagination.

Scott Cunningham is a biologist and sea kayaker who has explored the Atlantic coast by canoe and sea kayak for over two decades. In 1980 he circumnavigated the entire province of Nova Scotia in an open canoe. He has written extensively on the biology, geology and human history of the coastline for outdoor magazines and recently published *Sea Kayaking in Nova Scotia*, a detailed route guide. He is a senior instructor with the British Canoe Union, and a founding member and past president of the Association of Eastern Canadian Sea Kayaking Outfitters. He designed the sea kayak instructional program for the Canadian Recreational Canoeing Association. Dr. Cunningham lives in Tangier, Nova Scotia, where he operates Coastal Adventures.

David Finch is a professional historian specializing in Western Canadian history. He has a passion for the out-of-doors, especially the wilder reaches of Canadian rivers.

Maxwell W. Finkelstein currently works as the communications, marketing and education specialist for the Canadian Heritage Rivers System Secretariat. When he isn't paddling on a Canadian Heritage River, he usually can be found writing or talking about rivers. He is working on a television series about his travels on rivers. He lives, not surprisingly, beside the Ottawa River.

Toni Harting is a freelance writer-photographer specializing in canoeing-related nature topics. He is the editor of *Nastawgan*, the quarterly journal of the Wilderness Canoe Association. His book *French River: Canoeing the River of the Stick-Wavers* was published by the Boston Mills Press.

Bob Henderson teaches Outdoor Education at McMaster University and writes the Heritage column in *Kanawa* magazine.

Gwyneth Hoyle was taken on her first canoe trip in Algonquin Park by her teenaged sons, and since then has made a number of trips with Wanapitei, including a memorable one down the Thelon River. She lives in Peterborough and continues to search for a canoe light enough to permit solo trips beyond cottage country. She is co-author of *Canoeing North into the Unknown — A Record of River Travel: 1874 to 1974* (Natural Heritage/ Natural History Inc., 1994).

Stephan Kesting is a practising botanist and ecologist in British Columbia. He paddles rivers, lakes and streams wherever he goes.

Pat Mahaffey is a happy guy when he is canoeing on wilderness rivers with his wife, Colleen, and daughters, Fiona and Bridget, and being eaten alive by mosquitoes.

Sheena Masson is a writer canoe-tripper and kayaker who lives on the south shore of Nova Scotia. Her first book, *Paddle Lunenburg/Queens* (www.lunco.com/paddlelq), is a paddling guide to 31 routes in those two counties. She says it was the perfect job for a writer who paddles (or is it a paddler who writes?).

Keith Morton is a long-time paddler, hiker and backcountry skier who lives in Calgary. He instructs on a range of outdoor subjects and is the equipment and new products editor for *Explore* magazine. He is also the author of *Planning a Wilderness Trip in Canada and Alaska*, published by Rocky Mountain Books.

David F. Pelly grew up canoeing the waters of central Ontario, including Algonquin Park. He has since paddled thousands of miles on arctic rivers, forging a career of writing about the North, its wilderness, its geography, its history, its people. In 1988 David revived an old Canadian tradition when he used canoes as vehicles for scientific exploration on a major archaeological expedition down the Kazan River. His most recent book, *Thelon — A River Sanctuary*, was published in 1996.

Jim Price lives in Paradise, a small town just outside St. John's, and has paddled almost every river in Newfoundland. Owner of Eastern Edge Outfitters Limited, he divides his time between leading canoe and kayak trips and working as a resource planner with the Department of Environment and Lands.

Kevin Redmond is a CRCA master canoe instructor and co-author of the book *Canyons, Coves and Coastal Waters: Choice Canoe and Kayak Routes of Newfoundland and Labrador*. Along with his wife, Sophia, his frequent paddling partners include son Thomas and daughters Susan and Jacquelyn. Kevin is a freelance photographer and writer whose work has appeared throughout Europe, Asia and North America. His book is available through the CRCA.

Cliff Speer is a resident of Saskatoon, Saskatchewan. He operates an outdoor adventure company, CanoeSki Discovery Company, specializing in canoeing, nordic skiing instruction and wilderness touring (www.link.ca/canoeski or canoeski@link.ca). His pursuits also include freelance writing and photography.

John Stradiotto and **Martha Morris** live in Atikokan, Ontario, and operate Quetico Discovery Tours, specializing in canoe trips for families, photographers and novices in Quetico Park (www.atikokan.lakeheadu.ca/~jdstradi/index or jdstradi@atikokan.lakeheadu.ca).

Gaye Wadham lives by the sea. She kayaks the Gaspi coast in the summer and backcountry skis in the Chic Chocs in the winter.

Bob Waldon and his wife, **Carole**, have paddled the rivers flowing out of the wilderness east of Lake Winnipeg. On the smaller rivers they followed the old canoe routes used by the Aboriginal trappers and hunters, and developed a knack for finding long-overgrown portage trails. They have lived on Vancouver Island since 1991, but will soon divide their time between the North Island and their Manitoba retreat, 160 acres along the Pembina Valley northeast of Killarney, Bob's hometown.

Paula and Anton Zybach settled in Calgary after years of globetrotting. They now satisfy their appetites for adventure with hiking, skiing, snowshoeing, and canoeing.

Contributors

Topographical Maps

Information was gathered from resources of the Canada Centre for Topographic Information, Natural Resources Canada, including three index maps and this website: www.maps.nrcan.gc.ca.

Main River, Newfoundland
1:250,000 Sandy Lake: 12H.
1:50,000 Jackson's Arm: 12H/15; Hampden: 12H/11; Main River: 12H/14.

Terra Nova River, Newfoundland
1:250,000 Gander Lake: 2D.
1:50,000 Great Gull Lake: 2D/6; Kepenkeck Lake: 2D/7; Port Blandford: 2D/8; Glovertown: 2D/9.

Moisie River, Labrador
1:250,000 Shabogamo Lake: 23G; Lac Opocopa: 23B; Lac Fouquet: 22-O; Sept-Iles 22J.
1:50,000 Wabush Lake: 23G/2; Wightman Lake: 23G/1; Flora Lake: 23B/15; Lac Petite Hermine: 23B/16; Lac Opocopa: 23B/10; Lac Felix: 23B/7; 23B/2; Rapide Du Diable: 22-O/15; Lac Boudart: 22-O/10; Lac Du Brochet: 22-O/9; Grand Lac Au Sable: 22-O/8; Lac Nipissis: 22-O/1: Lac A L'Eau Doree: 22J/16; Rivere Vallee: 22J/9; Lac Des Rapides: 22J/8; Sept-Iles: 22J/1.

Harp Lake, Labrador
1:250,000 Mistastin Lake: 13M; Hopedale: 13N.
1:50,000 13M/1; Harp Lake: 13N/4; Shapio Lake: 13N/3; Ugjoktok Bay: 13N/2.

The Five Islands, Nova Scotia
1:50,000 Amherst: 21H.
1:250,000 Parrsboro: 21H/8.

Nova Scotia Waterways
Canoe Routes of Nova Scotia, published jointly by Canoe Nova Scotia and Camping Association of Nova Scotia, gives particulars on 70 canoeing areas

throughout the province. Contact Canoe Nova Scotia: 5516 Spring Garden Rd., Box 3010 South, Halifax, NS, B3J 3G6 or phone: (902) 425-5450, ext. 316.

PEI's North Shore
1:250,000 Charlottetown: 11L.
1:50,000 Malpeque: 11L/12; North Rustico: 11L/6; Mount Stewart: 11L/7; Souris: 11L/8.

Nepisiguit River, New Brunswick
1:250,000 Campbellton: 21-O; Bathurst: 21P.
1:50,000 Nepisiguit Lakes: 21-O/7; California Lake: 21-O/8; Nepisiguit Falls: 21P/5; Bathurst: 21P/12.

L'Eau Claire River, Quebec
1:50,000 Lac A L'Eau Claire: 34B; Lac Guillaume-Delisle: 34C.
1:250,000 34B/2; 34B/3; 34B/4; Ile Cairn: 34C/1; Belanger Island: 34C/2.

George River, Quebec
1:250,000 Lac Brisson: 24A; Lac Henrietta: 24H; Lac Saffray: 24G; Lac Ralleau: 24J.
1:50,000 Lac Cholmondely: 24A/14; Lac Bregent: 24A/13; Lac Fajot: 24H/4; Lac Qamanialuup: 24H/5; Lac Gelin: 24G/8; Lac Sivulijartalik: 24G/9; Lac Monceaux: 24G/16; Lac Tasirpaarusiq: 24J/1; Lac Tasivalliajuq: 24J/2; Riviere Danielou: 24J/7.

French River, Ontario
1:250,000 Sudbury: 41-I.
1:50,000 Noelville: 41-I/1; Delamere: 41-I/2.

Ottawa River, Ontario (Beachburg section)
1:250,000 Pembroke: 31F.
1:50,000 Cobden: 31F/10.

Algonquin Park, Ontario
Map of Algonquin Park ($4.95 plus tax) available by calling (toll-free): 1-800-667-1940 or writing The Friends of Algonquin Park, Box 248, Whitney, ON, K0J 2MO. For information about Algonquin Park, write to: P.O. Box 219, Whitney, ON, K0J 2MO or call (705) 633-5572.

The Kawarthas, Ontario
1:250,000 Lake Simcoe: 31D.

Rideau Waterway, Ontario
1:250,000 Ottawa: 31G; Ogdensburg: 31B; Kingston: 31C.
1:50,000 Ottawa: 31G/5; Kemptville: 31G/4; Merrickville: 31B/13;
Perth: 31C/16; Westport: 31C/9; Gananoque: 31C/8; Sydenham: 31C/7.

Lady Evelyn River, Ontario
1:250,000 Gogama: 41P.
1:50,000 Lady Evelyn Lake: 41P/8; Elk Lake: 41P/9.

Steel River, Ontario
1:250,000 Schreiber: 42D; Longlac: 42E.
1:50,000 Schreiber: 42D/14; Dickison Lake: 42E/3; Wintering Lake: 42E/6.

Quetico, Ontario
Map of Quetico Park ($8.70 plus tax) available by calling (toll-free):
1-800-667-1940 or writing The Friends of Quetico Park, P. O. Box 1959,
Atikokan, ON, P0T 1C0. For information about Quetico Park, write to:
c/o District Manager, Ministry of Natural Resources, Atikokan, ON,
P0T 1C0 or call (807) 597-2735.

Hudson Bay, Manitoba
1:250,000 Caribou River: 54M; Churchill: 54L.
1:50,000 Hubbart Point: 54M/7; The Knoll: 54M/2; Knife Delta: 54L/15;
Button Bay: 54L/9; Churchill: 54L/16.

Souris River, Manitoba
1:250,000 Virden: 62F; Brandon: 62G.
1:50,000 Souris: 62F/9; Dunrea: 62G/5; Wawanesa: 62G/12.

Drinking River, Saskatchewan
1:250,000 Lac La Ronge: 73P.
1:50,000 From Settee Lake: 73P/16 to Nistowiak Lake: 73P/8.

Churchill River, Saskatchewan
1:250,000 Ile-A-La-Crosse: 73-0; Mudjatik River: 74B; Lac La Ronge: 73P.

1:50,000 Lac Ile-A-La-Crosse: 73-O/5; Black Bay: 73-O/12; Shagwenaw Lake: 73-O/13; Little Flatstone Lake: 74B/4; Dipper Lake: 73-O/14; Bentley Bay: 73-O/15; Pinehouse Lake: 73-O/10; Sandfly Lake: 73-O/9; Belanger: 73-O/16; Black Bear Island Lake: 73P/12; Kavanagh Lake: 73P/11; Otter Lake: 73P/10; Stanley Mission: 73P/7; Nistowiak Lake: 73P/8.

William River, Saskatchewan
1:250,000 William River: 74K; Tazin Lake: 74N.
1:50,000 James Creek: 74K/3; Millard Lake: 74K/2; Payne Lake: 74K/7; Field Lake: 74K/10; Atchison Lake: 74K/15; Silverthorn Lake: 74K/14; William Point: 74N/3.

MacFarlane River, Saskatchewan
1:250,000 Cree Lake: 74G; Lloyd Lake: 74F; Livingstone Lake: 74J; William River: 74K; Tazin Lake: 74N; Fond-Du-Lac: 74-O.
1:50,000 Norseman Lake: 74G/13; Dunning Lake: 74F/16; Brudell Lake: 74J/4; Snare Lake: 74J/5; Kalln Lake: 74K/8; Birney Lake: 74J/12; Urton Lake: 74J/13; Davy Lake: 74K/16; Archibald River: 74N/1; Helmer Lake: 74-O/4.

Highwood River, Alberta
1:250,000 Kananaskis Lakes: 82J; Gleichen: 82-I.
1:50,000 Mount Rae: 82J/10; Mount Head: 82J/7; Stimson Creek: 82J/8; Turner Valley: 82J/9; High River: 82-I/12.

Sheep River, Alberta
1:250,000 Kananaskis Lakes: 82J.
1:50,000 Priddis: 82J/16.

Bowron Lakes, B.C.
For a map of Bowron Lakes Park, contact: BC Parks, Cariboo District, 281 – 1st Ave. North, Williams Lake, B.C. or phone: (250) 398-4414 or fax: (250) 398-4686.

Kicking Horse River, B.C.
1:250,000 Golden: 82N.
1:50,000 McMurdo: 82N/2; Golden: 82N/7.

Spatsizi and Stikine Rivers, B.C. and Alaska

1:250,000 Spatsizi: 104H; Toodoggone River: 94E; Cry Lake: 104-I; Dease Lake: 104J; Telegraph Creek: 104 G; Iskut River: 104B.

1:50,000 Tuaton Lake: 104H/8; Laslui Lake: 94E/5; Spruce Hill: 94E/12; Dawson River: 104H/9; Diamond Creek: 104H/16; Cambridge Creek: 104H/15; Cullivan Creek: 104H/14; Ealue Lake 104H/13; Beale Lake: 104-I/14; Stikine Canyon: 104J/1; Classy Creek: 104J/2; Buckley Lake: 104G/15; Telegraph Creek: 104G/14; Yehiniko Lake: 104G/11; Chutine River: 104G/12; Scud River: 104G/5; Flood Glacier: 104G/4; Great Glacier: 104B/13; Katete River: 104B/12. American maps include Petersburg C-1, C-2, B-2 and Bradfield C-6.

Tatshenshini River, B.C., Yukon and Alaska

1:250,000 Tatshenshini River: 114P; Dezadesh Range: 115A; Yakutat: 114-O.

1:50,000 Parton River: 114P/15; Takhanne River: 115A/2; Silver Creek: 115A/3; Survey Lake: 114P/14; Carmine Mountain: 114P/11; Pentice Ridge: 114P/6; Konamoxt Glacier: 114P/5.

Soper River, Nunavut

1:250,000 Armshow River: 25N; Lake Harbour: 25K.

1:50,000 25N/12; Mount Joy: 25N/5; Mount Moore: 25N/4; Lake Harbour: 25K/13.

Thelon River, N.W.T. and Nunavut

1:250,000 Artillery Lake:75-O; Hanbury River: 75P; Clarke River: 65M; Tammarvi River: 66D; Beverly Lake: 66C; Aberdeen Lake: 66B; Schultz Lake: 66A.

1:50,000 Ford Lake: 75-O/3; 75-O/2; 75-O/7; Heuss Lake: 75-O/6; 75-O/10; 75-O/9; Hanbury Lake: 75P/12; Hoarne Lake: 75P/11; 75P/14; Macdonald Falls: 75P/15; Ford Falls: 75P/10; The Gap: 75P/9; Axecut Lake: 75P/16; 65M/13; Hornby Point: 66D/4; 66D/5; 66D/6; Muskox Hill: 66D/7; Lookout Point: 66D/2; 66D/1; 66D/8; Ursus Islands: 66C/5; 66C/12; Thelon Bluffs: 66C/11; Hoare Point: 66C/10; 66C/8; 66B/12; Koangok Narrows: 66B/11; 66B/10; Qamanaugaq Bay: 66B/9; Aggattalik Narrows: 66A/12; Whalebone Hill: 66A/13; 66A/14; Ayaktuukvik Lake: 66A/10; Baker Lake: 66A/8.

Morse River, Nunavut (trip from Saskatchewan–N.W.T. border to Arctic Ocean via the Dubawnt, Thelon and Back rivers)
1:250,000 Pelly Lake: 66F.
1:50,000 Morse River: 66F/10.

South Nahanni River, N.W.T.
1:250,000 Little Nahanni River: 105-I; Glacier Lake: 95L; Flat River: 95E; Virginia Falls: 95F; Sibbeston Lake: 95G; Fort Simpson: 95H.
1:50,000 Mount Wilson: 105-I/13; Jones Lake: 105-I/14; 105-I/11; 105-I/10; Dozer Lake: 105-I/7; Mount Appler: 105-I/8; Black Wolf Mountain: 95L/5; James Macbrie: 95L/4; Dolf Mountain: 95L/3; Hole In The Wall Lake: 95E/14; Hell Roaring Creek: 95E/15; Flood Creek: 95E/16; 95E/9; 95F/2; Vera Creek: 95F/11; May Creek: 95F/6; Second Canyon: 95F/7; First Canyon: 95F/8; Twisted Mountain: 95G/4; Nahanni Butte: 95G/3; Dehdjida Island: 95G/2.

Snare–Coppermine Rivers, N.W.T.
1:250,000 Yellowknife: 85J; Rae: 85K; Wecho Lake: 85-O; Marian River: 85N; Indian Lake 86B; Winter Lake: 86A; Redrock Lake 86G; Hepburn Lake: 86J; Sloan River 86K; Dismal Lakes 86N; Coppermine: 86-O.
1:50,000 Yellowknife Bay: 85J/8; Ptarmigan Point: 85J/7; Old Fort Island: 85J/6; Trout Rock: 85J/11; Waite Island: 85J/12; Stagg River: 85J/13; Bedford Point: 85K/16; Shoti Lake: 85N/1; La Martre Falls: 85N/2; Tumi Lake: 85N/7; Strutt Lake: 85N/8; Labrish Lake: 85N/9; Snively Lake: 85N/16; Basler Lake: 85-O/13; Matterberry Lake: 86B/4; Norris Lake: 86B/5; Arseno Lake: 86B/12; Rodrigues Lake: 86B/13; Mesa Lake: 86B/14; Irritation Lake: 86G/3; 86G/2; 86G/1; 86G/8; Rocknest Lake: 86G/9; 86G/16; Fairy Lake River: 86J/1; 86J/8; Fontano Lake: 86J/7; 86J/10; Muskox Lakes: 86J/11; Stanbridge Lake: 86J/14; 86J/13; Qingaluk Lake: 86K/16; Rocky Defile Rapids: 86N/1; 86-O/4; Burnt Creek: 86-O/5; 86-O/12; Escape Rapids: 86-O/11; Richardson Bay: 86-O/14.

Bonnet Plume River, Yukon
1:250,000 Bonnet Plume Lake: 106B; Nadaleen River: 106C; Wind River: 106E.
1:50,000 106B/6; 106B/5; Duo Creek: 106C/8; Goz Creek: 106C/7; Bonnet Plume Pass: 106C/6; Corn Creek: 106C/11; Gillespie Creek: 106C/12; Fairchild Lake: 106C/13; Quartet Lakes: 106E/1; 106E/8; 106E/7; 106E/10; Chappie Lake: 106E/15.

Yukon River, Yukon (from Johnson's Crossing to Dawson City)
1:250,000 Teslin: 105C; Lake Laberge: 105E; Glenlyon: 105L; Carmacks:
115-I; Stevenson Ridge: 115J; Stewart River: 115-O; Dawson: 116B.
1:50,000 Teslin: 105C/2; Lone Tree Creek: 105C/7; Brooks Brook: 105C/6;
Mount Grant: 105C/11; Streak Mountain: 105C/12; Rosy Lake: 105C/13;
105C/16; Frank Creek: 105E/11; Twin Lakes: 105E/12; Mason Landing:
105E/7; Hootalinqua: 105E/10; Big Salmon: 105E/15; Claire Lake: 105E/14;
Mandanna Lake: 105E/13; Frenchman Lake: 105L/4; Yukon Crossing:
115-I/8; Merrice Lake: 115-I/7; Minto: 115-I/10; Dark Creek: 115-I/11;
Volcano Mountain: 115-I/14; Black Creek: 115-I/13; Cripple Creek:
115J/16; Britannia Creek: 115J/15; Coffee Creek: 115J/14; Thistle Creek:
115-O/3; Los Angeles Creek: 115-O/4; Stewart River: 115-O/6; Excelsior
Creek: 115-O/5; Ogilvie: 115-O/12; Garner Creek: 115-O/13; Swede Creek:
116B/4; Dawson: 116B/3.

Listings

Algonquin Bound Outdoor Store & Canoe Rentals
Box 228, Madawaska, Ontario, Canada K0J 2C0
Ph.: 1 (800) 704-4537 / (613) 637-5508 Fax: (613) 637-2054
Website: www.algonquinbound.com E-mail: info@algonquinbound.com

Algonquin Bound offers canoe rentals and a complete range of outfitting
services and equipment to help make your wilderness canoe or fishing trip
a memorable experience. We pride ourselves on offering top quality light-
weight rental equipment. Our staff will provide friendly service with a
personal touch. With their knowledge of Algonquin Park they are able
to help you plan a successful and enjoyable trip. Guided trips. Complete
outdoor store on site.

Algonquin Outfitters
R.R.#1, Oxtongue Lake, Dwight, Ontario, Canada P0A 1H0
Ph.: (705) 635-2243 Fax: (705) 635-1834
Website: www.algonquinoutfitters.com E-mail: canoe@muskoka.com

Algonquin Outfitters offers complete and partial outfitting for Algonquin
Park canoe trips. Guided and self-guided trips are available. For over
39 years, Algonquin Outfitters has been well known for experienced,
knowledgeable staff, ultra-lightweight canoes and high quality equipment.
Our retail store has an amazing selection of outdoor gear and canoe
tripping equipment. Contact us for a complete information package.
Open year round.

Bathurst Inlet Lodge & Outfitting
Box 820(kw), Yellowknife, Northwest Territories, Canada X1A 2N6
Ph.: (867) 873-2595 Fax: (867) 920-4263
Website: www.bathurstintellodge.com E-mail: canoe@bathurstintellodge.com

Canoe outfitting in the central NorthwestTerritories. The Burnside/Mara,
Hood, Back, Thelon River and more...One call does it all; we supply
canoes, spray skirts, paddles, radios, river reports/maps, other gear, plus
air transport. Rental camps available. Other expediting services available.
An Inuit Partnership – owner/operator. Before and after stay at the
spectacular Bathurst Inlet Lodge.

Beckers Lodge
Bowron Lake, Box 129, Wells, British Columbia, Canada V0K 2R0
Website: www.beckers.bc.ca E-mail: beckers@beckers.bc.ca

Becker's Lodge is located directly on beautiful Bowron Lake with a fantastic view of the snowcapped Cariboo Mountains. A great Canadian escape. Offering cozy log cabins and chalets for rent. Licensed restaurant and lounge. European cuisine. General store offering everything needed for your trip. We also rent camping equipment and hold over 120 canoes and kayaks in different brands, models, lengths and materials. Licensed outfitter for Bowron Lake Provincial Park. Guided canoe trips. Transfer to Quesnel and Barkerville Historic Town and much more. Visit our web site for details.

Blackfeather/Trailhead
1960 Scott St., Ottawa, Ontario, Canada K1Z 8L8
Ph.: (613) 722-9717 Fax: (613) 722-0245
Website: www.blackfeather.com E-mail: trips@blackfeather.com

Rentals or complete outfitting for guided trips on N.W.T.'s Mountain, Snake, Bonnet Plume, Natla, Keele, and Upper Keele tributaries. Quebec – all rivers, specializing in the Dumoine, Mistassibi N.E., Batiscan, Bazin, Lievre and Aguanus. Hiking trips and mountain biking on N.W.T.'s Canol Road, Baffin Islands and Mackenzie Mountains. Private trips anywhere $200/day - fully guided and outfitted canoe and kayak trips plus transportation cost. $175/day for hiking/mountain biking trips. 5:1 guide ratio.

Canoe Arctic Inc.
P.O. Box 130 CR, Fort Smith, Northwest Territories, Canada X0E 0P0
Ph.: (867) 872-2308
Website: www.auroranet.nt.ca/canoe

Remote, fly-in canoe trips in the Barren Lands of the Northwest and Nunavut Territories, including the Thelon and Back Rivers. Warm, arid summers. Muskoxen, white wolves (our specialty), moose, grizzlies and caribou herds half a million strong. All trips guided by Alex Hall, wildlife biologist and the Canadian Arctic's first and most experienced canoeing guide. Operating since 1974. Free brochure.

CanoeSki Discovery Company
Canadian Wilderness Canoeing & Skiing EcoExplorations
1618-9th Ave. N., Saskatoon, Saskatchewan, Canada SK7 3A1
Tel./Fax: (306) 653-5693
Website: www.link.ca/canoeski E-mail: canoeski@link.ca

CanoeSki offers small group, fully catered wilderness canoe tours with an eco focus. Expert interpreters and certified tour leaders facilitate learning adventures in wildlife watching, ecology, history, aboriginal culture, archaeology, and ethnobotany. Programs appeal primarily to mature eco-travellers seeking inspiration for both mind and body. Affiliated with the University of Saskatchewan Community Education Programs and accredited as a "Saskatchewan ecotour operator.

Coastal Adventures

P.O. Box 77, Tangier, Nova Scotia, Canada B0J 3H0
Ph./Fax: (902) 772-2774
Website: www.coastaladventures.com E-mail: coastal@dunmac.com

Coastal Adventures is Atlantic Canada's most experienced sea kayaking operation (19 years), offering something for every interest and skill level: Nova Scotia coastal islands, Cape Breton Highlands, PEI beaches, Fundy tides and currents, Newfoundland fjords and icebergs. Our tours emphasize the unique biology, geology and human history of this fascinating environment where the land meets the sea. In our sea kayaking school, we offer certification with the Canadian Recreational Canoeing Association (CRCA), the BCU and the Association of Eastern Canadian Sea Kayaking Outfitters.

Eastern Edge Outfitters Limited

Box 17, Site 14, R.R.#2, Paradise, Newfoundland, Canada A1L 1C2
Ph.: (709) 782-5925 Fax: (709) 773-2201
Website: www.kayakeeo@hypersource.com E-mail: kayakeeo@nfld.com

Awaken your spirit of adventure and come with us to explore the same rugged coastline that challenged the Vikings a thousand years ago. Paddle this unique and exotic land of boundless beauty and fascinating history with Newfoundland's first outfitter, specializing in sea kayak tours. We also organize canoe and white water kayak trips throughout the province.

Ecosummer Expeditions Ltd.

Box 1765, R.R.#1, Clearwater, British Columbia, Canada V0E 1N0
Ph.: 1(800) 465-8884 Fax: (250) 674-2197
Website: www.ecosummer.com E-mail: trips@ecosummer.com

Since 1976, our journeys of discovery pleased thousands of guests with top quality and performance: CANOEING – Bowron Lake Park, Wells Gray Park, North Tweedsmuir Park, Dease River, Yukon River, Teslin River, Big Salmon River. KAYAKING – Vancouver Island, Queen Charlotte Islands, Baja California, Bahamas, Belize, Tonga, Greenland and Ellesmere Island, Ecuador, Patagonia and Peru.

Great Canadian Ecoventures & Air Thelon Ltd.

Box 2481, Yellowknife, Northwest Territories, Canada X1A 2P8
Ph.: 1 (800) 667-9453 Fax: (867) 920-7180
Website: www.thelon.com E-mail: tundra@thelon.com

We offer escorted 8-16 day canoe, raft and kayak expeditions on some of
the most remote wild rivers in the Canadian Arctic, led by some of the
most qualified trip leaders in the North. We operate wildlife photography
base camps in the Thelon and Queen Maud Sanctuaries. We also provide
the service of canoe/equipment rentals and logistical support for most
remote tundra rivers with access offered from Yellowknife and Baker Lake.
For a copy of our escorted trip brochure, or our partial outfitting information (please specify which), contact Tundra Tom at above number.

Horizons Unlimited/Churchill River Canoe Outfitters

P.O. Box 1110, La Ronge, Saskatchewan, Canada K0J 1P0
Ph.: (306) 635-4420 Fax: (306) 635-4420
Website: www.lights.com/waterways/crco
E-mail: ric.crco@sk.sympatico.ca

Churchill River Canoe Outfitters is located on the Churchill River
in Northern Saskatchewan. We offer guided canoe trips on most
Saskatchewan rivers and many rivers in northern Manitoba and Nunavut.
CRCO also offers extensive canoe courses in whitewater, canoe camping
and river rescue. We have canoes and canoeing equipment for rent, maps
and route information available as well as cabins for rent.

Ron Johnstone Paddling Centre

446 Main St. West, Merrickville, Ontario, Canada K0G 1N0
Ph.: (613) 269-2910 Toll Free: 1-888-252-6292 Fax: (613) 269-2908
Website: www.crca.ca E-mail: staff@crca.ca

When paddling the Rideau Canal System between Ottawa and Kingston -
visit the Ron Johnstone Paddling Centre - the spectacular timberframe
headquarters of the Canadian Recreational Canoeing Association
(CRCA) on the shores of the Rideau in historic Merrickville. The Centre
boasts the largest collection of books, maps and videos on paddling
anywhere in the world (available on-line at www.crca.ca), as well as a
wilderness art exhibit, canoe and sea kayak rentals/instructional programs,
voyageur canoes for rent and the annual Canadian Canoe Symposium
events, (3rd weekend in August each year). A shuttle service along the
Rideau Canal System is also available. Call, write or visit our web site
for complete details.

Smoothwater Outfitters & Ecolodge
Temagami's Ecotourism Specialist (Est. 1984)
Box 40, Temagami, Ontario, Canada P0H 2H0
Ph.: (705) 569-3539 Fax: (705) 569-2710
Website: www.smoothwater.com E-mail: temagami@onlink.net

Temagami is the Canoe Capital of North America and birthplace of Grey Owl. With over 14,000 square kilometers of stunning wilderness, famous old growth pine forests and seven provincial parks, Smoothwater advises where to find the most remote lakes, wildest rivers and highest climbs. We specialize in canoe and kayak rentals, outfitting, consultation, shuttles, guides, organic cuisine and pre/post trip lodging. During winter, we're a haven for cross country skiers with 60 kilometers of trails and hut to hut skiing.

KANAWA Canada's Canoeing & Kayking Magazine
446 Main St. West, Merrickville, Ontario, Canada K0G 1N0
Ph.: (613) 269-2910 Toll Free: 1-888-252-6292 Fax: (613) 269-2908
Website: www.crca.ca E-mail: staff@crca.ca

KANAWA – Canada's Canoeing & Kayaking Magazine is your complete source of information on canoeing, whitewater kayaking and sea kayaking in Canada. Articles, features, destinations, outdoor cooking, clothing, gear and much more. Regular columns on equipment, events, instruction, heritage and photography keep paddlers informed. Subscriptions are $20 (+ 7%GST) in Canada ($20US in the U.S.A. and internationally) and can be ordered by telephone, fax, mail or e-mail. Visit www.crca.ca for complete details & ask for our free "Paddling Catalogue" of information.

Killarney Outfitters
Killarney, Ontario, Canada P0M 2A0
Ph.: 1 (800) 461 -1117 Fax: (705) 287-2691
Website: www.killarneyoutfitters.com E-mail: info@killarneyoutfitters.com

Explore Killarney Park and Georgian Bay by sea kayak or canoe. We offer personalized guided adventures and a unique resort stay before each trip. Killarney is famous for rugged red grand islands, windswept pines, dead blue waters and ancient white quartrite hills. We provide quality rentals, outfitting and food packages, trip-planning services, shuttles, wilderness guides, accommodation and great meals at Killarney Mountain Lodge.

Lakeland Airways Limited

Box 249, Temagami, Ontario, Canada P0H 2H0
Ph.: (705) 569-3455 Fax: (705) 569-3687
Website: www.lakelandthreebuoys.com E-mail: lakeland@onlink.net
Lakeland Airways is situated on Lake Temagami with fly-in access to many great canoeing areas such as the Smoothwater Wilderness Park. Our well equipped Beaver Cessna 185 aircraft will fly you into our remote outpost camps situated on different lakes with acess to many river systems, or we can fly you directly into any lake you prefer or river system. You can be picked up by plane at another destination or paddle your way out. We also rent Kevelar canoes as well as supply paddles and lifejackets.

Madawaska Kanu Centre

Box 635, Barry's Bay, Ontario, Canada K0J 1B0
Ph.: (613) 594-5268 Fax: (613) 234-4097
Website: www.owl-mkc.ca E-mail: paddle@owl-mkc.ca

Madawaska Kanu Centre provides highly personal instructions in both Whitewater kayaking and canoeing, leading to diplomas recognized worldwide. Located on the Madawaska River by Algonquin Park, Madawaska Kanu Centre offers all the comforts of a vacation resort in European style. Our classes are small and our rivers clean, warm and uncrowded. Excellent water flow is guaranteed all summer long. Join us for a weekend or five day course. www.owl-mkc.ca (613) 756-3620 • Before May 1st (613) 594-5268.

Mountain Equipment Co-op

149 W. 4th Avenue, Vancouver, British Columbia, Canada V5Y 4A6
Ph.: (604) 732-1989 Fax: (604) 731-6483
Website: www.mec.ca

Mountain Equipment Co-op is Canada's leading outdoor equipment retailer. We are a member owned and directed co-operative; a $5 share purchase entitles you to a lifetime membership. We sell and rent equipment for paddling, hiking, backcountry skiing, cycling, and climbing. We have retail stores in Vancouver, Edmonton, Calgary, Toronto, and Ottawa, and a Mail Order Department at 1-800-663-2776. Visit www.mec.ca.

Nahanni River Adventures

P.O. Box 4869, Whitehorse, Yukon Territory, Canada Y1A 4N6
Ph.: 1 (800) 297-6927 Fax: (867) 668-3056
Website: www.nahanni.com E-mail: nahanni@yknet.yk.ca

River expeditions from Alaska to Nunavut. Visit our extensive northern expedition web site. Natural history and wilderness adventures by canoe and raft. Options available for all ages and skill levels including 'mature' age segment and single travellers. Outfitted and accompanied by qualified and licensed guide/naturalists who are also superb cooks. Nahanni, Tatshenshini, Alsek, Firth, Stikine, Wind, Snake, Yukon, Taku and Horton rivers.

Nahanni Wilderness Adventures

Box 4, Site 6, R.R.#1, Didsbury, Alberta, Canada T0M 0W0
Ph.: 1 (888) 897-5223 Fax: (403) 637-3843
Website: www.nahanniwild.com E-mail: adventures@nahanniwild.com

Specializing in first class and fully outfitted canoe and raft adventures since 1985 for the north's most celebrated wilderness river, The South Nahanni! Nahanni Wilderness Adventures is owned and operated by David Hibbard, the Nahanni River's most active and experienced professional river guide. We also offer a trip planning service with canoe/raft and equipment rentals for self guided trips in the Nahanni region.

Narwal Adventure Training & Tours

#101, 5102, 51 Ave., Yellowknife, Northwest Territories,
Canada X1A 1S8
Ph.: (867) 873-6443 Fax: (867) 873-2741
Website: www.ssimicro.com/~narwal/index.htm
E-mail: narwal@ssimicro.com

NARWAL Adventure Training and Tours is a northern owned family business specializing in canoe and kayak instruction, rentals and tours. Join Titus and Cathy Allooloo for wildlife viewing and shore lunch featuring traditional northern delicacies. Nationally certified instructors with over 20 years experience offer quality instruction – lake and river applications. Tailor-made private, group and specialty courses. Licensed outfitter, Great Slave Lake and northern watershed.

Quetico Discovery Tours

P.O. Box 593, Atikokan, Ontario, Canada P0T 1C0
Ph.: (807) 597-2621
Website: http://atikokan.lakeheadu.ca/~jdstradi/index.html
E-mail: jdstradi@atikokan.lakeheadu.ca

Quetico Discovery Tours provides customized adventure canoe trips into
Quetico Provincial Park in Northwestern Ontario, a vast lakeland wilderness known for its beauty and voyageur history. Tours include: photography
and artist's tours and retreats; family tours for all ages and generations;
nature tours; seniors tours; year-round park guiding services; outfitting and
bed-and-breakfast services by reservation. You can start your trip Monday
morning and return Friday afternoon from mid-May through October.
No previous experience is required. Shorter or longer trips, or special
itineraries, can be arranged. Weekly fees in U.S. funds are: $375 Child
(12 and under) $500 Adult (taxes are extra). These rates include park
permits, complete outfitting, guiding and instruction in wilderness travel
skills, and food. You will enjoy fresh food and warm companionship on
the trail. All you will need to bring is a sleeping bag and personal items.

Rideau Canal – Parks Canada

Rideau Canal, 34A Beckwith St. S., Smiths Falls, Ontario,
Canada K7A 2A8
Ph.: 1 (800) 230-0016 / (613) 283-5170 Fax: (613) 283-0677
Website: www.parkscanada.gc.ca/rideau

Savour an excursion on 202 kilometres of waterway through this historic
corridor in Eastern Ontario between Ottawa and Kingston. With stretches
of secluded shoreline, thriving wetlands and scenic lakes, the Rideau
Canal links a variety of paddling environments within the Rideau and
Cataraqui watersheds. Our 24 lockstations offer drinking water, wash-
rooms, barbecue grills, picnic tables, parking and a place to pitch your
tent. Information disponible en français.

Simpson Air/Nahanni Mountain Lodge

Box 260, Fort Simpson, Northwest Territories, Canada X0E 0N0
Ph.: (867) 695-2505 Fax: (867) 695-2925
Website: www.cancom.net/~simpair E-mail: simpair@cancom.net

Simpson Air is the longest active flying business offering charter aircraft
on floats or wheels into the Nahanni National Park and surrounding area.
Let our experience help you to plan your Nahanni canoe trip.

Spanish River Outfitters

P.O. Box 390, Levack, Ontario, Canada P0M 2C0
Ph.: (705) 965-2701
Website: www.adventuretravelontario.com

Located minutes from "The Elbow on the Spanish River". Begin your trip with a relaxing night at the lodge prior to your canoe adventure on the Spanish River. Enjoy a voyageur dinner, paddler's breakfast, sauna, woodfired hot tub, shuttles, canoe rentals, guided trips, the "new waterproof" Spanish River Map. Contact Spanish River Outfitters at (705) 9652701 for details on your customized canoe adventure, or visit our web site at www.adventuretravelontario.com.

Temagami Wilderness Centre

R.R.#1, Temagami, Ontario, Canada P0H 2H0
Ph: 1 (800) 881-1189 / (705) 569-3733 Fax: (705) 569-3594
Website: www.temagami.com E-mail: info@temagami.com

Serving the Lady Evelyn River as well as over 4,800 kilometers of canoe waterways with every type of condition. We offer outfitting, instruction courses, bed and breakfast and guided eco-tours.

Tuckamor Trips Inc.

7123 Lac Noir Road, Ste-Agathe-des-Monts, Quebec, Canada J8C 2Z8
Ph.: (819) 326-3602 Fax: (819) 326-8617
Website: www.tuckamor.com E-mail: bill@tuckamor.com

There are more wonderful canoe trips in Quebec than this book would have you believe. We run fully guided and outfitted trips on many of them including the Dumoine, Coulonge, Batiscan, Upper Rouge, La Verendrye Wildlife Reserve, Lievre, and, of course the Moisie. Give us a try for family trips, instructional trips, trips for corporations, etc. Request our catalogue.

Valley Ventures

P.O. Box 1115, R.R.#1, Deep River, Ontario, Canada K0J 1P0
Ph.: (613) 584-2577 Fax: (613) 584-9016
Website: www.magma.ca/~vent E-mail: vent@magma.ca

Our complete and partial outfitting business provides support services for such rivers as the Dumoine, Noire, Coulonge and Petawawa. We provide guided trips and custom trips to many other areas such as Algonquin Park, Northern Ontario, Quebec and Manitoba. Our facilities include accommodation, outdoor retail supplies, equipment rentals, shuttles and certified instruction. We are located in the Upper Ottawa Valley along the Trans Canada Highway.

Voyageur Wilderness Programme Ltd.

P.O. Box 850, Atikokan, Ontario, Canada P0T 1C0
Ph.: (807) 597-2450 Off Season: (204) 233-2702 Fax: (204) 233-0153
Website: http://www.vwp.com E-mail: vwp@vwp.com

Discover Quetico wilderness park through it's premier canoe outfitter offering the traditional ambiance of voyageurs who once paddled these same waters. Voyageur Wilderness Programme, located on Voyageur Island, Nym Lake – has, for the past 40 years, provided eco-adventure canoe excursions to nature enthusiasts, schools, universities, youth and community groups. VWP provides a wide variety of eco-excursion services including: canoe routing, complete and partial outfitting, food and menu preparation and planning, bed and breakfast facilities (pre and post trip), sauna on the lake, special group and family trip planning. Contact our office or visit our web-site for complete details.

Wanapitei Canoe

"Canada's Oldest Canoe Trip Company"
17-393 Water St., Peterborough, Ontario, Canada K9H 3L7
Ph.: 1 (888) 781-0411 / (705) 745-3721
Website: www.wanapiteicanoe.com E-mail: trips@wanapiteicanoe.com
Paddle with the best when you join one of our great canoe adventures. 70 years of canoe tripping tradition tells you a great deal. Quality, professionalism, safety, fun and enjoyment are not just buzz words for us, they are what we have been all about for generations.

Western Arctic Adventures & Equipment

P.O. Box 1554, Inuvik, Northwest Territories, Canada X0E 0T0
Ph.: (867) 777-2594 Fax: (867) 777-4542
Website: www.inuvik.net/canoenwt E-mail: canoenwt@permafrost.com

Canoe and kayak sales and rentals for the western N.W.T. Trip consulting and logistic arrangements services. Covering the northern Yukon, northern Mackenzie Valley, Delta, Banks, and Victoria Islands. Canoes and kayaks available in Inuvik, Norman Wells and Cambridge Bay. Covering the Horton, Anderson, Hornaday, Thomson, Kuujjua, Nanook, Mountain, Keele, Natla, Peele, Snake, Eagle, Bell, Porcupine, Kugaluk and Mackenzie rivers.

CANOE & KAYAK CANADA

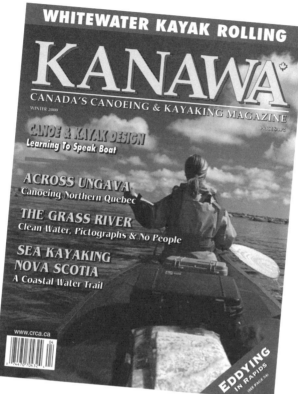

START SENDING ME
KANAWA°
Canada's Canoeing & Kayaking Magazine

❏ Please send me free Safe Paddling Information
❏ Please send me *KANAWA* (4 issues/yr) for: ❏ $40.66/2 yrs ❏ $21.40/yr (USA & Int'l in US Funds)
(NF/NS/NB ❏ $43.70/2 yrs ❏ $23.00/yr)
❏ Payment by: ❏ VISA ❏ MasterCard ❏ Cheque/Money Order

Card Number: _____ Exp. Date: _____

Signature: _____

Name: _____

Address: _____ City: _____ Prov./Terr./State_____

Postal/Zip Code:_____ Tel.: (H) _____ (B) _____

❏ This is a gift subscription from: _____Telephone: _____